ROCKY MOUNTAIN
MAMMALS

Wapiti, or Elk *(Gene Putney)*

ROCKY MOUNTAIN
MAMMALS

*A Handbook of Mammals of Rocky Mountain
National Park and Vicinity, Third Edition*

DAVID M. ARMSTRONG

UNIVERSITY PRESS *of* COLORADO
in cooperation with
THE ROCKY MOUNTAIN NATURE ASSOCIATION

© 1987, 2008 by the Rocky Mountain Nature Association
First edition 1975
Third edition 2008

Published by the University Press of Colorado
5589 Arapahoe Avenue, Suite 206C
Boulder, Colorado 80303

in cooperation with

The Rocky Mountain Nature Association
48 Alpine Circle
Estes Park, Colorado 80517

 The University Press of Colorado is a proud member of
the Association of American University Presses.

The University Press of Colorado is a cooperative publishing enterprise supported, in part, by Adams State College, Colorado State University, Fort Lewis College, Mesa State College, Metropolitan State College of Denver, University of Colorado, University of Northern Colorado, and Western State College of Colorado.

∞ The paper used in this publication meets the minimum requirements of the American National Standard for Information Sciences—Permanence of Paper for Printed Library Materials. ANSI Z39.48-1992

Library of Congress Cataloging-in-Publication Data

Armstrong, David Michael, 1944–
  Rocky Mountain mammals : a handbook of mammals of Rocky Mountain National Park and vicinity / by David M. Armstrong. — 3rd ed.
    p. cm.
  Includes bibliographical references.
  ISBN 978-0-87081-882-0 (pbk. : alk. paper) 1. Mammals—Colorado—Rocky Mountain National Park Region. 2. Rocky Mountain National Park Region (Colo.) I. Rocky Mountain Nature Association. II. Title.
  QL719.C6A75 2007
  599.09788'69—dc22

                                                                    2007032172

Design by Daniel Pratt

17   16   15   14   13   12   11   10   09   08   10   9   8   7   6   5   4   3   2   1

In memory of Maurice and Mayme Jessup of
Sylvan Dale Guest Ranch, Loveland, Colorado
Dear friends of the Greatest Generation

Contents

List of Tables

Checklist of Mammals of Rocky Mountain National Park and Vicinity

ORDER SORICOMORPHA—SHREWS AND ALLIES
Family Soricidae—Shrews

ORDER CHIROPTERA—BATS
Family Vespertilionidae—Vesper Bats

ORDER PRIMATES—PRIMATES
Family Hominidae—People

ORDER LAGOMORPHA—RABBITS AND ALLIES
Family Ochotonidae—Pikas

Family Leporidae—Rabbits and Hares

ORDER RODENTIA—RODENTS
Family Sciuridae—Squirrels

Family Geomyidae—Pocket Gophers

ORDER ARTIODACTYLA—EVEN-TOED HOOFED MAMMALS

[*] Extirpated from Colorado within historic time
[†] Introduced in Colorado
Notes: Because of dramatic and ongoing advances in systematic and evolutionary biology over the past generation, the higher classification of mammals is dynamic, and so are the names of some groups. The sequence of treatment of orders, families, and genera is roughly phylogenetic, following R. Baker, Bradley, Bradley, et al. (2003). Common and scientific nomenclature generally follows R. Baker, Bradley, Bradley, et al. (2003). Most generic, familial, and ordinal names have been updated to conform to Wilson and Reeder (2005).

ROCKY MOUNTAIN
MAMMALS

Moose Cow with Calf *(Gene Putney)*

1

INTRODUCTION

This is a handbook of mammals of Rocky Mountain National Park and adjacent areas. Its purpose is to help visitors increase their understanding and appreciation of the mammals of the area by describing their diversity, their habits, and their complex relationships with the natural environment.

The more we know about our surroundings, the more we can enjoy them. The more we enjoy any resource, the more tenacious we are in protecting it for our own continuing enjoyment and that of generations to come—generations of people and generations of pine squirrels! I hope that this handbook will not only serve visitors but will also serve our native fauna and its precarious habitat.

The fauna of any area is a dynamic assemblage. Some species undergo seasonal migrations. Others disappear to enter hibernation or dormancy.

Geographical ranges change on time scales of years or millennia, as climatic change leads to changes in the resource base. Superimposed on these natural patterns are changes in response to human involvement—deliberate or not—in native ecosystems.

Because of this dynamism—and because some species are simply difficult to observe—it is nearly impossible to list and describe accurately an entire fauna for a particular area, especially an area as complex and diverse as Rocky Mountain National Park. Of the seventy-two species described in this book, about sixty have been documented in Rocky Mountain National Park or Arapaho National Recreation Area by museum specimens and/or confirmed observations of animals or their certain sign. Of that number, at least four species (gray wolf, grizzly bear, river otter, bison, and perhaps the wolverine) have been extirpated within historic time. (The river otter now has been restored on the west side of the national park.) The moose was of occasional natural occurrence in northern Colorado in the latter half of the nineteenth century. The animals were introduced in North Park in recent years by the Colorado Division of Wildlife, and moose are now residents of Rocky Mountain National Park.

Organization—The bulk of this handbook is composed of accounts of the species of mammals occurring in or adjacent to Rocky Mountain National Park and Arapaho National Recreation Area (or are strongly suspected to occur or have occurred there within historic times). Accounts of most species treat distribution and habitat, appearance and field recognition, and natural history. Accounts (usually somewhat abbreviated) are provided for species not yet documented in the area but whose presence may eventually be detected, given ongoing habitat change, including direct and indirect human interference.

Wherever possible, data in accounts of species are from local studies. Selected references are provided for each species. These citations will lead interested readers to useful reviews or technical monographs. In keeping with an orientation toward a lay audience, text citations are few. For more information on any of the species described, see Fitzgerald et al. (1994). An attempt has been made to cite recent review papers and books. Fortunately, most of the species discussed in this book have been reviewed in *Mammalian Species*. That series is published by the American Society of Mammalogists. Accounts are authoritative and succinct and they cite the detailed sources from the primary research literature. All are available gratis on the Worldwide Web, from an archive maintained by Professor Virginia Hayssen at Smith College (http://www.science.smith.edu/departments/Biology/VHAYSSEN/msi/default.html).

Although our interest is focused specifically on mammals of Rocky Mountain National Park and immediately adjacent areas, this handbook has

Rocky Mountain
National Park

Cheyenne

Denver

Santa Fe

Sketch map of parts of Wyoming, Colorado, and New Mexico, showing in shaded relief the geographic context of this handbook—the Southern Rocky Mountains. After Adams (2003), used by permission.

far wider application (see map). It applies without exception to mountainous parts of north-central Colorado and adjacent Wyoming. Elsewhere in the Southern Rockies a similar fauna is present, although there is a gradual attenuation of the ranges of some species southward. In mountainous areas to the north and west (in the Middle Rocky Mountains of Wyoming and Utah), our coverage becomes progressively less complete. The reader interested in mammals of Colorado as a whole should consult Fitzgerald et al. (1994), or Lechleitner (1969). Mammals of the Great Plains to the east were treated by

Jones et al. (1983, 1985), and Armstrong (1982) described mammals of the Colorado Plateau to the west.

A rather extensive, general introduction precedes the accounts of species. What Is a Mammal? describes mammals in general and attempts to put the local fauna in temporal perspective with respect to other vertebrate animals. Mammalian Distribution establishes the fauna in its spatial context. Comments on ecological distribution are intended to aid the reader in selecting those areas of Rocky Mountain National Park best suited to the development of certain mammalian communities. How to Observe Mammals offers a few hints for the would-be mammal watcher.

Explanation of Terminology—This is intended as a popular handbook. By "popular" I do not imply that it is intended as a "best seller" but that it was written for laypeople without extensive formal training in biology. Nonetheless, some scientific vocabulary has been used, and scientific names are included for each species. Why?

First, why not? Certainly not to impress—and not to discourage—the interested amateur. As paleontologist H. E. Wood once observed, "The justification for the technical terminology of any specialty is not to serve as a hog latin by which initiates may mystify and exclude *hoi polloi.*" Rather, technical vocabulary allows precise statements where the simpler or more familiar words of everyday language might be misleading. Technical terms are defined in a glossary (Appendix II) near the end of this handbook.

What about scientific names? Here again, precision is the overriding criterion. A scientific name permits unequivocal reference to a particular species. Vernacular ("common") names often do not. Consider as an example the vernacular name "gopher." To the biologist, the word "gopher" connotes a pocket gopher, any member of the family Geomyidae. "Gopher" in this sense is not a very restrictive term—there are some forty species of pocket gophers. However, some people use the term "gopher" to designate any burrowing rodent. The "Golden Gopher" of Minnesota is not a geomyid but the 13-lined ground squirrel. That same species is called "gopher" (or "picket-pin") in northeastern Colorado. In northwestern Colorado, however, the 13-lined ground squirrel is called "corn weasel"; in that area "picket-pin" designates the Wyoming ground squirrel, a widely different kind of ground squirrel. In Florida, "gopher" does not refer to a mammal at all but designates a kind of tortoise. That leaves the Floridian pocket gopher without a common name, so some locals call them "salamanders"!

Scientific names prevent the confusion inherent in a loose system of common names. Scientific names are formulated and proposed under stringent international rules to which the systematic biologists of the world all subscribe voluntarily. Each species of animal or plant has a unique name. The complete name of a species consists of two words. The first word (capitalized) designates the genus to which a species belongs. The western jumping mouse is in the genus *Zapus*. Often a genus comprises several species and the generic name in common indicates close evolutionary affinity of one species with another. The second word (not capitalized) is unique and refers to a single species, such as *Zapus princeps*. Because they are written in a foreign language, Latin, scientific names are conventionally printed in italic type.

What is an animal species? To the layperson (and to most zoologists on a day-to-day basis), species are groups of individuals that look alike. In most— but by no means all—cases this definition is quite adequate. Some species look very much alike, especially externally (the Colorado and Uinta chipmunks are examples in Rocky Mountain National Park). However, individuals within a species may look very different from one another. Siblings from the same litter may differ widely in color or pattern. For example, Abert's squirrels (*Sciurus aberti*) may be black, brown, or gray. "Red" foxes (*Vulpes vulpes*) may be reddish, grayish (the "cross" phase), or "silver" (actually a "frosted" black). "Black" bears (*Ursus americanus*) may be brown, whereas brown bears (*Ursus arctos,* also called grizzly bears) may be blonde.

In addition to local differences between individuals, species vary geographically; in the eastern United States and Canada, our "red" squirrels, *Tamiasciurus hudsonicus* (also called chickarees or pine squirrels) are indeed reddish in color, but in the Southern Rockies, most individuals are not red at all but a sort of bluish brown. Clearly, a criterion for species more meaningful than mere appearance is needed. Today zoologists consider species to be groups of actually or potentially interbreeding individuals, reproductively isolated from other such groups. That is, species are defined by reproductive continuity, not merely by appearance.

This book is about species of mammals (with brief comments on the families and orders in which the species are classified). Recognized scientific names are used to allow a fixed point of reference for those who might wish to read more about a particular species in the technical literature. For those who are interested, the derivations of scientific names (where known to me) are included in Appendix III. Vernacular names usually follow R. Baker, Bradley, Bradley, et al. (2003). (That checklist is available online, gratis, from the Museum of Texas Tech University; http://www.nsrl.ttu.edu/publications/opapers/ops/op229.pdf.) Where appropriate, alternative common names are included to facilitate conversation with local naturalists.

Orders, families, and genera are treated in traditional phylogenetic sequence (following R. Baker, Bradley, Bradley, et al. 2003). Ordinal names and comments on diversity within orders follow Wilson and Reeder (2005). Species within genera are arranged alphabetically. Descriptions of continental ranges are based on Hall (1981) and those of ranges in Colorado are based on Fitzgerald et al. (1994), which updated maps from Armstrong (1972).

Measurements—Measurements are of Coloradan animals (generally following Armstrong 1972). Some incidental measurements are in the so-called English system, but measurements of mammals are given in metric units, the so-called SI System (abbreviated from the French Système International d'Unités because the system was invented by the French during the Enlightenment). Abbreviations for SI units are as follows: mm = millimeter, cm = centimeter; m = meter; km = kilometer; g = gram; kg = kilogram. This two-system arrangement should not prove confusing, and it may be instructive. The metric system is the world scientific standard and, except in the United States, has become the official commercial standard as well. Philosophically, the metric system is far more satisfying than our traditional system of measurement. The meter is based (roughly) on the circumference of Earth rather than on the length of some forgotten monarch's arm. Also, once one gets accustomed to "thinking metric," it is a much easier system to use than the English system because everything is based on multiples of ten: 10 millimeters to the centimeter, 100 centimeters to the meter, 1,000 meters to the kilometer, 1,000 grams to the kilogram, 1,000 kilograms to the metric tonne. Conversion factors and a table of English-metric equivalents appear in the back of this book.

Acknowledgments—Numerous readers made comments or corrections on earlier editions of this book (see Armstrong 1975, 1987). For this revision, Catherine Driscoll provided recent observations on status of bighorn sheep; Park Service resource manager Jeff Connor facilitated access to the observations of numerous visitors and Park Service personnel who have contributed to the wildlife observation files at RMNP-HQ. Dr. James B. Benedict of the Center for Mountain Archeology, Ward, Colorado, provided literature and insights on human prehistory.

As always, in all ways, I thank Susan for her patience.

2

WHAT IS A MAMMAL?

Historical—Mammals are vertebrate animals with hair. Mammals arose from the therapsid reptiles in the Triassic period, over 200 million years ago. Earliest mammals mostly were small animals and they probably were of relatively little importance in the ecosystems of their day. In the Triassic period, the ruling reptiles (the archosaurs, commonly called "dinosaurs") were beginning to dominate the land and shallow seas, a position they would occupy for over 100 million years. During the Age of Reptiles, mammals remained obscure and relatively unimportant, all the while honing the adaptations that are the hallmarks of the mammalian grade of organization. Toward the end of the Cretaceous period (about 65 million years ago) the vast majority of archosaurs became extinct. Today they are survived only by the crocodiles and their kin (and a specialized side branch, the birds).

Mammals seized upon the demise of ruling reptiles and diversified rapidly, rising quickly to a dominant position on the land and assuming an important role in freshwater and marine communities as well. Because of this dominance, the Cenozoic era, the past 65 million years, is aptly termed the Age of Mammals.

Anatomical—To define mammals as "vertebrate animals with hair" is an obvious understatement. Mammals certainly are far more than reptiles glorified with hair, but hair was a most important evolutionary "invention." In the first place, hair is an insulator. With a hairy coat separating the body from the environment, maintenance of a high and relatively constant body temperature is possible. Endothermy, or warm-bloodedness—as such temperature maintenance usually is called—allows an animal to remain active despite the ambient temperature. The "cold-blooded" (ectothermic) reptiles, on the other hand, can be active only when environmental temperatures rise well above freezing. Today reptiles are diverse only in tropical and subtropical areas of Earth. Mammals, on the other hand, have successfully occupied the cold environments of high latitudes and high elevations, areas completely beyond the tolerance of most reptiles. Only a single species of reptile (the common garter snake, *Thamnophis elegans*) is documented in Rocky Mountain National Park.

Coupled with the insulation provided by hair, mammals have evolved a highly efficient circulatory system. As in birds, the heart consists of four chambers. There are completely separate routes for blood to the body and blood to the lungs. Blood arriving at the tissues is rich in oxygen, allowing high rates of metabolism and a high level of activity.

The name "mammal" is derived from the Latin word *mamma*, "teat," and alludes to another hallmark of the class. Female mammals produce milk to nourish their young. Milk is secreted by specialized glands thought to represent highly modified sweat and sebaceous glands. Because sweat glands are peculiar to mammals and sebaceous glands are associated with hair follicles, the elaboration of mammary glands reemphasizes the importance of the skin, and especially hair, in the evolution of the mammalian condition.

Milk is the food of young mammals immediately after birth. Milk contains fats, sugar, and proteins and varies in proportional composition from species to species. On this rich diet—balanced to the needs of each particular species—young mammals grow until they are able to obtain their own food. But suckling allows more than a mere head start. It permits a period of contact between the mother and her offspring. The lactation period allows the parent to train the young. By complex means such as imitative play, the young receive information learned through experience by the parental generation.

In animals that show no parental care, communication between generations can only be by way of the genes, the biological inheritance. In mammals (and to a lesser extent in birds) training can take place.

The possibility for training during a period of maternal dependence has made it advantageous for mammals to increase the size and complexity of learning centers in the brain, generally at the expense of lower centers concerned with innate (inborn or instinctive) behavioral patterns. Mammals as a class have a behavioral plasticity unmatched by other animal groups.

Another advance of mammals over their reptilian forebears is the presence of specialized teeth. Mammalian teeth are set in sockets (a condition termed "thecodont"). This structure provides mechanical strength for tearing, gnawing, and grinding. From front to back within the toothrow, the teeth are specialized for various functions ("heterodont"). Incisors are adapted to gnawing and nipping; molars are superior for grinding and crushing. Specialization of individual teeth within the toothrow allows far greater efficiency in collecting food and preparing it for digestion than does a dentition in which all teeth are the same ("homodont"). Four sorts of teeth are recognizable in most mammals: incisors, canines, premolars, and molars. Teeth of mammals are described numerically in terms of a "dental formula," which describes the upper and lower dentition in one side of the jaw. Thus, the dental formula of ancestral mammals was incisors, 3/3; canines, 1/1; premolars, 4/4; molars, 3/3; total teeth, 44. Dental formulas of mammals of Rocky Mountain National Park are shown in Table 1.

Mammalian teeth differ greatly with feeding habits. The cheekteeth of grazers, from meadow mice to elk, grow throughout life, an adaptation to their abrasive diet of grasses. The teeth of squirrels are suited to crushing and grinding seeds. Rodents have no canine teeth, because the food of most species is plants. Mammals that feed on other animals (most members of the order Carnivora, for example) have well-developed canine teeth to grasp and hold the prey. The cats (and to a lesser extent, other carnivores as well) have a highly efficient shearing mechanism between upper and lower cheekteeth. The diversity of mammalian teeth is a classic example of "adaptive radiation." Adaptive radiation is the evolution from a common ancestor of divergent lineages adapted to specialized ecological roles.

Adaptive radiation also has occurred in locomotion. Ancestral mammals have five toes on each foot, both fore and aft. In modern mammals the number of toes may be reduced to one on each foot (and in some of the marine mammals, toes are lost completely). The primitive stance probably was plantigrade (as in humans and bears), with the toes, foot bones, and parts of the ankle and wrist in contact with the ground. The stance of modern mammals may be digitigrade (only the digits on the ground, as in dogs) or unguligrade

Table 1. Dental formulas of mammals of Rocky Mountain National Park and vicinity (I = incisors, C = canines, P = premolars, M = molars).

I 3/3, C 1/1, P 4/4, M 2/3 = 42	*Ursus,* * *Canis, Vulpes, Urocyon*
I 3/3, C 1/1, P 4/4, M 2/2 = 40	*Procyon, Bassariscus*
I 2/3, C 1/1, P 3/3, M 3/3 = 38	*Myotis*
I 3/3, C 1/1, P 4/4, M 1/2 = 38	*Martes, Gulo*
I 2/3, C 1/1, P 2/3, M 3/3 = 36	*Lasionycteris, Corynorhinus*
I 3/3, C 1/1, P 4/3, M 1/2 = 36	*Lontra*
I 3/3, C 1/1, P 3/3, M 1/2 = 34	*Mustela, Mephitis, Neovison, Taxidea, Spilogale*
I 0/3, C 1/1, P 3/3, M 3/3 = 34	*Cervus*
I 2/2, C 1/1, P 2/2, M 3/3 = 32	*Homo*
I 2/3, C 1/1, P 1/2, M 3/3 = 32	*Eptesicus*
I 3/1, C 1/1, P 3/1, M 3/3 = 32	*Sorex*
I 1/3, C 1/1, P 2/2, M 3/3 = 32	*Lasiurus*
I 0/3, C 0/1, P 3/3, M 3/3 = 32	*Odocoileus, Alces, Bison, Antilocapra, Ovis, Oreamnos*
I 3/3, C 1/1, P 2–3/2, M 1/1 = 28 or 30	*Lynx, Puma*
I 2/1, C 0/0, P 3/2, M 3/3 = 28	*Lepus, Sylvilagus*
I 2/1, C 0/0, P 2/2, M 3/3 = 26	*Ochotona*
I 1/1, C 0/0, P 2/1, M 3/3 = 22	*Marmota, Spermophilus, Neotamias, Tamiasciurus, Cynomys, Sciurus* *
I 1/1, C 0/0, P 1/1, M 3/3 = 20	*Castor, Erethizon, Thomomys*
I 1/1, C 0/0, P 1/0, M 3/3 = 18	*Zapus*
I 1/1, C 0/0, P 0/0, M 3/3 = 16	*Neotoma, Phenacomys, Myodes, Microtus, Peromyscus, Lemmiscus, Ondatra*

*May have one upper premolar missing.

(only the tips of the toes—protected by an ungule or hoof—on the ground, as in horses and cattle).

Diversity has evolved not only in stance but in the mode of progression, or gait. Ancestral mammals probably were ambulatory (walkers). In open habitats, swift cursorial (running) locomotion is at a premium among larger animals, and smaller mammals in such situations often are saltatory (jumping). Natatory (swimming) mammals represent a number of groups; the whales are so modified to marine life that they are completely helpless ashore. Invading the trees, some mammalian groups became scansorial (climbers). Some scansorial groups (for example, the flying squirrels) have adapted for efficient glissant (gliding) locomotion, but only one order, the bats, is volant (that is, capable of true, powered flight). The diversity of locomotor adaptations points out how plastic the basic mammalian body plan has been. Mammals compete successfully not only with other terrestrial groups but with birds and fishes as well.

Reproductive and Developmental—Reptiles advanced over their amphibian ancestors and successfully invaded the land with the evolution of the shelled egg. The land egg has a number of membranes. Just within the shell is the chorion, which protects the developing embryo from desiccation. Two membranous bags attach to the belly of the embryonic reptile. The yolk sac contains stored food and the allantois serves to collect wastes from the embryo. Closely surrounding the embryo is another membrane, the fluid-filled amnion. Amnionic fluid provides the developing reptile with protection from temperature change, chemical insult, and mechanical shock. In short, the land egg provides the embryonic reptile with its own "private pond."

Mammals took the basic structure of the reptilian egg and went a few steps farther. Among living mammals, only the monotremes (the duck-billed platypus of Australia and the spiny anteaters of Australia and New Guinea) lay reptile-like shelled eggs. In all other mammals the embryos are retained to some extent within the reproductive tract of the mother, and the egg shell is gone. The membranes of the reptilian embryo, however, remain. The amnion and its fluid protect the developing mammals, and parts of the allantois and yolk sac form the umbilical cord. The chorion—the outer membrane of the reptilian egg—comes into contact with the wall of the uterus. The chorion and the adjacent allantois are well supplied with blood vessels and through these vessels essential nutrients and oxygen pass from the blood of the mother to that of the embryo. Waste gases and fluids pass back in the opposite direction. The complex of embryonic and maternal membranes that permits this two-way exchange of materials is called the placenta. A placenta is characteristic of the largest group of mammals, the Eutheria; the marsupials (Metatheria—pouched mammals, such as the opossum) lack a true placenta. In many mammalian groups the placenta is passed with the newborn young at birth and is termed the "afterbirth."

In most mammals, reproduction occurs during only a part of the year, the "breeding season." In females, hormones secreted by the ovaries and the pituitary gland regulate the reproductive cycle. Interplay of these hormones produces a sequence of events known as the estrous cycle. Estrus (commonly called "heat") often coincides with ovulation, the release of eggs from the ovaries. During estrus, the female is receptive to the male. An interval termed proestrus precedes the period of heat. During proestrus, follicles on the ovaries are stimulated by pituitary hormones to produce egg cells (ova). The ovarian follicle produces a hormone (estrogen) that stimulates the growth of the lining of the uterus. After the ovum is shed from the follicle, the ruptured follicle forms a structure known as a corpus luteum ("yellow body"), which secretes the hormone progesterone. Progesterone causes the uterus to become quiescent, ready for the implantation of the embryos should fertilization occur. If fertilization does take place, the embryos develop within the uterus for a variable length of time, the gestation period. During gestation, progesterone is secreted by the placenta to help maintain the quiescence of the uterus.

The length of the gestation period of placental mammals varies from less than three weeks in some small rodents to nearly two years in the African elephant. In a number of mammals, embryonic development does not begin immediately after fertilization. Rather, the fertilized egg (zygote) undergoes a few cell divisions and then development is suspended, frequently for a number of months. Later the early embryo is implanted in the uterine wall and development continues. This phenomenon is known as delayed implantation, which occurs in bears and some species of weasels in Rocky Mountain National Park.

Mammals that breed but once a year are termed "monoestrous"; those that breed more than once a year are described as "polyestrous." In polyestrous mammals the estrous cycle ceases temporarily during gestation and often during lactation (nursing). However, some rodents exhibit a postpartum estrus and mate immediately after giving birth (parturition). Females with postpartum estrus can be lactating and gestating at the same time.

Generally the sexual activity of males also is seasonal. Sperm are produced only during the time of the year when females are reproductively active. Active testes are situated in a sack, the scrotum, outside the body cavity. Here the cooler temperatures optimal for sperm production can be maintained. When active spermatogenesis (sperm production) is not taking place, the testes of many species migrate from the scrotum to lie within the abdominal cavity.

The timing of reproduction depends on specific annual rhythms. The annual cycle may be endogenous (that is, it may be specifically encoded in the genetic program of the animal). Endogenous rhythms continue in the laboratory in the absence of external environmental stimuli. Other rhythms are exogenous. Exogenous rhythms depend upon environmental cues, such as day length (photoperiod) and environmental temperature. Annual rhythms control not only the reproductive cycle but also other periodic phenomena such as hibernation and migration.

Selected General References—S. Anderson and Jones (1984); Eisenberg (1981); Feldhamer et al. (2004).Vaughan et al. (2000).

3

MAMMALIAN DISTRIBUTION

The Ecological Context—Mammals are not distributed at random over the Earth. On a broad scale, long-term evolutionary sequences and geologic accidents determine which species occur where. More locally, the most important factor in mammalian distribution is the character of the vegetation. Vegetation provides mammals with cover and food (whether directly or indirectly). The best predictor of the presence or absence of a species at a particular locality is the character of the local plant community. Thus, description of mammalian habitats in Rocky Mountain National Park (as indicated in Table 2) is important. Within the local species population, distribution of mammals is nonrandom also. The area covered by an individual in its daily round of activity is called its "home range." The home range differs in size from a fraction of a hectare for some small mammals, such as shrews and some rodents, to many square kilometers for some large carnivores, such as mountain lions and grizzly bears.

A part of the home range may be defended against other members of the species. The defended area is termed a "territory." Two basic kinds of territories are commonly observed: the breeding territory and the foraging territory. Territoriality results in dispersion of individuals over available habitat. Consequently, the resources of the ecosystem are not overtaxed by an over-concentrated population. In Rocky Mountain National Park, where some populations may have access to artificially great resources (campgrounds, picnic areas, and scenic viewpoints, for example), unnatural concentrations of animals may congregate. Under such circumstances normal territorial behavior may break down.

The kind of ecosystem in which a mammal lives is termed its "habitat." Because the habitat requirements of any particular species tend to be rather narrow, the experienced observer can simply look at a natural community and predict with considerable accuracy the kinds of animals that might occur. Major criteria involved in the description of habitats are vegetation, cover, soil, and moisture relationships. A complete description of a habitat would involve all characteristics of an animal's physical and biotic surroundings. Two or more species may share the same basic habitat. For example, both porcupines and Abert's squirrels occupy the trees of the ponderosa pine woodland.

The functional role of an animal in a community is termed its "ecological niche." The terms "habitat" and "niche" sometimes are used interchangeably, but that is unfortunate. "Niche" is a complex concept. Eminent English ecologist Charles Elton contrasted habitat and niche nicely: habitat is a species' "address"; niche is that species' "occupation." Description of habitat may be relatively simple; description of a niche is notoriously complex. The role of any species is sufficiently complicated that it probably is fair to say that for no species has the niche been described thoroughly.

A given ecological niche is occupied by a single species. Where two or more species have the same or closely similar demands on the environment (broad niche overlap), one species will eventually displace the other, a phenomenon known as competitive exclusion. The result may be the extinction of one species, its restriction to areas from which the competing species is absent, or changes in behavioral patterns that allow coexistence without direct competition. In this manner, the resources of an ecosystem are partitioned among the species that occupy the system.

Elevational Distribution—Traveling from the eastern plains (at Loveland, Longmont, or Boulder, for example) to the top of Trail Ridge Road, one will have passed in a space of tens of kilometers (and about 2,000 meters of elevation) through a remarkably wide range of ecological conditions. To encom-

Ponderosa pine woodland (Rocky Mountain National Park)

pass a comparable range of conditions traveling northward with no change in elevation, one would need to go nearly 3,200 km (2,000 miles), from Colorado to the Canadian Arctic. When approaching the park from the west, the effects of elevation are less apparent (because elevational change is less abrupt), but the effects are there nonetheless.

A striking effect of increasing elevation (or increasing latitude) is the zonation of biotic communities. Approaching the park from the east, for example, one passes from plains grassland through a narrow shrub zone, upward through various kinds of forest, to the alpine zone. Why are biotic communities zoned? For a start, recall that each species has a genetic program. That program specifies a range of tolerance for the species, a range of conditions (within the broader range of environmental conditions) within which it can exist. Each species-specific range of tolerance is characterized by a minimum, a maximum, and (in most cases) an optimum—a point on the scale where conditions are best for survival and reproduction. The environment provides a range of resources and conditions. For virtually any environmental factor that one might wish to investigate—temperature, rainfall, growing season, sunlight, available minerals, and so on—a range of conditions could be discovered. Species array themselves along resource gradients by occupying those areas that are most favorable.

A natural community usually is a complex web of competitive interactions. Under those circumstances, species tend to be restricted to a relatively narrow set of conditions ranging around the optimum. Toward the extremes of its range of tolerance, a species may be less competitive than a different species with a different genetic optimum.

In mountainous areas, many environmental factors vary with elevation. Doubtless the most obvious of these is temperature, but the amount of sunlight, actual and effective precipitation, composition of the atmosphere, texture of the soil, and other factors also change with elevation and direction of slope. Even relatively obscure factors, such as the mineral content of soils, may vary with elevation, for water is the great natural transport medium in ecological systems, and water flows downhill, changing concentrations of materials as it goes.

Physical factors of the environment are zoned with elevation. Organisms respond to the gradient of physical factors by occupying areas where they are most competitive, where conditions range closely about the optima for their needs. Where physical factors occur as elevational belts or bands so, as a direct consequence, do biotic communities.

Early workers in Colorado (and elsewhere in western North America) described elevational zonation in terms of formal "life zones": Sonoran, Transition, Canadian, Hudsonian, and Arctic-Alpine. Recently, less formal systems of zones have been developed that are applicable to our area. The lowest of the vegetational zones is the montane woodland or forest, a relatively open community dominated by ponderosa pine or Douglas-fir, depending on local conditions and history. The montane zone occurs at elevations from about 6,000 to 9,000 feet (roughly 2,000 to 3,000 m). Between 9,000 feet and about 11,500 feet (300–3,700 m) is a zone of subalpine forest, dominated by Engelmann spruce and subalpine fir. The upper limit of the subalpine is treeline. Above treeline is the alpine zone.

Within the broad elevational zones, local conditions dictate development of a diversity of habitats, which we may call biotic community types. Description of community types helps to point out the diversity of mammalian habitats in Rocky Mountain National Park. The list here is not exhaustive. It simply includes those sorts of communities—distinctive patches in the living landscape—that are most important from the standpoint of mammalian distribution. Under that criterion, nine community types seem worthy of brief description. Let us consider each of these in turn, listing a few of the mammalian species characteristic of each (see Table 2).

Montane forest is the relatively open forest of moderate elevations in the park, dominated by ponderosa pine (*Pinus ponderosa*) on drier, more exposed sites and by Douglas-fir (*Pseudotsuga menziesii*) in moister locations. As the name implies, this is the forest community of the montane zone. In favorably moist areas, blue spruce (*Picea pungens*) may occur. In general, we may consid-

Table 2. Ecological distribution of mammals in Rocky Mountain National Park and vicinity (after Armstrong 1972).

	Ponderosa Pine Woodland	Subalpine Forest	Meadows	Aspen Woodland	Riparian & Shoreline	Alpine Tundra	Mountain Brush	Sagebrush
Masked shrew	X	X	X	X	X	X		
Pygmy shrew		X			X	X		
Merriam's shrew								X
Montane shrew	X	X	X	X	X			
Dwarf shrew	X	X	X	X		X	X	X
American water shrew				X	X			
Western small-footed myotis							X	
Long-eared myotis	X							
Little brown bat	X		X	X	X		X	
Fringed myotis	X							
Long-legged myotis	X			X	X		X	
Hoary bat	X	X		X	X			
Silver-haired bat	X	X		X	X			
Big brown bat	X			X			X	
Townsend's big-eared bat	X						X	
Humankind	X	X	X	X	X	X	X	X
American pika						X		
Mountain, or Nuttall's, cottontail	X	X	X	X	X		X	X
Snowshoe hare		X		X	X			
White-tailed jackrabbit	X	X	X	X		X	X	X
Least chipmunk	X	X	X	X		X		X
Colorado chipmunk	X						X	
Uinta chipmunk		X	X					
Yellow-bellied marmot	X	X	X	X		X		X
Wyoming ground squirrel			X					X
Golden-mantled ground squirrel	X	X	X	X		X	X	X
Rock squirrel	X						X	
Abert's squirrel	X							
Eastern fox squirrel					X			
Pine squirrel, chickaree, or red squirrel	X	X						
Northern pocket gopher	X	X	X	X		X	X	X
American beaver				X	X			
Deer mouse	X	X	X	X	X	X	X	X
Northern rock mouse	X						X	
Bushy-tailed woodrat	X	X				X	X	
Mexican woodrat	X						X	
Southern red-backed vole		X						

continued on next page

Table 2—*continued*

	Ponderosa Pine Woodland	Subalpine Forest	Meadows	Aspen Woodland	Riparian & Shoreline	Alpine Tundra	Mountain Brush	Sagebrush
Western heather vole		X						
Long-tailed vole	X	X	X	X	X	X		X
Montane vole			X	X	X	X		X
Sagebrush vole								X
Muskrat					X			
Western jumping mouse		X	X	X	X			
North American porcupine	X	X				X	X	X
Coyote	X	X	X	X	X	X	X	X
Gray wolf*	X	X	X	X	X	X	X	X
Red fox		X	X	X				
Gray fox	X						X	
Black bear	X	X		X	X		X	
Grizzly, or brown, bear*	X	X	X	X	X	X	X	X
Northern raccoon				X	X			
Ringtail	X						X	
Marten		X				X		
Ermine		X	X	X	X	X	X	
Long-tailed weasel	X	X	X	X	X	X	X	X
Black-footed ferret				X				X
American mink					X			
Wolverine		X						
American badger	X		X			X	X	X
Northern river otter					X			
Western spotted skunk	X						X	
Striped skunk	X	X	X	X	X	X	X	X
Mountain lion	X						X	
Canada lynx		X						
Bobcat	X	X				X	X	X
Wapiti, or elk	X	X	X	X	X	X	X	X
Mule deer	X	X	X	X	X	X	X	X
White-tailed deer					X			
Moose†					X			
Pronghorn								X
Bison*			X			X		X
Mountain goat‡						X		
Mountain, or bighorn, sheep	X		X			X	X	

* Extirpated within historic time.
† Introduced near Rocky Mountain National Park, resident.
‡ Introduced near Rocky Mountain National Park, occasional.

er the montane forest to be a ponderosa pine woodland with local variations depending on soil moisture, microclimate, and fire history.

In some parts of Colorado, it is appropriate to separate ponderosa pine woodland and the more dense and complex montane forest as distinct community types, but in our area such distinction is difficult so not especially useful. Montane forest occurs along the western edge of Estes Park. Most of the private resort development in the vicinity is in this community type, as is the National Park Headquarters southwest of Estes Park. Typical mammals of the community-type include bats, such as the long-eared myotis (*Myotis evotis*) and the long-legged myotis (*Myotis volans*), and Abert's squirrel (*Sciurus aberti*). In the foothills just east of the national park a number of species of Mexican affinities reach their high elevation limits near the northern and western extremes of their geographic ranges. With climatic warming, which seems to be under way, several of those species (the rock squirrel, Mexican woodrat, and northern rock mouse, for example) may be able to expand into the national park.

Subalpine forest constitutes a relatively closed stand composed chiefly of Engelmann spruce (*Picea engelmannii*) and subalpine fir (*Abies lasiocarpa*). Limber pine (*Pinus flexilis*) occurs locally. The forest frequently is interrupted by bogs, ponds, and stands of quaking aspen. Tree species of the subalpine forest are stunted at high elevations to form an elfin woodland or Krummholz, familiar to the traveler on Trail Ridge Road or the higher hiking trails of the park. The upper limit of subalpine forest is treeline. Few mammals are restricted to subalpine forest. The snowshoe hare (*Lepus americanus*) and two species perhaps extirpated from the park, the wolverine (*Gulo gulo*) and the lynx (*Lynx lynx*), would be characteristic of such forests. Other species of the diverse fauna of subalpine forest are also typical of adjacent communities.

Stands of *lodgepole pine* are found in the park mostly on flat to gently rolling sites with well-drained soils, especially glacial moraines. Lodgepole pine stands are favored by periodic fire. The trees form nearly pure stands, and a young forest presents an almost impenetrable maze of trees. For consumers, this is a challenging place to make a living and is thus suitable mostly for specialists. The dense growth of trees prevents much light from reaching the forest floor, so herbaceous plants are minimal. Most of the community's resources are tied up in trees. Among herbivorous mammals, only pine squirrels (or chickarees, *Tamiasciurus hudsonicus*) are found in any numbers. Southern red-backed voles (*Myodes gapperi*) may be associated with chickaree middens and American martens (*Martes americana*) feed extensively on chickarees.

Throughout Rocky Mountain National Park are openings in the forest where *montane* and *subalpine meadows* have developed. Such meadows often are called "parks" locally, and when sufficiently large may be dignified with

Subalpine forest, Kawunchee Valley (Rocky Mountain National Park)

proper names—for example, Estes Park, Moraine Park, Horseshoe Park. Many of the larger parks (and some lesser meadows as well) develop in areas of fine-grained (hence poorly drained) soils and high water tables. Herbs (including both grasses and forbs) are sufficiently well established that the access of trees to the areas is precluded or slowed to an imperceptible pace. The consequences of these meadows for mammals are immense. For one thing, meadows provide optimal foraging habitat for grazing mammals. For many years, elk competed with cattle for dominance in the major parks. Formerly, bison utilized the mountain parks as prime summer range. Also, meadows break up the continuity of forests. There is a tendency for an increase in the diversity of species and in biotic productivity at the interface between adjacent communities. This is termed the "edge effect." The edge effect is due in part to the juxtaposition of the protective cover of forest and the greater productivity of the well-lighted meadow. By increasing the extent of "edge" in the mountain ecosystem, meadows increase local diversity, productivity, and aesthetic interest to people.

   Species of mountain meadows include the Wyoming ground squirrel (*Spermophilus elegans*), northern pocket gopher (*Thomomys talpoides*), and long-tailed vole (*Microtus longicaudus*). In tall-grass meadows, the western jumping mouse (*Zapus princeps*) is common. Species of the forest edge include the yellow-bellied marmot (*Marmota flaviventris*), the golden-mantled

Krummholz *(Rocky Mountain National Park)*

ground squirrel (*Spermophilus lateralis*), Nuttall's cottontail (*Sylvilagus nuttallii*), the least chipmunk (*Neotamias minimus*), and—at higher elevations—the Uinta chipmunk (*Neotamias umbrinus*). Generally speaking, montane parks are drier than subalpine meadows and have a less extensive fauna. When adequately moist, however, montane meadows have essentially the same fauna as their subalpine counterpart.

Aspen woodland, dominated by *Populus tremuloides,* occurs throughout the park, usually as small- to moderate-sized stands in relatively moist areas. In the Southern Rockies, aspen reproduces from root-suckers rather than from seed. Hence aspen woodland is an important stage in reforestation after fire on many sites, and it also typifies avalanche tracks in the high country. The dappled shade and moist soil of an aspen woodland encourage the development of a luxuriant understory of herbs. This provides excellent habitat for such species as the montane vole (*Microtus montanus*) and the western jumping mouse (*Zapus princeps*). There are many similarities between the fauna of the aspen woodland and that of streambank and shoreline communities.

Streambank and shoreline communities develop along streams and about ponds and lakes, and in them occurs a typical mammalian fauna. Beaver (*Castor canadensis*) feed on willows, alder, and aspen near the water's edge. Marshy grasslands are inhabited by shrews (*Sorex cinereus, S. monticolus*), the muskrat (*Ondatra zibethicus*), and the western jumping mouse (*Zapus princeps*). Water shrews (*Sorex palustris*) occur about streamside rocks and fallen

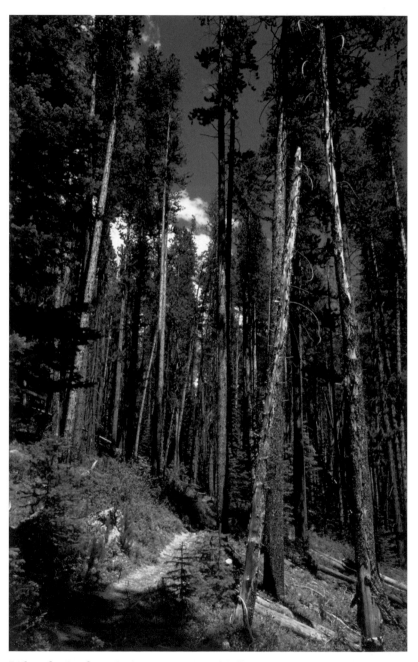

Lodgepole pine forest *(Rocky Mountain National Park)*

Montane meadow *(Rocky Mountain National Park)*

timber. Such communities are found through much of the park, from can-yon-bound streams of lower elevations, to quiet ponds of the high forests, to snow-fed rivulets above timberline.

Alpine meadows and fellfield occupy much of the area above timberline. Within this community-type, which corresponds to the alpine zone, is a complex array of habitats. Alpine meadows consist of mats of low grasses, sedges, and forbs overlying a thin soil. On well-watered sites, thickets of dwarf willows prevail. Fellfield is a common term derived from the German word for rock (*Fels*) and refers to boulder fields, stabilized talus slopes, and any other very rocky terrain. Thanks to the presence of Trail Ridge Road, alpine habitats in the park are more accessible to the casual visitor in Rocky Mountain National Park than almost anywhere else in the Southern Rockies. The more serious student of the alpine zone may follow such communities virtually uninterrupted along the Continental Divide over the entire length of the park.

No mammalian species is restricted to the alpine zone, although the pika (*Ochotona princeps*) may find optimal conditions there, and yellow-bellied marmots (*Marmota flaviventris*) and northern pocket gophers (*Thomomys talpoides*) are abundant. The community provides summer range for large grazers, especially elk.

"Saxicoline" means "rock-inhabiting" and *saxicoline brush* refers to a community developed on broken, rocky terrain. Bitterbrush (*Purshia tridentata*) is perhaps the most important shrub in this community in Rocky Mountain

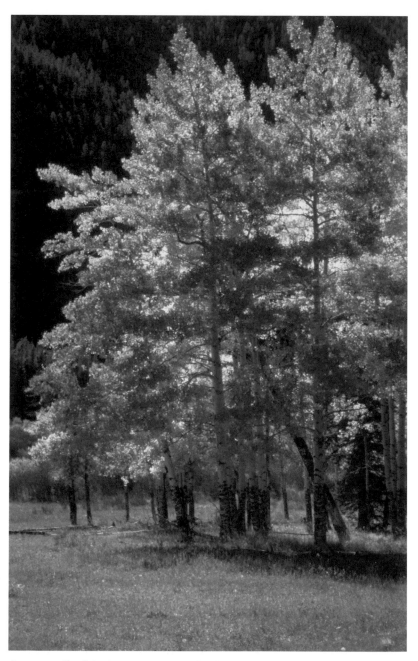

Aspen woodland (Rocky Mountain National Park)

Streamside habitat *(Rocky Mountain National Park)*

National Park; to the east and north, mountain mahogany (*Cercocarpus montanus*) is important. A widespread community-type in Colorado, saxicoline brush is best developed in the park at lower elevations on the Eastern Slope, in particular on the western edge of Estes Park. It is also prevalent in the canyons leading to the park from the east and in the lower, rougher, more exposed parts of the foothills. Mammals typical of saxicoline brush include the dwarf shrew (*Sorex nanus*), western small-footed myotis (*Myotis ciliolabrum*), Colorado chipmunk (*Neotamias quadrivittatus*), rock squirrel (*Spermophilus variegatus*), northern rock mouse (*Peromyscus nasutus*), Mexican woodrat (*Neotoma mexicana*), western spotted skunk (*Spilogale gracilis*), and gray fox (*Urocyon cinereoargenteus*).

Sagebrush communities are characterized by shrubs of the genus *Artemisia*. Sagebrush occurs as small stands at widely scattered localities in the park. Extensive sagebrush stands occur in Arapaho National Recreation Area. Such communities appear as broad expanses of grayish green shrubs, often with a profusion of herbs beneath. Sagebrush communities are generally continuous from our area westward into Middle Park and other open country in the upper Colorado drainage. Mammals that typify the sagebrush community include the Wyoming ground squirrel (*Spermophilus elegans*) and the pronghorn (*Antilocarpa americana*). Farther west, the sagebrush vole (*Lemmiscus curtatus*) and white-tailed prairie dog (*Cynomys leucurus*) are important and conspicuous.

Willows in bloom *(Rocky Mountain National Park)*

    Faunal Relationships of Rocky Mountain National Park—Zoogeography is the study of the distribution of animals. Among other things, zoogeographic studies may provide clues to the character of ecosystems of the past. Often, species are not continuously distributed but occur as a patchwork or mosaic. Areas of habitat suitable for a given kind of animal may be separated from each other by tracts of unsuitable country.

    In general terms, the closest faunal relationships of the mammals of Rocky Mountain National Park are to the north. A broad band of coniferous forest—sometimes called by its Russian name, "taiga"—stretches across North America and Asia. The mammals of the taiga often are circumboreal (also termed holarctic); that is, they occur in both the New and Old Worlds. The grizzly bear, gray wolf, lynx, wolverine, short-tailed weasel, and elk all are circumboreal species. In other cases, closely related species occupy similar niches in the taiga of Eurasia and North America. For example, there are species of red-backed voles in both Eurasia and North America. Southward, taiga is increasingly restricted to areas of high elevation. Temperature decreases with increasing elevation so that, in many respects, habitats of high elevation are comparable to those of high latitudes. At medium elevations in the Colorado Rockies, a zone of taiga occurs. Above timberline, habitats are somewhat comparable to those of the Arctic tundra. The farther south one proceeds, the higher one must go to reach conditions suitable for the development of taiga or tundra. In Colorado the taiga is more or less con-

Sagebrush (Rocky Mountain National Park)

tinuous along the main ranges of the Rockies. Continuity is interrupted for only short distances at major passes or breaks in the mountain chain. Alpine tundra, however, occurs only on high mountains. Patches of tundra are isolated from one another, forming a chain of "islands." Farther south, taiga also becomes discontinuous. With ongoing climatic warming, this situation may be expected to intensify. As life zones creep upslope, what are now "peninsulas" of habitat will become islands, and eventually some of those islands will become too small to support viable populations.

Although the taiga in Colorado is essentially continuous, it is separated from similar habitats in areas adjacent to the north (such as northern Utah and northwestern Wyoming) by appreciable ecological barriers. How did mountain mammals get to the forested "island" of the Colorado Rockies?

The Cenozoic era—the past 65 million years of geological time—has been marked by major changes in world climate. Throughout most of the era there has been a gradual cooling trend over the Earth. The most recent episode in this history is called the Quaternary period. The Quaternary period comprises approximately the past 1.6 million years and includes the Pleistocene epoch, or Ice Age, and Recent or Holocene times. The Pleistocene was characterized by the recurrence of glacial advances both at middle and

Treeline (Rocky Mountain National Park)

high latitudes and at high elevations. Glacial intervals were separated by inter-glacial periods in which deglaciation was complete. For all we know, "recent" might simply turn out to be an interglacial interval.

The continental ice sheets that scoured much of Canada and the northern United States did not reach Colorado. There were, however, recurrent episodes of alpine glaciation. Glaciation and accompanying erosion carved the spectacular alpine scenery of Rocky Mountain National Park. Indeed, the physical landscape as we know it throughout much of North America is mostly a product of the Pleistocene epoch.

During the Pleistocene, valley glaciers occurred as low as about 2,100 m (7,000 feet) in Colorado. At high elevations, some valley glaciers sometimes coalesced to form cap ice. The effects of glaciation on the distribution of biotic communities were immense. In particular, cooling allowed an increase in effective precipitation. With moister conditions, forest communities typical of the mountains today could have occurred at lower elevations. The biotic zonation so readily observed in mountainous areas apparently was depressed, perhaps by as much as 1,000 to 1,200 m (3,000 to 4,000 feet). With a depression of biotic zones, forest was continuous (at least intermittently) across areas that are not forested today. It was during glacial intervals that forest-adapted mammals made their way to Colorado, from the Middle Rocky Mountains of northern Utah and western Wyoming.

Fellfield (Rocky Mountain National Park)

Tundra above treeline in Forest Canyon (Rocky Mountain National Park)

Selected References—Armstrong (1972); Cary (1911); Elias (2002); Fitzgerald et al. (1994); Kurtén (1971); Kurtén and Anderson (1980); Martin (2005); Mutel and Emerick (1992); Willard and Foster (1990); Zwinger and Willard (1972).

Bighorn rams *(Gene Putney)*

4

HOW TO OBSERVE MAMMALS

Wild mammals can be difficult to observe. Perhaps that is why we hear more about bird watchers than we do about "mammal watchers." Most mammals could be described as "shy" or "retiring." Of course those are human terms describing human traits. Nonhuman animals have nonhuman adaptations, but their habits earn them anthropomorphic descriptions. Mammals are seldom "shy" when facing their environments on their own terms. They are simply hungry or they are not. Under usual conditions, many species are quite "curious," and the successful mammal watcher uses this fact to advantage.

A majority of mammals are active at night (nocturnal) or during the twilight hours (crepuscular). The squirrels, which are active by day (diurnal), are the obvious exceptions to this rule in northern latitudes. Squirrels are

Beaver lodge *(Rocky Mountain National Park)*

interesting and entertaining subjects, a good group on which aspiring mammal watchers can sharpen their skills.

Select a comfortable spot at the edge of a meadow. If you remain quiet, the squirrels in the neighborhood soon will resume their usual activity. Wyoming ground squirrels scurry about in open, grassy areas. From beneath a boulder or fallen log, marmots venture forth to feed on leaves or sun themselves on warm rocks. Least chipmunks dart about, busily seeking seeds or insects to eat. In the forest, chickarees bark their excited territorial alarm and then accept your presence and go about their daily round of activities. With practice, you will come to recognize individuals by distinctive scars, molt patterns, or behavioral peculiarities. Soon the complexities of social life will begin to be familiar. The most useful tool for the mammal watcher is patience. For observing marmots and tree squirrels, field glasses may be useful, but chipmunks move too rapidly to follow easily with binoculars.

Early morning and evening are the best times to observe the mammals of Rocky Mountain National Park. A beaver pond may appear lifeless during the day, save for the ripple of an occasional trout or the whispering sound of a garter snake moving through a shoreline marsh. But return to the pond at dusk. Wear a warm jacket and insect repellent so that you can sit quietly and watch the pond. Soon beaver will begin to ply the pond, moving silently from lodge to shore to dam, feeding, repairing the dam, or storing winter food. Muskrats are also more active at dusk, usually using beaver ponds in the mountains.

Stay alert for mule deer and elk coming to the pond to drink. At lower elevations you may see raccoons beginning their nocturnal rounds. Overhead, bats flutter about, taking their evening's toll of insects. The bats of the park can often be distinguished by their typical patterns in flight and characteristic times of emergence. A musty smell in the willows near the water's edge may hint of a wet porcupine.

The sign of mammals—tracks, droppings (scat), nests, trails—provides unmistakable evidence of a species' occurrence even though the animal itself may never be seen. The observant naturalist can piece together an image of mammalian activity in a community without ever seeing the animals themselves.

Nearly everyone recognizes an aspen or willow gnawed by a beaver. Claw marks on tree trunks are evidence of the black bear. Bark removed from high on the trunk of a ponderosa pine tells of porcupines in the neighborhood. Chickarees make their presence known by leaving piles of unopened spruce, fir, or lodgepole pine cones neatly cut from the branches and by accumulating middens of cone scales and other debris. Abert's squirrels clip and drop bundles of needles from ponderosa pines. In moist meadows, look for tunnels in the grass, the runways of the montane vole. Often, short, neatly cut pieces of grass litter the trails of these mice. Old runways may be used by other small mammals, especially deer mice and shrews. Grass stems from which the seeds have been stripped points to the activity of jumping mice. Look for small trees and shrubs from which the tender young branches have been removed. This may be the work of deer or may point to browsing by rabbits. At higher elevations, grasses and forbs are harvested by pikas and piled in unmistakable "haystacks" to serve as winter food.

Scat, or droppings, is another useful mammalian sign. The round fecal pellets of rabbits are familiar to most people as are the larger, elliptical droppings of deer. The minute scat of shrews frequently is deposited on conspicuous (from the shrew's point of view) objects in the environment, such as the tops of fallen leaves or a negligent visitor's paper plate. Coyote droppings are abundant along trails in many habitats and frequently contain feathers, fur, and bits of broken bone.

Owls regurgitate pellets of fur, bone, and other indigestible materials. At first, these may be confused with the scat of a mammal, but owl pellets are far looser in their construction and they often contain unbroken bones, including intact skulls. Owl pellets are an excellent source of evidence of the small mammals of an area. Frequently, owls are "the better mousetrap," providing

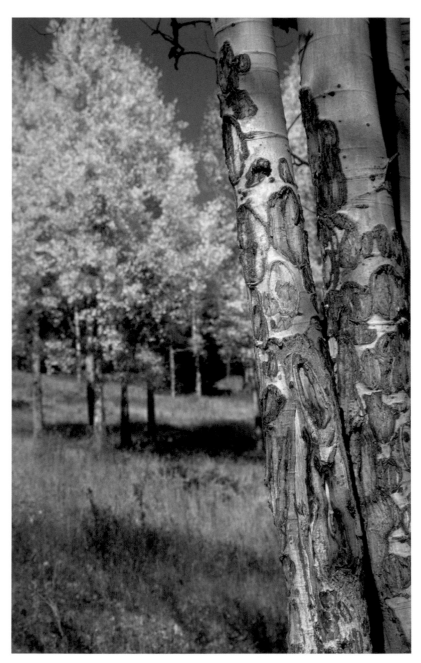

Aspen scraped by wapiti, or elk (Rocky Mountain National Park)

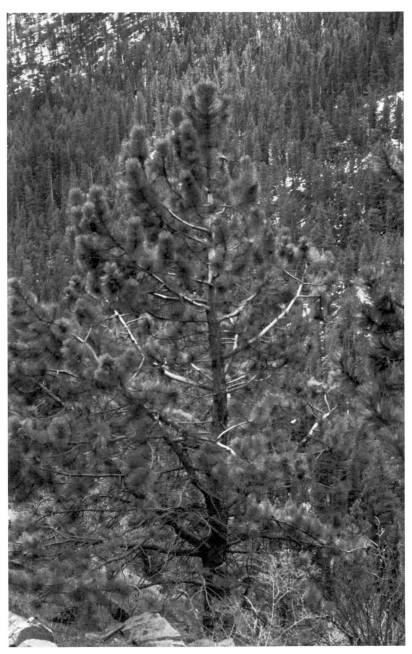

Ponderosa pine branches stripped by porcupine (Rocky Mountain National Park)

Elk droppings (Rocky Mountain National Park)

evidence of the occurrence of secretive small mammals that would not be obvious otherwise.

Tracks are perhaps the most commonly observed sign of mammals. With practice, one can read detailed stories of the intricacies of mammalian activities and interactions simply by careful observation of tracks. You may see tracks of a coyote, for example, superimposed upon those of a rabbit. The evidence should indicate the point at which the rabbit sensed the presence of the coyote, where instinct and experience told the rabbit to take flight, and whether the coyote captured the rabbit or turned elsewhere for dinner. Tracks of deer tell not only that deer are present but how many have passed by, which direction they went, and how fast they were going.

For most would-be mammal watchers the best place to look for tracks is in the firm mud around a pond or along a streambank. Dusty trails and rocky areas are more difficult to work and tracks are less obvious. The best place of all is in fresh, wet snow. Here, tracks of the larger, more familiar species are readily seen. In addition, however, the tracks of smaller mammals—a scurrying mouse and a bounding weasel—are preserved. The sight of myriad mammal trails on fresh snow is just one of the rewards reserved for those who venture out to observe the mountain world in winter on skis or snowshoes.

Making casts of tracks is an excellent way to "collect" mammals in the national park, where all species enjoy well-deserved protection. Plaster of Paris (available at paint and hardware stores) is the commonest and most practical material for making casts of tracks. A form or collar of sheet metal or cardboard (sections of paper milk cartons are excellent) is placed firmly in the mud around the track. A thick (but fluid) paste of plaster and water is poured into the form. Gentle stirring will remove bubbles and fill in details with plaster. In a few minutes the plaster will set sufficiently to allow the cast to be removed. In a few hours it will have cured and any attached mud or soil can be gently brushed away.

Photography is the other method of choice for "collecting" mammals in the national parks. At its best, of course, wildlife photography is a highly sophisticated art form, but that fact should not prevent the amateur from trying. The rewards are great long before any pictures are printed. The simplest camera will capture the larger mammals. For detailed photos of smaller species, a telephoto lens may be necessary. For nocturnal species, elaborate setups may be employed to trick an unsuspecting mammal into taking its own picture. Like any art, wildlife photography is learned only by doing it (preferably alongside an experienced artist), is fun because it is creative, and is to be entered upon only with due trepidation, for it may become a consuming passion.

Selected References—Halfpenny (1986); Murie (1954). The Rocky Mountain Nature Association (www.rmna.org) frequently offers excellent workshops on wildlife photography.

5

ORDER SORICOMORPHA
Shrews and Allies

The order Soricomorpha—the "shrew-shaped" mammals—occurs almost worldwide except for Australia. The order includes the shrews, among the smallest of mammals. The pygmy shrew and the dwarf shrew, both of which doubtless occur in Rocky Mountain National Park, are among the smallest of the shrews. Other well-known temperate zone soricomorphs are the moles (which do not occur in the mountains of Colorado). The Soricomorpha includes part of the former order Insectivora. Recent analyses suggest that the "insectivores" are not all close evolutionary relatives and so do not belong in a single order. All told, there are four living families in the Soricomorpha and over 400 species. All soricomorphs in the mountains of Colorado are members of the family Soricidae.

FAMILY SORICIDAE—SHREWS

Five or six kinds of shrews occur in Rocky Mountain National Park. Shrews in general are readily recognizable by their very small size and their relatively long, pointed snouts. Particular species of shrews may be difficult to identify in hand in the museum, let alone in the field. This is the most diverse family of soricomorphs, with some 375 species. Nine kinds of shrews occur in Colorado and about thirty species inhabit North America north of Mexico.

Masked Shrew
Sorex cinereus

Description—The masked shrew is of medium size, slightly smaller than the montane shrew but larger than the dwarf shrew. Adults range in total length from 90 to 105 mm; the tail is about 37 to 45 mm long. Weights typically are 3 to 5 g. The color is grayish to medium brown above and slightly paler below. The sparsely haired tail is typically unicolored to obscurely bicolored. *Field Recognition*—Medium-sized, brownish shrew. In the field, the masked shrew is hardly distinguishable from the montane shrew. For comparison of the two species, see the account of the montane shrew.

Distribution and Habitat—The masked shrew, sometimes called the "common shrew," occurs widely in continental North America, from the Arctic Slope of Alaska and Canada southward to the north-central United States, and in mountainous regions to southern Utah, central New Mexico, North Carolina, and Tennessee.

This is a common mammal in moist habitats throughout the Colorado Rockies. Typically, individuals occur in moist meadows, in bogs, about springs, and along the shores of ponds, lakes, and streams. No differences have been reported between the habitats of masked and montane shrews, although the animals occur together over wide areas in the West. It is a canon of ecology (to which no substantial exception has been demonstrated) that two species cannot occupy the same ecological niche simultaneously. Eventually, competition forces the exclusion of one or the other. Perhaps slight differences in size reduce the overlap of niches in this case. The two species may occur in a mosaic pattern, one species occurring in a given patch of habitat to the exclusion of the other. Whatever the underlying mechanism, these two shrews manage to share an apparently common habitat in our area. Of course, competitition may not occur because because their common insect prey is not a limiting resource.

Natural History—The masked shrew, like other shrews, is highly active throughout the year. It forages with rapid, darting movements for invertebrates and other prey, relying mostly on touch and smell to locate food.

Masked Shrew *(James F. Parnell)*

Probably the tiny eyes can sense differences between dark and light. The animals forage above ground or beneath the surface of loose litter, either in burrows of their own making or in those of other animals. The masked shrew has a voracious appetite.

Animals as small as shrews are prey for almost any meat-eating animal, although they provide a staple for none. Frogs, fish, and snakes all have been reported to eat shrews of one kind or another. Probably the most effective predators on shrews are hawks and owls. Weasels also take a toll. Other carnivores catch and kill shrews, but many (including house cats) will not eat them. Presumably they are unpalatable because of the strong scent from the flank glands and other secretions of the skin.

Female masked shrews are polyestrous, bearing and rearing several litters of four to ten young through the warmer months of spring and summer. Some females apparently breed late their first summer, although this has not been observed in Colorado. Young are born blind and helpless, are well-furred in about ten days, and leave the nest, completely self-sufficient, at three to four weeks of age. They overwinter as young adults, and breed the following summer. Few individuals survive a second winter.

Selected References—Brown (1967a); Forsyth (1976); Spencer and Pettus (1966); Whitaker (2004).

Pygmy Shrew
Sorex hoyi

Description—The pygmy shrew vies with the dwarf shrew for the distinction of being the smallest mammal in the Southern Rocky Mountains. The total length of the pygmy shrew (75 to 85 mm) is less than that of the dwarf shrew, but the tail (26 to 29 mm) is relatively much shorter, so the body of the pygmy shrew is somewhat longer than that of the dwarf shrew. Adult pygmy shrews in reproductive condition weigh less than 4 g (more than a U.S. penny, but less than a nickel). The animals generally are dark brown in color, darker than the other brownish shrews in the region. *Field Recognition*—Small size with relatively short tail; dark brown color.

Distinguishing species of shrews in the museum is tricky enough, even for an experienced mammalogist with a taxonomic key and a microscope at hand; identification in the field may be impossible. If circumstances permit close examination, however, the teeth of each species clearly are distinctive. In the case of the pygmy shrew, the third and fifth unicuspid teeth are small, barely (if at all) visible when viewed from the side.

Distribution and Habitat—The pygmy shrew occurs in the taiga of Alaska, Canada, and the north-central and northeastern United States. In the East, the animals follow the Appalachian Mountains southward to North Carolina. In the West, the species occurs—apparently as disjunct, isolated, relict populations—in the Rocky Mountains as far south as central Colorado. To date there are no records of the pygmy shrew in Rocky Mountain National Park, but the species is to be expected there in suitable habitat; records are available from near Cameron Pass, just north of the park, and from Rabbit Ears Pass, west of the park in Grand County.

The animals seem to favor upland forests over boggy situations, perhaps moving from wetter areas to drier ones seasonally. With regard to moisture requirements, the species seems to be intermediate between the masked and montane shrews (which apparently require a moist habitat) and the dwarf shrew (which may occupy dry, brushy areas well away from water). In view of its seemingly adaptive nature and relatively broad tolerances, it seems peculiar that the pygmy shrew has so narrow a geographic range in our area. Perhaps this anomaly will one day be found to be an artifact of our meager knowledge of our surroundings, and no fault of the shrew's.

Natural History—Like most of its relatives, the pygmy shrew is a highly active mammal, foraging day and night, year-around. The diet is composed mostly of insects but includes virtually anything that moves and is small enough to apprehend and swallow. Captives have been reported to consume quantities of food in excess of twice their own weight each day. Such tremendous amounts of food are necessary because of their high rate of metabolism and the high ratio of heat-radiating surface to heat-producing volume. The movements of this and other shrews are rapid and erratic. The appearance of nervousness is heightened by a constant twitching of the snout, with its ample touch-sensitive whiskers. Smell and touch are probably the keenest senses, but hearing may also be acute. Foraging activities may be interrupted suddenly by brief periods of deep sleep.

A thorough study of the biology of *Sorex hoyi* has yet to be made, and there is disagreement as to whether females produce one or several litters of young. The animals breed during the warmer months. A typical litter comprises five or six young, with a maximum of seven reported.

Selected References—Long (1974); Spencer and Pettus (1966). The pygmy shrew is sometimes placed in the genus *Microsorex.*

Merriam's Shrew
Sorex merriami

Merriam's shrew has not been documented in Rocky Mountain National Park, but judging from its known ecological distribution, one would strongly suspect it to be found there eventually, especially in the vicinity of Estes Park. Nearest records of occurrence are in the foothills near Fort Collins and Boulder. The most drought-adapted of Coloradan species of *Sorex,* this species may be expected to expand its range with ongoing climatic change.

Merriam's shrew is of moderate size, much larger than the dwarf shrew and considerably smaller than the water shrew, just slightly larger than the montane shrew and the masked shrew. They are paler in color than other shrews in our area, grayish drab above grading to paler grayish on the flanks and becoming white below.

The animals occur in the western United States, from western Nebraska and the Dakotas to California, and from Washington and Montana southward to Arizona and New Mexico. In Colorado, records are scattered at moderate elevations both east and west of the Continental Divide. Preferred habitat includes sagebrush, coniferous woodland, and grasslands. The elevational range of the species in Colorado is about 1,500 to 2,850 m (5,000 to 9,500 feet).

Selected References—Armstrong and Jones (1971).

Montane Shrew
Sorex monticolus

Description—This is the largest brown-colored shrew in the park. Adults range in total length from 95 to 115 mm, and the tail ranges from 42 to 48 mm long. Weights of breeding animals range around 7 g, and nonbreeding adults are about 2 g lighter. The animals are medium to dark brown in color above, paling to drab or pale brown below; the tail is obscurely bicolored. *Field Recognition*—Medium-sized, brownish shrew. The montane shrew is easily confused in the field with the masked shrew, with which it apparently shares its habitat. The montane shrew averages somewhat darker in color than the masked shrew and is heavier-bodied, but only by examining the teeth can certain identification be made. Merriam's shrews may be as large as montane shrews, but they are consistently paler in color and occupy pronouncedly drier, upland habitats. Here again, dental characteristics (as outlined in the key to soricomorphs, Appendix I) allow certain identification.

Distribution and Habitat—The montane shrew occurs in western North America, from northern Alaska southward at increasingly high elevations to central Mexico and from Colorado to the eastern foothills of the Sierra Nevada. It was only in the 1970s that this species was demonstrated to be distinct from the wandering, or vagrant, shrew, *Sorex vagrans*; the older literature on the montane shrew in Colorado will be found under the latter name. Montane shrews occur in mountainous parts of Colorado at elevations to above 3,350 m (11,000 feet). The animals occur in suitable habitat throughout Rocky Mountain National Park. This is an animal typical of moist habitats in forested country. One may encounter the animals or their signs (tracks and minute brownish scat) in marshes, bogs, the edges of swamps, and around springs. The montane shrew also occupies moist microhabitats in the forest proper, especially the rich accumulations of humus around fallen trees or piles of debris. In Colorado, the species is known to follow riparian communities into the foothills as low as 5,300 feet. They also occur beneath dwarf willows above timberline.

Natural History—The montane shrew is a rather abundant animal over much of its range and (relative to other shrews) has been studied fairly extensively. Individuals may be active at any time, day or night, throughout the year. The shrews may move about over light snow, but when deep snows form a continuous blanket, they forage in the litter beneath the snow, protected from harsh winds and severe temperatures. During the winter, their diet consists mostly of "resting" stages of insects (larvae, eggs), worms, and spiders. Plant material is found commonly in stomach analyses, but this may be taken unintentionally, simply ingested along with animal matter. (These animals eat in a hurry.) Vertebrates are not a mainstay of the shrew's diet, but captives will eat mice and—under crowded conditions—will even attack and eat other shrews.

A voracious, meat-eating animal like a shrew needs a fairly large foraging area. The home range of individual montane shrews is only about 0.04

hectare (0.1 acre). Spacing is promoted by mutual avoidance and nest defense. Actual combat is expensive in terms of energy demand and is avoided by behavioral rituals in this and many other kinds of mammals. The social life of these animals apparently is limited to brief contacts of mother and offspring. Immatures seek contact with each other and with the mother to an age of six or seven weeks; then the juvenile behavior ceases and the young disperse.

There are distinct winter (darker) and summer (paler) pelages, with spring and fall molts. The spring molt occurs from April to June and the fall molt takes place in September and October. Molt is patterned; that is, replacement of hair is gradual and sequential over the body and does not occur erratically or all over at the same time. Molting individuals exhibit a pronounced molt line between new and old pelage.

Montane shrews are reproductively active in spring and summer, but whether individual females are polyestrous is not known. In Colorado, most breeding appears to be in the period from June through mid-August. Males become sexually active in February and March.

The gestation period is about twenty days. The young are born blind and naked. A female carries two to nine (the average is 6.4 in Montana) embryos, and the size of litters doubtless is somewhat smaller, perhaps about five. The young develop rapidly, sheltered in a ball-shaped nest of grass and debris. Females apparently do not breed until their second summer. Very few individuals survive a second winter; fifteen months marks old age for a shrew. Occasionally one finds an animal that obviously is very old—the teeth are worn to the gums and the pelage is ragged and patchy. Such aged animals most often are males. Flank glands, which seem to function in sexual attraction, are well-developed in males, more so during the breeding season. The glands are less conspicuous in females and immature animals.

Selected References—Brown (1967a); Hennings and Hoffmann (1977); M. Smith and Belk (1996); Spencer and Pettus (1966; as *Sorex vagrans*).

Dwarf Shrew
Sorex nanus

Description—This is the smallest of mammals in Rocky Mountain National Park and one of the smallest anywhere in the world. The pygmy shrew may be shorter overall, but it has a longer body than does the dwarf shrew. These two species contend only with the lesser shrew (*Sorex minutus*) of Europe for the distinction of being the smallest mammal known. Adult dwarf shrews range in total length from 90 to 100 mm, and the tail is 39 to 42 mm long. Weights vary from 2.5 to 3.5 g, about the weight of a copper penny. The dorsal color is medium brown, paling slightly beneath. The relatively long tail is bicolored. The teeth are arranged as in the montane shrew—the third unicuspid is markedly smaller than the fourth—but the dentition is much less robust. Also, the dwarf shrew inhabits drier habitats than does any other local shrew except Merriam's shrew, a relatively large, pale-colored species. *Field Recognition*—Tiny size and relatively long tail.

Distribution and Habitat—The dwarf shrew occurs in the western United States—in and near the Central and Southern Rocky Mountains—from Montana southward to New Mexico and Arizona and eastward to western South Dakota. In Colorado, the species is known from the mountains and foothills of central and southwestern parts of the state and it may be expected in suitable habitat throughout Rocky Mountain National Park. The species is known from a variety of ecological situations and apparently has a wider range of tolerance than do several of its larger relatives. In Colorado and southern Wyoming, the animals are known to inhabit forests (both unbroken and partially cleared); open woodland; rocky, shrubby foothills slopes; and alpine and subalpine rockslides. The elevational range of specimens in our area is from 1,675 to 3,050 m (5,500 to 10,000 feet).

Natural History—The dwarf shrew has the dubious distinction of being the least known of our mammals—not only locally, but over its range. No modern study of the species has been made; the meager available data are derived from incidental notes of collectors. A study conducted in Larimer County, Colorado, just north of Rocky Mountain National Park, indicated that numbers of dwarf shrews peaked in mid-August, suggesting that this is the time that the young begin to forage about on their own, adding to the trappable population. There is some evidence that females are polyestrous and have postpartum estrus. Breeding takes place during the warmer months, with the first litter produced about the end of July and second litters born a month later. Published embryo counts range from six to eight.

The type locality of *Sorex nanus* is Estes Park. (In taxonomy, the type locality is the place where the holotype is collected. The holotype is the particular museum specimen designated by the author of a new scientific name of a species or subspecies as the official name-bearer.)

Selected References—Armstrong et al. (1973); Brown (1967a); Hoffmann and Owen (1980); Muths (1999); Spencer and Pettus (1966).

American Water Shrew
Sorex palustris

Description—The water shrew is the largest and most strikingly colored shrew in Rocky Mountain National Park, and the shrew most frequently seen by visitors. Adults range in total length from about 150 to 170 mm. The tail is

American Water Shrew *(R. B. Forbes/ASM Mammal Images Library)*

approximately the same length as the head and body. Adults weigh from 12 to 18 g. The upper parts are a rich, velvety, grayish black and the belly is silvery gray to white. The tail has a distinct black stripe above and is grayish white below. The relatively large hind feet (about 20 mm long) are fringed with stiff hairs. *Field Recognition*—Pond margins or streamside habitat; relatively large size for shrew; dark color; hind foot fringed with stiff hairs.

Distribution and Habitat—The water shrew occurs in the coniferous forests of North America, from southern Alaska and British Columbia eastward to Labrador and Nova Scotia. The species ranges southward in forested mountains to central California, Arizona, and New Mexico in the West and to Tennessee in the East. In Colorado and adjacent states, the water shrew is confined to the mountains, where it occurs along streambanks, around the margins of lakes and ponds, and in marshes. They frequently are seen around exposed roots of streamside trees or shrubs or under cover of rocks or overhanging banks.

Natural History—Like other kinds of shrews, water shrews are voracious. Captives reportedly consume a quantity of food equal to their own weight each day. In the wild, water shrews feed mostly on insects, both aquatic and terrestrial. In addition, some small fish are captured, and carrion is eaten when available. The vegetable matter seen in stomachs of some specimens may be taken inadvertently along with more typical animal food. Water shrews are active at any time of the day or night, foraging excitedly for short periods and suddenly dropping off to sleep. Vision is poorly developed, but senses of touch, hearing, and smell apparently are acute.

Water shrews are excellent swimmers. Skimming across the water on fringed feet, they sometimes appear to run on the surface and, in fact, do so for short distances. These animals also swim beneath the water or actually scramble along the bottom, clinging to rocks. The velvety fur holds bubbles of air and thus resists wetting. This gives shrews swimming underwater a striking, silvery appearance. Activity continues throughout the year. Water levels of mountain streams frequently fall in winter, and the water shrew is able to forage along streambanks beneath a cover of ice, yet above the winter waterline.

The water shrew undergoes two molts annually. The spring molt begins in late winter or early spring and is complete by June. The autumnal molt takes place in late July or August. In common with many small mammals, water shrews are short-lived. In natural populations, few individuals survive their second winter.

Male water shrews become sexually active in about January and breeding continues until August. As in other species of *Sorex,* breeding males have glands on the sides, midway between the front and hind legs. The hairs over the glands are oily and matted. Presumably, the flank glands produce a substance that attracts females. Ovulation is induced by copulation. The gestation period probably is between two and three weeks. Litter size varies from four to eight, the usual number being six. Pregnancy may recur while a female is nursing a litter, but such pregnancies seldom reach term. Nonetheless, several litters may be reared successfully over the relatively long breeding season. Growth of the young is rapid; females born early in the season sometimes breed late in the same season, although most do not breed until the following spring.

Selected References—Beneski and Stinson (1987); Conaway (1952).

6

ORDER CHIROPTERA
Bats

Bats are the only mammals capable of true flight. "Flying" squirrels and the "flying lemurs" of Southeast Asia are highly efficient gliders, but they cannot actually fly (and furthermore, flying lemurs are not even lemurs!) As fliers, bats are members of an elite group: only four groups of animals have successfully evolved aerial niches. Many kinds of insects can fly, of course, and once there were flying reptiles (including the well-known pterosaurs). Birds evolved flight independently of other flying reptiles. And bats represent the fourth independent line of flying animals, having evolved from shrew-like mammals. Like pterosaurs—and unlike the birds—bats have wings formed by a membrane stretched between greatly elongated finger bones. The principal flight surface of a bird, by contrast, is formed by feathers attached to the arm.

The earliest fossils of bats have been collected from shales of Eocene age (some 50 million years old) in southwestern Wyoming. The earliest known bats were already perfectly good fliers and in many respects resemble groups now living. Intermediate stages between ground-dwelling insectivores and flying bats are unknown. There are about 1,100 living species of bats arrayed in 18 families, making this the second most diverse order of mammals.

For a number of reasons, bats have fascinated humans down through the ages. In the early days, we humans shared our rock shelter domiciles with bats. Bat bugs and bed bugs (family Cimicidae—order Hemiptera) are barely distinguishable, and this common ectoparasite of bats and people is probably traceable to a former common cave dwelling. Early in human cultural evolution, bats became the subject of myth and superstition. Misinformation about bats continues to the present day, even among otherwise enlightened peoples. Bats are mostly secretive and nocturnal. They navigate with unerring accuracy in tight, dark places. To us this ability is remarkable, although today we know that bats navigate by echolocation—a natural "sonar"; to our ancestors it must have seemed mysterious and perhaps frightening.

Recently there has been a great deal of scientific research on bats. Much has been learned about echolocation and the role of bats as vectors of disease. The physics and physiology of flight have been studied in a number of species. Despite this new information, much remains to be learned. For example, many kinds of bats are migratory. A particular species may be abundant in a locality in summer but absent in winter. And no one knows where they have gone. In other cases, maternity colonies are well-studied, but the whereabouts of males remains a mystery. These and other basic questions about the biology of bats remain unanswered. Table 3 summarizes some natural history information on local bats.

Many kinds of bats form large colonies throughout the year, during the breeding season, or during hibernation. Sometimes these aggregations are in places readily accessible to people—occupied or abandoned buildings, mines, and caves. In such places, roosting bats are often molested wantonly. Such molestation is to be strongly discouraged. First, it is unlawful. Moreover, as active and voracious predators on insects, bats are firm allies of humans. The reproductive potential of most kinds of bats is low. Females of most species produce just one young per year. Once decimated, colonies may takes years to reestablish, if they ever recover. If bats are roosting in large numbers in an occupied building, they may become a nuisance, of course. Under these circumstances one would be wise to notify the biology department of a nearby college or university. Inquiry will eventually lead to a specialist on bats who can suggest a solution to a specific problem that will spare the bat colony. In the long run, extermination by a commercial pest control service will probably

Table 3. Comparative summary of natural history characteristics of bats of Rocky Mountain National Park and vicinity.

Species	Day Roost	Night Roost	Foraging Habitat	Foraging Style	Foraging Height
Myotis ciliolabrum—Western small-footed myotis	buildings, mines, crevices	buildings, mines, crevices	among boulders, shrubs	fluttering, maneuver-able pursuit	1–2 m
Myotis evotis—Long-eared myotis	under bark, mines, structures		near trees over water	gleaner	
Myotis lucifugus—Little brown bat	attics, mines	tree hollows, buildings	over water	erratic pursuit on repeated circuit	3–6 m
Myotis thysanodes—Fringed myotis	cave, mines, buildings	cave, mines, buildings	woodlands	gleaner	
Myotis volans—Long-legged myotis	rock fissures, under bark, buildings	caves, mines	over ponds, streams	relaxed foraging flight	3–4 m
Lasionycteris noctivagans—Silver-haired bat	mostly trees, also open caves	open buildings	over clearings	repeated circuit	
Eptesicus fuscus—Big brown bat	buildings, caves, crevices	buildings	open areas	strong, straight	6–10 m
Lasiurus cinereus—Hoary bat	trees	trees	openings in forest	fast, direct	
Corynorhinus townsendii—Townsend's big-eared bat	mines, caves, structures		near vegetation	gleaner	

continued on next page

Table 3—continued

Species	Foraging Time	Food	General Habitat	Hibernal Activity
Myotis ciliolabrum—Western small-footed myotis	early, still light	flying insects	shrubs, woodland	locally in mines, tunnels, caves
Myotis evotis—Long-eared myotis	after dark	moths, flies, spiders, beetles	coniferous woodland	unknown
Myotis lucifugus—Little brown bat	dusk	aquatic insects, moths, flies	riparian woodland	locally migratory to mines, caves?
Myotis thysanodes—Fringed myotis	full dark	wide variety of insects	ponderosa pine woodland	locally migratory to caves, buildings
Myotis volans—Long-legged myotis	early, still light	moths	woodland	locally migratory to caves, mines?
Lasionycteris noctivagans—Silver-haired bat	late, full dark	moths, flies	forest	migratory, winter range unknown
Eptesicus fuscus—Big brown bat	dusk	insects, especially flying beetles	riparian woodland, urban	sedentary or local migrant; caves, mines, tunnels, buildings
Lasiurus cinereus—Hoary bat	late, full dark	moths, beetles, grass-hoppers, small bats	forest, woodland	migratory, winter range unknown
Plecotus townsendii—Townsend's big-eared bat	late, full dark	moths, beetles, flies	broken, rocky country	sedentary, hibernates locally in mines, tunnels

be more harmful than beneficial. Locally, the Colorado Bat Society is an excellent source of information, as is the Colorado Division of Wildlife. Adams's (2003) *Bats of the Rocky Mountain West* is strongly recommended.

Selected References—Adams (2003); Allen (1939); Armstrong et al. (1995); Barbour and Davis (1969); Gannon (2003); J. Hill and Smith (1984); Humphrey (1982); Kunz (1982b); Ross (1967).

FAMILY VESPERTILIONIDAE—VESPER BATS

Probably eight species of vespertilionid bats occur in Rocky Mountain National Park, and an additional eight or more species occur elsewhere in Colorado. In the continental United States, the family is represented by about thirty species. This is the only family of bats with representatives in the park, and—with over 300 species in over 30 genera—vespertilionids make up the bulk of the bat fauna throughout the North Temperate Zone, both in North America and Eurasia.

Western Small-footed Myotis
Myotis ciliolabrum

Description—The small-footed myotis is the smallest bat in the park. Total length ranges from 76 to 88 mm, and the tail from 35 to 39 mm. The forearm ranges in length from about 31 to 34 mm. The hindfoot (7 to 8 mm long) is noticeably smaller than that of other local bats. This is the palest of the brown bats in our area. Although the color is variable, the dorsal hairs are predominantly pale to medium brown, the venter tan to nearly white. The ears are black and the wings and membranes are dark brown, contrasting strongly with the pale fur. The tips of the dorsal hairs are burnished, lending the pelage a metallic sheen. *Field Recognition*—Small size; low, fluttering flight pattern.

Distribution and Habitat—The small-footed myotis is fairly common in western North America, ranging from southern Canada to northern Mexico. These bats apparently occur statewide in Colorado in suitable situations at lower to moderate elevations. No specimens of the small-footed myotis are available from the park, but the species doubtless occurs in rocky areas at lower elevations and probably also west of the Continental Divide in Arapaho National Recreation Area. Rocky, broken country provides habitat for the small-footed myotis. Locally, the bats are commonest in the foothills, but they occur in the mountains to about 2,450 m (8,000 feet). To the east of the Rockies, the small-footed myotis occurs locally near rocky breaks in the otherwise featureless terrain of the Great Plains. Pawnee Buttes in northeastern

Western Small-footed Myotis *(J. Scott Altenbach)*

Colorado is one such locality. This bat roosts in and around buildings and in caves, mines, and fissures—in short, in just about any sheltered place.

Natural History—Despite its diminutive size, the small-footed myotis is the hardiest species of *Myotis* in our area and apparently the only one that overwinters here. In late fall, after most bats have left the area, the animals enter hibernation, hanging singly in caves, mines, and tunnels. Often such shelters are shared with Townsend's big-eared bat (*Corynorhinus townsendii*) and the big brown bat (*Eptesicus fuscus*). The latter species are more than twice the size of the western small-footed myotis. How tiny *Myotis ciliolabrum*—with its small heat-producing volume and relatively great radiative surface—survives the hostile, cold, and dry conditions of its hibernacula is not known.

These bats forage, generally near or over water, in a slow, fluttering movement. Slow flight is atypical of bats of such small size. No detailed study of food habits of the small-footed myotis has been made, although, as other vespertilionids, they are insectivorous.

Reproductive data for the western small-footed myotis are few. Small nursery colonies (to about two dozen individuals) are formed. Single births are the rule, and the gestation period is about two months. In north-central Colorado, the young are born in July

Selected References—Adams (2003); Holloway and Barclay (2001); Turner (1974); Tuttle and Heaney (1974). In some older literature, this species was called *Myotis subulatus* and, more recently, *Myotis leibii*.

Long-eared Myotis
Myotis evotis

Description—This species has the longest ears (about 25 mm long) of any North American myotis. The ears, wings, and interfemoral membrane are black, contrasting sharply with the medium brown fur of the dorsum. The underparts are tan. Total length ranges from 88 to 95 mm, length of tail from 42 to 46 mm, and the forearm from 37 to 40 mm. Adults weigh about 5 to 7 g.

Field Recognition—Medium brown color with long, black ears.

Distribution and Habitat—The long-eared myotis is a bat of western North America, ranging from British Columbia southward to Arizona, New Mexico, and Baja California. In Colorado, the species occurs in wooded areas in the western three-fifths of the state and at moderate elevations throughout Rocky Mountain National Park on either side of the Continental Divide. They may roost by day in buildings or tree hollows, and caves and tunnels are used as night roosts. They forage in woodlands, frequently over ponds.

Natural History—Little has been recorded about the habits of this pretty bat, despite the fact that the animals are widespread and not uncommon in the West. They emerge late in the evening to feed, after full darkness. In such areas as Hollowell Park and Moraine Park, the species forages in the company of the hoary bat, the silver-haired bat, and the big brown bat—all of which are larger animals. The little brown bat and the long-legged myotis may also share such a communal feeding ground.

There is a single annual molt in mid-summer (July–August). As is usual among mammals with a cyclic molting schedule, males molt before females that have borne young.

No detailed study has ever been made of reproduction in this species. Small maternity colonies apparently form in buildings. A single young is born, probably in early July. The gestation period is undocumented but probably is seven to eight weeks.

Selected References—Adams (2003); Black (1974); Husar (1976); Manning and Jones (1989).

Little Brown Bat
Myotis lucifugus

Description—*Myotis lucifugus* is of medium size for the genus. Total length of females is about 90 to 100 mm, and the length of the tail is 37 to 44 mm. The forearm is 37 to 42 mm in length. The color is variable, from medium to dark brown above and paler below. Hairs of the upper parts are usually glossy or even metallic in appearance. The dark brown ears are relatively short (14 to 16 mm) and have rounded tips; the rather blunt tragus is less than half the length of the ear. (In short, the little brown bat is rather nondescript; perhaps it is best identified by a process of eliminating those more distinctive species it is not.) *Field Recognition*—Dark brown, metallic fur; erratic flight for medium-sized bat.

Distribution and Habitat—The little brown bat occupies a wide range in North America, from central Alaska eastward across Canada to Newfoundland, southward in the West to Chihuahua and in the East to Georgia. Over parts of its range, this is the commonest bat. In Colorado, the species is common in forested areas and woodlands at moderate elevations in and near the mountains and is known from elevations to 3,350 m (11,000 feet). The little brown bat probably ranges throughout the park and adjacent areas in suitable habitat. Our population is migratory, but the winter range is unknown. Nursery colonies of little brown bats roost in buildings, especially warm attics. Single males will roost in almost any sheltered place, including crevices in buildings and holes in trees. They generally forage over water, streetlights, or high yard lights in resort communities such as Estes Park, Allenspark, Glen Haven, and Grand Lake.

Natural History—*Myotis lucifugus* is a common bat (perhaps the reason for the rather unimaginative vernacular name). Because of its abundance around major population centers (hence, around major universities), the biology of this species is as well-known as that of any bat in the world. Indeed, many of the pioneering studies of echolocation were conducted on the little brown bat.

As with other species of *Myotis,* the little brown bat feeds mostly on flying insects. Prey in the range of 3 to 10 mm is most common, and aquatic insects are a frequent staple, especially when insects congregate in mating

Little Brown Bat *(J. Scott Altenbach)*

swarms. The animals begin to forage at about dark and continue to feed intermittently until dawn. While feeding, the bats remain 3 to 6 m above the ground, and an individual usually follows a similar zigzag path through the feeding area night after night.

The animals locate their prey by sonar, then knock the insect off balance with a wingtip, and then scoop the insect with the wing into a "basket" formed by curling forward the tail and uropatagium (or interfemoral membrane—the membrane extending between the hind limbs and including the tail). The insect thus netted is then taken into the mouth. This remarkable acrobatic movement occurs in about one-tenth of a second, a human "eyeblink."

The little brown bat mates in the fall on the winter range. Sperm are stored through the hibernation period in the uterus of the female. Actual fertilization of the egg cell occurs upon emergence from hibernation in the spring. Returning to the summer range, pregnant females establish nursery colonies that may include several hundred individuals (although in Colorado, colonies of a few dozen are more common). After a gestation period that varies with environmental temperature from 50 to 60 days, the naked, blind young are born in late June or early July. A single young is the rule. To give birth, the female hangs with the head up (upside down for a roosting bat). The uropatagium is extended to form a basket to catch the young; parturition occurs in the space of a half hour. The newborn bats weigh 1.5 to 2.0 g, nearly one-fourth the weight of the mother. When disturbed, the female will fly with the newborn young clinging to the nipple. The young learn to fly and forage beginning at about three weeks of age. These bats are long-lived for so small an animal. Ages in excess of thirty years have been reported (and the maximum known age for a bat is forty-one); reports of ages over ten years are common. However, given mortality from predation, wanton molestation, and the stress of hibernation, average longevity is probably between one and three years.

Selected References—Adams (1997, 2003); Fenton and Barclay (1980); Storz and Williams (1996).

Fringed Myotis
Myotis thysanodes

The fringed myotis has not been reported from Rocky Mountain National Park. It is a species found in western North America, from British Columbia to Chiapas, Mexico. The local distribution of the animals along the eastern margin of their range in Colorado, Wyoming, and western South Dakota is poorly documented. Because the fringed myotis often has been found in open ponderosa pine woodland, it may be expected along the eastern boundary of the national park. The closest records of occurrence are from near Fort Collins, in the foothills above Boulder, and along Cedar Creek, just east of Drake.

The animals have dark membranes and rather long ears, although not as long as those of *Myotis evotis*. The fringed myotis is so-called because of a conspicuous fringe of stiff hairs along the trailing edge of the interfemoral membrane.

Selected References—Adams (2003); O'Farrell and Studier (1980).

Long-legged Myotis
Myotis volans

Description—The long-legged myotis is slightly larger than other species of *Myotis* in the park. Adults range from 96 to 106 mm in total length, and the tail is 38 to 46 mm long. The forearm is about 37 to 40 mm in length. Adults weigh 8 to 12 g. As in many other kinds of bats, females average slightly larger than males. The upper parts are medium to dark brown in color, the underparts somewhat paler.

Even when close at hand, this bat might be confused at first glance with *Myotis lucifugus,* the little brown bat. The long-legged myotis differs in its slightly larger size; broader, more rounded ears; less glossy pelage; keeled calcar; and in the fact that the fur of the belly extends on the underside of the wing to the level of the elbow. The last-mentioned characteristic allows certain identification of an animal in hand. *Field Recognition*—Short, rounded ears; "relaxed" flight pattern.

Distribution and Habitat—Like the long-eared myotis, the long-legged myotis is a species of western North America, ranging from extreme south-

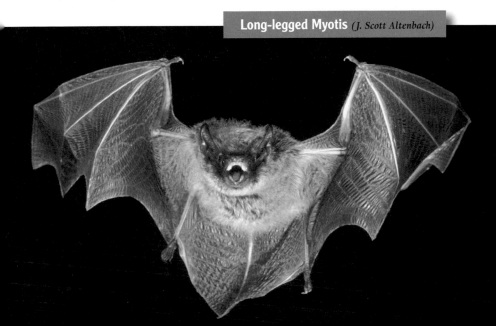

Long-legged Myotis *(J. Scott Altenbach)*

eastern Alaska southward to central Mexico and reaching the eastern limits of its range in western parts of Texas, Nebraska, and the Dakotas. In Colorado, the species occurs in summer in suitable habitat in the mountainous western three-fifths of the state. The winter range of our population is unknown. The long-legged myotis occurs mostly in wooded areas and may be expected throughout forested parts of the park. They sometimes occupy buildings; for example, the animals occur in some structures at the YMCA of the Rockies southwest of Estes Park. This is thought to be the highest-elevation North American bat; the highest record of occurrence of the species is at over 4,240 m (14,000 feet) on Mount Evans.

Natural History—As is the case with many of our bats, the habits of this species are poorly known. The long-legged myotis emerges to feed well before full darkness, the first of the species of *Myotis* to appear. The flight pattern is slower and more erratic than that of the little brown bat.

By day, the species roosts in trees, buildings, or crevices. Maternity colonies form in similar situations, commonly beneath the loose bark of trees. Tunnels and caves are used as night roosts. The foraging habitat is similar to that of the little brown bat and the long-eared myotis. Feeding flights are over woodland ponds or small openings in the trees. Activity peaks three to four hours after sunset. Moths are the principal food, but insects of many other groups are also taken. The long-legged myotis captures its prey in rapid, direct pursuit.

No thorough study of reproduction in this species has been made, but apparently the timing of parturition is highly variable geographically—in New Mexico the single young is born in early June, in northern Colorado in early August. The timing of birth may be related to latitude, elevation, or both, or may stem from characteristics of the winter range that are unknown. Nursery colonies may consist of hundreds of individuals, but the whereabouts of these animals after the breakup of the colonies remains to be learned. Maximum reported longevity is in excess of twenty years.

Selected References—Adams (2003); Armstrong et al. (1995); Turner (1974); Warner and Czaplewski (1984).

Hoary Bat
Lasiurus cinereus

Description—This is the largest of our local bats. Adults measure 120 to 145 mm in total length, and the tail is 50 to 60 mm long. The forearm is 50 to 56 mm in length. Adults weigh 24 to 32 g. In flight, the hoary bat is recognizable by its fast, straight-line foraging pattern and large size (the wingspread is about 400 mm). The fur is dark reddish brown, mostly tipped

Hoary Bat *(J. Scott Altenbach)*

with white, giving the animals their unique "hoary," or frosted, appearance. The dorsal surface of the interfemoral membrane is densely furred, as are the short, rounded, black-rimmed ears. *Field Recognition*—Large size; white-tipped hairs; fast flight pattern.

Distribution and Habitat—The hoary bat is the most widespread American bat, ranging from the islands of Hudson Bay southward to Argentina and Chile. These bats are strong fliers and are the only land mammals native to the Hawaiian Islands. In Colorado, the animals occur statewide as migrants and are summer residents in the mountains, including places at moderate elevations in Rocky Mountain National Park on either side of the Continental Divide to elevations of about 2,900 m (9,500 feet). Hoary bats live in wooded areas, roosting in trees. Migratory individuals sometimes are captured in riparian woodlands on the plains of eastern Colorado.

Natural History—Little is known of the natural history of this beautiful mammal, perhaps because it roosts singly in trees and thus is usually observed only by accident. The animals are mostly insectivorous, feeding largely on moths, although they occasionally feed on smaller bats. By day, the animals hang under cover of leaves or branches, 3 to 5 m above the ground. They emerge to feed, often over water, only well after dark. Among local bats only the big brown bat and the hoary bat make distinctly audible chirps in flight. The flight sounds of other species are mostly above the range of human hearing.

Obviously the hoary bat is migratory, but the winter range of Coloradan animals is uncertain. Probably it is in the southwestern United States and Mexico, but routes of migration have not been discovered. Migrating hoary bats seem to move in flocks of several dozen to several hundred individuals. Flight is swift and strong. The animals tend to arrive in Rocky Mountain National Park about May and leave in late August or September.

Breeding habits of this species are largely unknown. Mating probably occurs on the winter range, with fertilization or implantation delayed until spring. Most records indicate that females bear and rear the young in Canada and the northeastern and north-central United States. A few females do bear young in Colorado, but most summer residents are males. The young are born in June. Twins seem to be the norm, but litters of one to four young have been reported. Until a week old, the young may be carried by the mother in flight; older offspring are left hanging in a tree as the mother feeds because older sucklings are so heavy that the mother cannot get airborne with them clinging to her teats. Not infrequently, a helpless mother with her large young is found beneath a tree from which she has been dislodged.

Selected References—Adams (2003); Shump and Shump (1982). Sometimes this species is placed in the genus *Nycteris*.

Silver-haired Bat
Lasionycteris noctivagans

Description—The silver-haired bat is of medium-size, about the size of a large myotis. Total length ranges from about 95 to 105 mm, the tail from 36 to 40 mm, and the forearm from about 39 to 43 mm. Adults weigh 9 to 13 g. The fur is black, as are the ears and membranes. The hairs of the back are tipped with silver or white, making this one of our most strikingly colored bats.

In hand, there is no mistaking this beautiful bat. Only one other bat in our area, the hoary bat (*Lasiurus cinereus*), has white dorsal hairs. Hoary bats are distinguished by large size (forearm 50 to 56 mm) and have short, rounded, black-rimmed ears and an interfemoral membrane that is heavily furred. *Field Recognition*—Silver-tipped pelage; very slow flight, usually only a few feet above the ground.

Distribution and Habitat—The silver-haired bat is a widespread species, present either as residents or migrants from southern Alaska, across southern

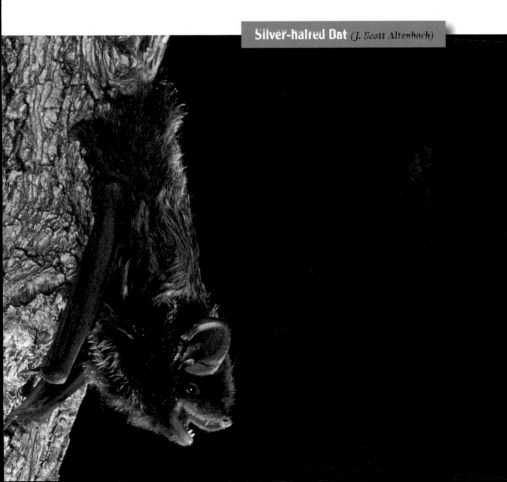

Silver-haired Bat *(J. Scott Altenbach)*

Canada, and throughout the conterminous United States (except peninsular Florida). In Colorado, the species may be expected statewide as migrants, and males are summer residents in the mountains. The silver-haired bat is a forest-dwelling species. The animals are rarely found in open country, although they do pass over such areas as migrants. Preferred foraging habitat is streams, ponds, and woodland clearings. In Colorado, records range to over 3,050 m (10,000 feet) in elevation, and this bat may be encountered in wooded areas throughout the park on either side of the Continental Divide.

Natural History—Resident silver-haired bats roost primarily in trees—beneath loose bark, in rotting snags and wind-throws, in tree holes, and even in birds' nests. During migration, the animals will occupy virtually any kind of shelter, including buildings, trees in riverbank woodlands, and even woodpiles.

Silver-haired bats migrate in spring and fall. Most of Colorado apparently lies on the migratory path. The domestic arrangement is an enviable one in some respects: males summer in the mountains of Colorado, arriving in early spring; females generally migrate farther north along the Rockies to bear and rear the young. An individual was captured at Boulder on 21 March 1914 in "zero weather." In warm years, the animals may remain in Colorado until early winter. The winter range of the local population is unknown, and general patterns of migration are poorly understood, although they probably winter in the southern United States or northern Mexico.

The silver-haired bat emerges relatively late in the evening to commence its slow, low-altitude foraging pattern. Usually the animals feed over water, but clearings are also exploited as feeding areas. Campers may see these bats as they come to feed on the insects attracted to the light of a campfire. The animals are mostly solitary while foraging. Moths have been shown to be prominent in several studies of food habits, but a wide range of flying insects is taken. By day the silver-haired bat apparently roosts in trees behind loose bark, and they are rarely seen.

Contrary to the usual situation in bats, twin births are the rule in this species. Young silver-haired bats are born on the northern summer range in late June or early July, weighing about 2 g. Fertilization occurs in the spring, accomplished by sperm stored over the winter in the reproductive tract of the female after a pre-hibernation breeding season in August and September. Gestation takes seven to eight weeks. Most young mature sexually their first summer. Nursery colonies may be formed, but evidence for them is equivocal and the breeding habits of this species are poorly known.

Selected References—Adams (2003); Armstrong et al. (1995); Hayes (2003); Kunz (1982a).

Big Brown Bat
Eptesicus fuscus

Description—The big brown bat is the largest of the several brown-colored bats in the park. Total length ranges from 105 to 125 mm, length of tail from 40 to 52 mm, and length of the forearm from 45 to 50 mm. Adults weigh 14 to 20 g. Save for its size, the big brown bat is rather nondescript. Our population varies in color from pale grayish brown to nearly russet. The round-tipped tragus is less than half the length of the ear. The dark-colored wings are relatively broader than those of the much smaller *Myotis* species. *Field Recognition*—Large size, brown color with black membranes; leisurely wingbeats.

Distribution and Habitat—The big brown bat is a widespread species with broad ecological tolerance, ranging from the forests of central and southern Canada southward through Panama and the Caribbean into South America. In Colorado, the species is distributed essentially statewide from the eastern plains to elevations above 3,350 m (11,000 feet) in the mountains, and it may be expected widely in the park. Big brown bats are as nearly ubiquitous as any kind of bat. They may be encountered in rural or urban areas, in open country or woodlands, in deserts or riparian forest. The foraging habitat is comparably diverse and may be over water, above open vegetation, or along a lighted street.

Natural History—They may not be the most abundant bat in North America (certain cave bats form immense local colonies), but big brown bats are probably those seen most often by people, because they often roost in occupied buildings. Attics and lofts may be preferred, but any protective crevice may be utilized. The bats may also roost in hollow trees, caves, mines, and tunnels; beneath bridges; and in storm sewers.

The big brown bat feeds on flying insects. Studies in the eastern United States suggest that beetles, flying ants, wasps, and flies make up the bulk of its diet; moths are not utilized to any great extent. Experienced animals can fill the stomach within an hour; the inexperienced young animals have more difficulty detecting and catching flying insects and may take far longer to gather a full meal. In captivity, big brown bats will eat a variety of prepared foods, including ground beef and canned pet food. Obviously, their prey need not be flying.

These bats emerge to feed at dusk. They may share a common feeding ground with other species, but of these other species, only the hoary bat (*Lasiurus cinereus*) is obviously larger. The hoary bat begins to feed later than the big brown bat, after full darkness, and flies much more swiftly. Porches, eaves, and similar relatively exposed night roosts are used intermittently by foraging big brown bats.

Big Brown Bat *(J. Scott Altenbach)*

Some big brown bats have been thought to be sedentary, although the whereabouts of many individuals in winter is unknown. It was known that the animals hibernate in our area in mines, caves, tunnels, and cellars. Recently, animals that summered and reared their young in Fort Collins were radio-tracked and found to winter along the Cache la Poudre River at elevations above 2,900 m (9,500 feet). That suggests that hibernation may occur in Rocky Mountain National Park, at least along the eastern boundary, especially in the Big Thompson and Saint Vrain drainages. High, northwest-facing canyon walls with deep crevices provide optimal conditions for hibernation:

consistently cold but with temperatures above freezing. The hibernaculum must remain cool so that the bats can remain torpid. Winter activity places great demands on energy reserves, reserves that cannot be replaced when insects are unavailable. If the temperature in the hibernaculum dips below freezing, the bats arouse, shivering and moving about, burning stored fat to maintain the body temperature at a tolerable level. As with many other bats, big brown bats are long-lived for small mammals, the known age record being eighteen years.

Mating takes place in the winter roost, between October or November and March. Sperm is stored by the female until the time of ovulation in April. The gestation period is about sixty days, and the young are born in late June. The young weigh about 4 g at birth and gain at the rate of 0.5 g per day. Development is rapid, and juveniles are able to fly within a month. In the West, a single young is the rule, but in the East, twinning is the mode. Western mothers often carry their single offspring when foraging, but eastern mothers leave the young in the roost.

Selected References—Adams (2003); Kunz (1974); Kurta and Baker (1990); Neubaum et al. (2006).

Townsend's Big-Eared Bat
Corynorhinus townsendii

Description—Townsend's big-eared bat is of small size—about 82 to 102 mm in total length, with the tail 35 to 50 mm long and the forearm 39 to 45 mm in length. Adults weigh 9 to 14 g. The color is brown, varying from grayish through medium to dark brown in our area. The venter is slightly paler than the dorsum. The snout bears a pair of rather prominent, rounded lumps above the nostrils. The magnificent ears save the species from being just another small, nondescript, brown-colored bat. There are prominent transverse ridges on the backs of the ears. When the animal is at rest, the ears are folded back like ram's horns. When the bat is aroused from torpor, the ears unfold, often one at a time, and move about semaphore-style, allowing the animal to orient to its acoustic environment. *Field Recognition*—Long ears; irregular pursuit flights in full darkness.

Distribution and Habitat—Townsend's big-eared bat occurs in western North America, from southern British Columbia southward to southern Mexico. East of the Rockies, distribution is disjunct and localized in areas with caves, eastward through the Arkansas and Ohio valleys to West Virginia. In Colorado, the species inhabits the rough, broken country of the western, central, and southeastern parts of the state. In the park, this bat occurs at lower to moderate elevations. *Corynorhinus townsendii* is an animal of rough, broken country, where caves and fissures (and mines) provide suitable roosting sites. Vegetation on such terrain typically is brush or open woodland. Day and night roosts may be in buildings. The highest elevation in Colorado from which records are available is 2,900 m (9,500 feet); in Rocky Mountain National Park, the animals may be expected at moderate elevations on either side of the Continental Divide but especially in areas like Lumpy Ridge and Twin Sisters along the eastern boundary of the park.

Natural History—Townsend's big-eared bat apparently feeds mostly on moths. The bats are excellent echolocators and (like their prey) have highly maneuverable flight, perhaps more so than any other local species. They emerge late, only in full darkness, often foraging over water.

This is mostly a cave bat. In our area, mines and tunnels are used as day roosts in summer and as hibernacula. Buildings may be utilized as night roosts, for rest between feeding flights, but heated structures are too warm (and unheated buildings too cold) to be suitable for hibernation. Males are mostly solitary, but females form nursery colonies in summer. A single overall molt occurs annually in about August.

Mating takes place in the hibernaculum, beginning in October and lasting intermittently through the winter months. Sperm are stored until the onset of ovulation in spring. Gestation is highly variable, depending on roost temperature, among other things, and ranges from 50 to 100 days, with an average of about 73 days. A single young is born in early summer. Nursery colonies consist of ten to a few hundred females with young. While foraging, females leave their offspring hanging in a cluster. Returning to the colony, the mother locates the proper infant in the cluster. The young bat clings to the mother during the day. The young fly at about three weeks, reach full size at about one month, and are weaned by six weeks of age.

Selected References—Adams (2003); Humphrey and Kunz (1976); Kunz and Martin (1982). For a time this species was included in the genus *Plecotus*, a group now considered to be restricted to the Old World.

Humans *(James Frank)*

7

ORDER PRIMATES
Monkeys, Apes and Allies

The Primates constitute a group of rather generalized mammals descended from an early, primitive insectivore stock. Early in their history, competition with rodents seems to have been keen. However, the groups diverged and both prevail today (although in terms of diversity and numbers, the rodents are by far the more successful). Recent Primates are arranged in 10 families, including over 150 species, mostly tropical or subtropical in distribution.

FAMILY HOMINIDAE—PEOPLE
In traditional classifications, the family Hominidae includes a single living member, the human species. *Homo sapiens* is the most widespread biological species, permanently inhabiting all continents save Antarctica.

Humankind
Homo sapiens

Humans need no description, and perhaps an objective description is impossible. All of us recognize each other as part of a single, diverse species. In fact, why mention us at all? There is a single, but compelling, reason: humans are a part of the native mammalian fauna, probably established locally as long as any species and longer than many. Nearly everyone knows, of course, that we people are mammals, strangely "naked apes." But too often our relationship to the rest of the fauna is forgotten, our place in ecosystems (upon which we are utterly dependent) poorly understood. We allow the egocentric pressures of a burdensome humanity to obscure our basic "animality." Recognizing our fundamental animality makes us no less unique—each biological species is unique. It does, however, reemphasize an important and immutable fact—we are a part of nature, not apart from it.

When human beings first came to the area now known as Rocky Mountain National Park is not known. Paleoindians occupied the margin of the plains to the east during the last glacial period ten millenia ago. Parts of the park bear evidence of Indian occupation a thousand years ago. More recently, the Utes—a mountain tribe—hunted over the area, to be replaced by the plains-dwelling Arapaho in the nineteenth century. Amerindian cultures left their mark on the landscape—fire scars, camp circles, artifacts—but in many respects their long-term effects are less obvious than those of the beaver, the porcupine, the pine bark beetle, or the spruce budworm. They lived as nomadic, opportunistic omnivores, emphasizing hunting. Local populations adjusted to the resources of the region. Imports and exports of materials and energy were minimal.

The first Europeans to visit the region were fur trappers, the legendary "mountain men." Rufus Sage may have been the earliest of them; he described a place in 1840 that could very well have been Wild Basin. Enos Mills believed that Kit Carson entered the park in 1841. In 1860, Joel Estes brought his family to the park that now bears his name and stayed for six years. The area finally passed to the Earl of Dunraven, a wealthy British nobleman. Mining opened the area west of the Continental Divide, spawning towns such as Teller, Lulu City, and Grand Lake in the 1870s. The pioneer economy of the entire region was extractive, exploitative—trapping, mining, market-hunting, and grazing. Biological production and physical resources were exported from the area. Fortunately for us, the mines played out and Lord Dunraven guarded his domain like a medieval manor. In January 1915, through the persistent efforts of naturalist-writer Enos Mills and numerous others, Rocky Mountain National Park was established to preserve the region's most precious and fragile resource: a breathtakingly scenic landscape, a monumental mosaic of ecosystems, each with uniquely coevolved communities of plants and animals linked by endless cycles of resources and a ceaseless flow of energy. The objective of management here is to minimize the effect of mankind on native ecosystems. This goal should be a personal commitment on the part of each visitor.

Selected References—Benedict (1992, 1996, 1999); Buchholtz (1983); Cassells (1997); Drummond (1995); Estes (1939); Mills (1914); Stiger (2001); Trimble (1984); Wishart (1979).

Mountain, or Nuttall's, Cottontail *(Gene Putney)*

8

ORDER LAGOMORPHA
Rabbits and Allies

Four kinds of lagomorphs occur in Rocky Mountain National Park. An additional three species occur elsewhere in Colorado. Lagomorphs once were considered to be rodents, but now it is realized that, although rather similar in their dental adaptations for gnawing plant material, the orders have long independent evolutionary histories. Probably the lineages do have a common ancestor early in the Age of Mammals, so modern classifications group the orders together in a superorder Glires. Lagomorphs are native to all continents except Australia (and there they have been introduced, much to the detriment of natural biotic communities). There are approximately ninety species of living lagomorphs, arranged in two major families (both of which occur in the park).

FAMILY OCHOTONIDAE—PIKAS

The family Ochotonidae includes a single genus, *Ochotona*. The genus is Holarctic in distribution and includes two closely related North American species and two dozen or more Asian species with a wide variety of lifestyles.

American Pika
Ochotona princeps

Description—Superficially, pikas look more like grayish guinea pigs than like their cousins the rabbits and hares. The ears are short and rounded, and the tail is a mere vestige, so short that it is obscured by the fur. Pikas range in total length from about 175 to 200 mm, and weights range to about 200 g. The color is highly variable, often approaching the color of the rock in a given mountain range. In the park, most are "dirty gray," sometimes washed with buff, paling to grayish white below. Molting individuals may appear to be darker because the lead-gray bases of the hairs are exposed. Pikas can be confused with no other mammal, although the casual observer may mistake them for rocks—until they "chirp." *Field Recognition*—Diurnal habit; habitat in talus slides; metallic, nasal call note.

Distribution and Habitat—The American pika occurs in western North America, from central British Columbia southward to California, Utah, and northern New Mexico. The closely related collared pika (*Ochotona collaris*) occurs in southern Alaska and adjacent Canada. North American pikas are narrowly restricted to mountainous areas where talus slopes provide suitable cover. Some of the Old World species, by contrast, live in the vast open steppes and exhibit social behaviors reminiscent of North American prairie dogs and some open-country ground squirrels.

Locally, pikas live from well above timberline down into the subalpine forest to elevations as low as about 2,590 m (about 8,500 feet), wherever suitable rock slides exist. Occasional exceptional animals are found living under piles of boards or timbers or in burrows (probably made by other mammals), but broken rock (including mine tailings) is the usual habitat. Not just any rock pile will suffice—the rock must be sufficiently large that the spaces between provide corridors for movement, the slide must be of sufficiently recent origin that the spaces have not filled with debris from higher ground, and in optimal habitat the talus is interspersed with meadow vegetation. There are innumerable patches of habitat in the park suitable for pikas, and all but the most hurried visitor should expect to see them (or at least hear them) along Trail Ridge Road or on any of the high-country trails.

American Pika *(Gene Putney)*

Natural History—The pika (pronounced "pee-kuh" by purists; the name is taken from a Siberian dialect) has an intriguing variety of common names: little chief hare, rock rabbit, calling hare, cony, and "cooney," to list a sampling. Remarkably little is known of the biology of this fascinating little mammal, perhaps because its haunts are largely inaccessible through much of the year. Its best-known habitat is the vegetation it gathers into "haypiles."

These rounded stacks usually contain about a bushel of "hay," but they may be twice that size. In our area, building of haypiles begins in mid-July and continues in earnest for the remainder of the short growing season. Haypiles often are built under at least partial shelter of overhanging rocks. Presumably the animals are active through the winter beneath the snow, using stored hay as food, but direct observations in winter are meager.

Pikas eat a wide variety of plant material depending on local abundance. Typically, foliage makes up the bulk of the diet, although seeds are eaten in season. Forbs usually are more important in the diet than are grasses, and twigs, leaves, and bark of trees and shrubs may be eaten. The animals seem to have little (if any) need for free water, presumably meeting their requirements by eating succulent foliage. The urine is highly concentrated and viscous, frequently staining the rocks a chalky white to brown.

Like other lagomorphs, pikas produce two kinds of feces. True feces are round, fibrous, and hard, like those of rabbits but much smaller (BB-sized). A second kind of feces appears as an amorphous, elongate mass and is termed "soft feces." The hard fecal pellets actually are waste matter; soft feces, by contrast, are not waste. They are high in protein and energy and perhaps vitamins. As much as one-fourth of such soft feces is reingested, that is, swallowed and passed through the digestive tract a second time.

Pikas are diurnal and readily observable. An hour of pika-watching is an hour well spent, for these are interesting and highly entertaining animals. One is first made aware of their presence by the characteristic metallic call. Several calls are produced. They may function as alarm notes as well as a warning to neighbors approaching the territory. There is also a distinct mating call. Scent-marking also is practiced. Scents are placed on rocks by rubbing with chin glands and also with characteristic piles of feces and deposits of urine. Females are more likely to mate with familiar males, and familiarity appears to be a function of odor. Territories are closely guarded. Spacing is maintained mostly by vocalization, but intruders are also chased. Territories average about 400 square meters in extent, but the usual foraging range is somewhat smaller. When undisturbed, pikas spend their time in summer basking on the rocks (where they may be difficult to spot) and scampering about feeding. The animals are remarkably quick and agile but seldom jump. Toward fall, building the haypile for winter becomes the overriding concern.

In early summer the animals undergo a conspicuous patterned molt, beginning on the head and progressing backward. The summer pelage is much shorter and less fluffy than the winter coat. Summer pelage is worn for only about two months and then the fall molt begins. In any population, during the warmer months some individuals are sure to be undergoing one of these seasonal molts.

Predation on pikas is poorly documented, but weasels (both the long-tailed and short-tailed weasel, or ermine) have been observed to capture pikas. Martens also prey on them, as do some of the larger carnivores—such as coyotes—that venture high into the mountains. Birds of prey, especially hawks, eagles, and falcons, also must take a toll.

The breeding season begins in late March or April, and the last young are born in August. After a gestation period of a bit over thirty days, two to four (usually three) young are born, each weighing about 10 g. The young are reared in a nest under cover of rocks and are weaned at about 60 g. Immediately after giving birth, the female comes into heat (postpartum estrus). A single litter of young is usual in Rocky Mountain National Park. Environmental conditions affect survival and reproduction. There is evidence to indicate that in severe winters with late-lying snowpack and a late growing season, survival and reproductive success are lower than in other years. Maximal longevity has been reported from four to seven years.

Selected References—D. Johnson (1967); Meaney (1983); A. Smith (1975, 1978); A. Smith and Weston (1990); Southwick et al. (1986); Svendsen (1979).

FAMILY LEPORIDAE—RABBITS AND HARES

The family Leporidae includes the rabbits and hares. Of some sixty species of leporids, six occur in Colorado, and three of these occur in various habitats in Rocky Mountain National Park.

Mountain, or Nuttall's, Cottontail
Sylvilagus nuttallii

Description—Nuttall's cottontail is a rather small rabbit, ranging in total length from about 380 to 410 mm, of which 35 to 50 mm is tail. The ears are densely haired inside and short for a rabbit, 55 to 65 mm long. Weights range around 1 kg. This is the most richly colored lagomorph in the park. From a distance, the upper parts appear to be dark brown, but closer at hand the hairs are seen to be reddish, mostly tipped with black. The nape is rusty red and the underparts and tail are white. Nuttall's cottontail cannot be confused easily with other lagomorphs in Rocky Mountain National Park, but two closely related species do occur nearby. The desert cottontail (*Sylvilagus audubonii*) is about the same size as Nuttall's cottontail but has longer, sparsely haired ears and is considerably paler in color. Another confusingly similar nearby species is the eastern cottontail (*Sylvilagus floridanus*), somewhat larger than Nuttall's cottontail and slightly darker in color. The best way to distinguish the cottontails in the field is probably habitat preference—Nuttall's cottontail

Mountain, or Nuttall's, Cottontail *(Gene Putney)*

occurs in forest edge situations (and in sagebrush country in Middle Park and elsewhere in central and western Colorado); the desert cottontail occurs in open, semiarid grassland and in shrub communities in the foothills of the Eastern Slope; the eastern cottontail occurs in deciduous, riparian woodland on the eastern plains. Only Nuttall's cottontail is to be expected in and adjacent to Rocky Mountain National Park. *Field Recognition*—Small size, short ears, dark dorsal color.

Distribution and Habitat—Interior western North America is the range of Nuttall's cottontail, from the Rockies to the Sierra Nevada and from southern Alberta and Saskatchewan to Arizona. In Colorado, the species occurs over most of the western three-fifths of the state. Nuttall's cottontail is a mammal of brushy, forest edge situations in the Southern Rockies. Elsewhere in the West, stands of sagebrush are occupied as well. The species occurs throughout the park, from lowest elevations to about treeline.

Natural History—No comprehensive study of the life history of Nuttall's cottontail has been made. The animals are largely nocturnal. During the day they huddle to rest in rather deep depressions, called "forms," in dense shrubbery or in other sheltered spots, including hollow logs, piles of brush or logging slash, and burrows abandoned by other animals. When startled, the animals may leave the form during the day, but they quickly find alternative cover. Predators include coyotes, bobcats, foxes, weasels, and owls. Snakes take nestling young. Internal parasites include flatworms and roundworms, and the animals host fleas and ticks and are susceptible to tularemia (a microbial disease transmissible to humans by contact). Cottontails begin to feed in the evening. They are active throughout the year, and the diet varies with availability of food. During the growing season, succulent grasses and forbs are preferred, but in winter dry grasses, twigs, and bark are eaten. As in other lagomorphs, the upper and lower molar teeth of cottontails do not occlude directly. Chewing is by a side-to-side motion of the jaws, unlike the circular grinding motion seen in rodents.

Nuttall's cottontail probably is polyestrous, breeding throughout the warmer months. Four to eight (usually, four or five) young are born after a gestation period of about four weeks. As is true generally of rabbits, the young are altricial—born blind, naked, and highly dependent. Such offspring require more careful attention than do young hares. They are bedded in a nest in a burrow, hollow log, or other protected place. The nest is lined with fine grasses, leaves, and hair that the mother has plucked from her belly and chest.

Selected References—Chapman (1975); Chapman et al. (1982); Chapman and Litvaitis (2003).

Snowshoe Hare
Lepus americanus

Description—Snowshoe hares are of moderate size, somewhat larger than cottontails but markedly smaller than white-tailed jackrabbits. Total length ranges from 400 to 450 mm, the tail from 30 to 60 mm. The ears are relatively short for a hare, 65 to 70 mm, but the hindfeet are relatively large (hence the common name), 140 to 155 mm in length. Adults weigh about a kilogram. In summer, snowshoe hares are rusty brown, darkest along the dorsal midline and grading to grayish brown along the sides. The chin and belly are white to grayish, and the nape is grayish brown. The tail is black above, white below. In winter, the pelage is white except for black tips on the ears. *Field Recognition*—Moderate size; combination of rather short ears and large feet; in winter, combination of white pelage and forested habitat.

Distribution and Habitat—The snowshoe hare is a boreal mammal, occurring the breadth of North America, from New England and Maritime Canada to the Pacific Coast. The species occurs from north of the Arctic Circle southward through Canada and along the principal mountain ranges to California, New Mexico, and Tennessee. In Colorado, the snowshoe hare is confined to the mountains, and it occurs throughout Rocky Mountain National Park in suitable habitat. These are animals of thickets and dense forests in Colorado and are commonest where an understory of brush or shrubs is present. When a tract of forest has burned, shrubs soon invade, and such areas provide ideal habitat for local snowshoe hares. The elevational range in our area is from about 2,450 to 3,350 m (8,000 to 11,000 feet).

Natural History—The snowshoe hare is sometimes called a "rabbit," but it is a true hare. Rabbits bear altricial young—naked, blind, highly dependent. Young hares, however, are precocial—furred, alert, and able to move about soon after birth.

Snowshoe hares are largely nocturnal. During the day they rest in "forms"—unlined depressions under cover of shrubbery—and they move only if disturbed. At night they move away from the form over well-worn paths to feed or to dust themselves for ectoparasites in communal dust-baths.

The diet consists largely of grasses and forbs when available, but in winter the bark and young twigs of woody plants are eaten. Winter feeding by snowshoe hares leaves many saplings stripped of bark at the snowline. Such saplings cannot survive if girdling is complete, because nutrients cannot move from the leaves downward to nourish the roots. Although seemingly destructive, the hares actually may help the forest by removing occasional young trees, thus thinning the stand and improving conditions for the survivors. Unlike most other lagomorphs, snowshoe hares are known to eat carrion

Snowshoe Hare *(David Dahms)*

occasionally. Reingestion of soft feces occurs, as is true in other lagomorphs in the park. Water needs seem to be met by the moisture in the food and the lapping of dew. Snowshoe hares also eat snow.

The snowshoe hare, as a herbivore, is an important link in the food web, converting vegetation into food for coyotes, bobcats, and the larger birds of prey. Weasels prey on the young. Farther north, the Canada lynx is highly dependent upon snowshoe hares for food. Populations of hares are subject to wide fluctuation with about ten years between "crashes," and the lynx is subject to a closely related cycle of abundance. In Colorado, populations of snowshoe hares may fluctuate also, but this pattern has not been studied in any detail.

Adult snowshoe hares are solitary animals. During the reproductive season, males fight among themselves, and pregnant females are actively hostile toward males. Only on choice dusting spots does there appear to be any mutual tolerance.

The molt of snowshoe hares from "brush brown" to "snow white" is well-known. The autumnal molt begins in September and takes two to three months to complete. Timing is controlled (in part at least) by day length. Molt begins on the legs, then progresses to the back, and occurs last on the shoulders and crown. The short underfur is not molted. In March or April, prevernal molt begins, with a pattern opposite that seen in autumn. In years with early or late snowfall, the pelage may be out of phase with the background, leaving brown animals conspicuous against the snow or white animals obvious among dry, brown leaves. The timing of molt is adapted to regional climate, not local weather, and for the most part cryptic coloration must be adequate insurance against over-predation. In addition to color change, winter pelage has much better insulative value.

Snowshoe hares are polyestrous and exhibit postpartum heat. Breeding occurs from March to August, and females may bear one to three litters, with two being the most common number in Colorado. Litters of one to seven (average about three) precocial young are born—well-furred, the eyes open—after a gestation period of some thirty-eight days. The young huddle together in the unlined form, but by the second day they can move well if disturbed. Growth is rapid. Birth weights double in eight days, and when the young are weaned at about one month they have been eating some vegetation for at least two weeks and birth weights have increased nine times. By three to five months of age the animals reach adult weight. Young of the year do not breed, however.

Selected References—Bittner and Rongstad (1982); Murray (2003).

White-tailed Jackrabbit
Lepus townsendii

Description—The white-tailed jackrabbit is by far the largest lagomorph in the park. Adults are about 550 to 600 mm long, of which the tail comprises 75 to 85 mm. Females are somewhat larger than males. The ears are long, 90 to 115 mm from notch to tip. The hindfoot is about 140 to 165 mm long, only slightly longer than that of the much smaller snowshoe hare. Weights range to a maximum of 5 kg, but 2 to 4 kg is more usual.

In summer, the white-tailed jackrabbit is pale buffy gray above, pale gray to white below. The tail is white but may be marked with an obscure gray or black line. (This character is highly variable in our area.) The ears are white behind and tipped with black. In winter, most individuals don a white pelage, although the extremities and face often have a buffy tinge and the tips of the ears remain black. *Field Recognition*—Large size, long ears; habitat in relatively open country.

Distribution and Habitat—The white-tailed jackrabbit is a mammal of the Great Basin and the central and northern Great Plains, ranging from Alberta to New Mexico and from California to Iowa. This hare occurs almost statewide in Colorado and throughout Rocky Mountain National Park. White-tailed jackrabbits occupy open grasslands in summer and tend to move into shrubby country in winter. In Colorado, these animals have as wide an elevational range as any mammal, from below 1,220 m (4,000 feet) on the eastern plains to over 4,270 m (14,000 feet) in the alpine tundra. Because of their habitat preferences, white-tailed jackrabbits probably are more abundant at lower elevations in Arapaho National Recreation Area than elsewhere locally, but they range throughout the park in suitable habitat.

Natural History—Jackrabbits are not rabbits; they are hares, giving birth to precocial young. These are large lagomorphs, adapted to life in open habitats. Speed is useful insurance in such situations, and when pursued, white-tailed jackrabbits may cover short distances at 65 km (40 miles) per hour. The animals rely on cryptic coloration for concealment in their forms, however, and often can be approached quite closely before they flush.

As with preferred habitat, diet changes with season. In summer, herbs (mostly forbs) compose up to 90 percent of the diet, but in winter three-fourths of forage is shrubs. As in other lagomorphs, reingestion of soft feces occurs. The pellets are produced during the day (while the animals are resting) and are taken from the anus and swallowed. Reingestion allows the extraction of additional energy from the vegetable diet. The pellets also contain protein, as well as B vitamins, probably produced in the intestine by bacteria but not absorbable there.

White-tailed Jackrabbit *(Fi Rust)*

Jackrabbits are mostly crepuscular, being active in early morning and again in late afternoon and evening. Young jackrabbits are preyed on by coyotes, foxes, weasels, and birds of prey. The larger carnivorous mammals and birds also surprise and capture adults, but perhaps disease, parasites, and destruction of habitat by humans are more important enemies.

The breeding season lasts from about March through August. Groups of three or four males may follow a female in heat. Gestation takes about six weeks. There is a postpartum estrus, but a single litter of about five young (range, one to eleven) seems to be the general rule. The young are precocial and are reared in a simple form or in a burrow abandoned by another animal. Growth is rapid, and the mother's milk is quickly supplemented by vegetation.

Selected References—Bear and Hansen (1966); Dunn et al. (1982); Flinders and Chapman (2003); Hansen and Flinders (1969); Lim (1987).

Yellow-bellied Marmots *(Gene Putney)*

9

ORDER RODENTIA
Rodents

About two dozen species of rodents occur in Rocky Mountain National Park or sufficiently near the park that their occurrence should be considered likely. These species represent six families and utilize a broad range of habitats—in the trees, in the water, among the rocks, above and below ground. Rodents exceed all other mammals in the park in terms of numbers of species and numbers of individuals, and the same may be said of most terrestrial ecosystems throughout the world. The order Rodentia includes about one-third of living mammals (nearly 2,300 species), arranged in over 30 families. The incisors of rodents grow in length throughout life and are continually worn down by incessant gnawing on coarse plant materials. Further, because the face is hard enamel and the rear is softer dentine, the continual wear of upper against lower incisors sharpens them. These teeth are a key to the extraordinary evolutionary success of rodents.

FAMILY SCIURIDAE—SQUIRRELS

All squirrels in Rocky Mountain National Park are diurnal; hence, they are among the best known (and most appreciated) of rodents. There are about 280 species of squirrels in the world arranged in some 50 genera. Of the eighteen species of squirrels that occur in Colorado, nine live in or near Rocky Mountain National Park.

Selected References—MacClintock (1970).

Least Chipmunk
Neotamias minimus

Description—The least chipmunk is aptly named; it is our smallest squirrel. Adults range in total length from 190 to 215 mm, with a rather narrow tail 80 to 100 mm long. The hindfoot is 29 to 32 mm long, and weights range from 40 to 60 g.

The color of least chipmunks in our area is variable, because the park is a zone of integration between a brightly colored eastern subspecies and a dusky, less reddish western one. The back is marked with well-defined black and white stripes, and stripes also mark the face. The tail is clothed with black-tipped hairs with reddish bases. The sides are reddish brown to brown and the underparts are grayish buff to white.

Species of chipmunks are not easy to distinguish in the museum and they are difficult or impossible to identify in the field. For starters, however, be sure that the "chipmunk" has stripes on its face. If it does not, it is not a chipmunk at all but a golden-mantled ground squirrel. Next, look at its size. A decidedly small, animated chipmunk probably is the least chipmunk. Both the Uinta and Colorado chipmunks are larger and somewhat bolder and more deliberate in their movements.

The Uinta and Colorado chipmunks are even trickier to distinguish. There are subtle differences in color, the proportions of the skull are different, and the bacula differ in shape, but overall the species are remarkably similar. In our area, the best criterion for identification may be habitat. The Colorado chipmunk occurs in rocky areas with shrubby vegetation or sparse woodland, mostly below 2,300 m (7,500 feet) in elevation. The Uinta chipmunk occupies openings in heavier forests of higher elevations, generally above 2,450 m (8,000 feet). A warning: in intermediate areas, don't agonize over the specific identity of a chipmunk and risk losing your perspective and enthusiasm for squirrel watching. The important thing is that the chipmunks can tell themselves apart (by inscrutable means of their own). *Field Recognition*—Small size, bright color; rapid, nervous movements; habitat mostly in openings in wooded country.

Least Chipmunk *(Gene Putney)*

Distribution and Habitat—The least chipmunk is widespread, occurring from the Yukon eastward to Wisconsin, Upper Michigan, western Quebec, and southward—especially in mountainous areas—to southern New Mexico. The species lives throughout central and western Colorado and is an abundant and conspicuous mammal through most of Rocky Mountain National Park. The least chipmunk has the broadest ecological tolerance of local chipmunks, ranging from lowest elevations to timberline and above. Elsewhere, these animals occupy a diversity of habitats—shrub deserts, badlands, openings in damp coniferous forests. One seldom sees a chipmunk in unbroken forest, but any opening—even a tree-fall gap—will support a few, and greatest numbers are found at the forest edge, the ecotone between forest and meadow.

Natural History—This is one of the most familiar small mammals in the park, but surprisingly little is known of its natural history. Perhaps the difficulty of identifying species has made naturalists wary of chipmunks as subjects for field study; some older published observations cannot be attributed with certainty to any of the species presently recognized by taxonomists.

As with most squirrels, this is a diurnal mammal. Least chipmunks are more nervous and animated than our other chipmunks and less easily approached. When startled they dart beneath the nearest rock or into their burrows. Sometimes they climb trees to avoid danger and they seem to climb better and more readily than our other chipmunks.

Chipmunks are adapted to a diet of seeds, but this and other species have rather catholic diets overall. Seeds—especially those of the daisy family—form the bulk of the diet in season and they are stored in the burrow for winter, but other plant material, insects, and some carrion also are eaten. In the park, the animals eat table scraps, but they are by no means as proficient panhandlers as are the larger chipmunks or the golden-mantled ground squirrel. A study of the least chipmunk at Rainbow Curves found densities of least chipmunks seven times greater than more natural populations reported in the literature. Also, home ranges were smaller in the "subsidized" population. Artificial feeding of chipmunks and other wildlife is rightly discouraged for the sake of the animals' health and that of visitors as well.

Least chipmunks burrow beneath rocks, logs, shrubs, and other such shelters. Abandoned burrows of larger squirrels and pocket gophers may also be used. At the end of the complex tunnel is a nest chamber, used at night and through the long winter. With the first heavy snows, in October or early November, the animals enter a state of torpor and they remain below ground through the winter over much of the park. The winter sleep is not true hibernation, however, for the animals arouse periodically to feed on stored food. At lower elevations they may emerge from the burrow during warm spells for brief periods.

Males emerge in spring in breeding condition, and females come into estrus in about a week. Thus, the timing of reproduction varies widely, depending (in part at least) on the timing of snowmelt and the availability of fresh food resources. Breeding in our area takes place from May to early June, and the young are born by early July after a gestation period of four to five weeks. A typical litter comprises five or six young, with extremes of three to eight reported locally. The young are highly altricial and do not leave the nest until about four weeks of age. In our area, at any rate, females are monoestrous and young of the year do not breed.

Selected References—W. Carleton (1966); Friedrichsen (1977); Skryja (1974); Telleen (1978); Vaughan (1969); Verts and Carraway (2001). This and other species of western chipmunks have been listed under the generic names *Tamias* and *Eutamias*.

Colorado Chipmunk
Neotamias quadrivittatus

Description—The Colorado chipmunk is of moderate size, larger than the least chipmunk and of slightly stockier build than the Uinta chipmunk. Total length ranges from about 210 to 240 mm, the tail is 90 to 110 mm long, and the hindfoot is 33 to 36 mm in length. Weights range around 70 g.

The color is brighter overall than is that of the Uinta chipmunk and thus is very similar to that of the least chipmunk. The black and white stripes of the dorsum and head are well-defined, and the sides are reddish, grading to buff. For comments on distinguishing chipmunks in our area, see the account of the least chipmunk. *Field Recognition*—Large size, bright color; habitat in rocky country, generally below 2,290 m (7,500 feet).

Distribution and Habitat—The Colorado chipmunk is aptly named, for it occurs only in Colorado and neighboring parts of Arizona and New Mexico. The species has not been documented in Rocky Mountain National Park but may be expected at lower elevations about Estes Park. In northern Colorado, it occurs mostly in the foothills, in the canyons leading to the park from the east. The Colorado chipmunk is a mammal of rocky areas, finding suitable cover beneath rocks and shrubs and about the bases of scattered conifers. Records in our area are all from below 2,450 m (8,000 feet), roughly the elevation at which open woodland "closes up" into true forest and the lower limit of gravelly glacial soils.

Natural History—Most of the meager information published under the name "Colorado chipmunk" for our immediate area probably pertains instead to the Uinta chipmunk. It was not until 1953 that the two species were recognized as distinct here. The Colorado chipmunk has a restricted distribution in northern Colorado. Along with the rock squirrel, the Mexican woodrat, and the northern rock mouse, it occurs in a narrow band along the foothills, entering the mountains proper mostly on south-facing canyon walls and rocky, broken terrain.

Like other chipmunks, this species prefers seeds and berries, but it eats a variety of plant materials as available and takes occasional insects as well. Burrows are excavated beneath rocks, shrubs, and the exposed roots of trees. The home range is 5 ha (12 acres) or more.

Colorado Chipmunk *(Justin W. Moore)*

Mating occurs in late April or May. Gestation takes about thirty days and there is one litter of about five young per year. Newborns are altricial and weigh only about 3 g, gaining about 0.5 g per day for the first three months of life. The ears unfold after two or three days and the eyes open after about four weeks. Newborn chipmunks are hairless except for facial vibrissae ("whiskers"), but body hair appears quickly, and the dorsal stripes are evident in ten days. The dentition is complete at about five weeks, and the young are weaned at six to seven weeks of age. Young animals commonly appear above ground in August.

Selected References—Bergstrom (1988); Best et al. (1994); White (1953).

Uinta Chipmunk
Neotamias umbrinus

Description—This is a moderate-sized chipmunk, obviously larger than the least chipmunk, with a slightly fuller tail, but not as heavy-bodied as the Colorado chipmunk. The color is hardly distinctive, but generally the Uinta chipmunk has the dullest dorsal color and the least distinct lateral stripes of local chipmunks. Often the hindquarters are grayish, with the stripes obscure. For further comparisons, see the account of the least chipmunk.

Uinta Chipmunk *(Ann & Rob Simpson)*

Adults range in total length from 215 to 235 mm, and the tail is 90 to 110 mm long. The hindfoot measures 33 to 35 mm. Weights range around 65 g. *Field Recognition*—Relatively large size (hindfoot 33 mm or more), dusky color often with poorly defined stripes; habitat forest edge situations, generally above 2,450 m (8,000 feet).

Distribution and Habitat—The Uinta chipmunk has an erratic distribution in mountainous parts of the western United States, with disjunct populations in Colorado, northwestern Wyoming, Utah, and Nevada. The Coloradan population occurs in the north-central and northwestern parts of the state and is not known to overlap with the Colorado chipmunk. There are no obvious differences in habitat between the Uinta and least chipmunks. However, of the two, the Uinta chipmunk has the narrower elevational range (from about 2,450 meters to timberline or slightly above) and seems to be more closely restricted to rocky areas (although less so than the Colorado chipmunk). Although less retiring than the least chipmunk, this is mostly an animal of forest edge habitat in the park. Especially look for them in rocky openings in lodgepole pine forests.

Natural History—As with other chipmunks, these animals excavate burrows beneath rocks and shrubs. At the end of the tunnel is a nest chamber. During summer, individuals feed on seeds and berries, supplementing the diet with other plant material and insects. Birds' eggs and carrion are eaten occasionally, but these items are hardly staples. In autumn, seeds and berries are stored in the burrow. Uinta chipmunks in the park clean up after careless visitors. Often they bury a crust of bread or some other delicate morsel beneath a thin layer of soil near the source of supply and then sally forth for more booty, which is carried in capacious cheek pouches. Although more tame than least chipmunks, they are less brazen than the larger golden-mantled ground squirrel.

In winter the animals are dormant in the burrow under a protective blanket of snow. Their habitat is such that it usually holds snow through the winter, but occasionally animals on favorably warm slopes arouse during warm, snow-free periods and appear above ground. Others arouse and feed on stored food but do not leave the burrow.

There is considerable social interaction between individuals. Apparently a dominance hierarchy exists, and one animal may drive another from a bit of food without any show of physical force. There seems to be a repertoire of calls, but vocalizations have not been studied in any detail. The calls of the Uinta chipmunk are typically higher in pitch than those of the least chipmunk.

The presence in the same area of two species of chipmunks and the golden-mantled ground squirrel may puzzle amateur naturalists, because they look very much alike. In fact, professional naturalists are puzzled as well. No trenchant differences are known in the ecological needs of these species, yet a fundamental rule of ecology is that two species cannot coexist indefinitely in the same niche. How such similar species manage to live in such close proximity is unknown, but perhaps one day we will learn that available resources are neatly, if subtly, partitioned, just as has been demonstrated in other complex communities, by the firmest of arbiters—the process of natural selection.

Soon after the animals emerge in spring there is a flurry of activity so seemingly irresponsible that it can only be associated with courtship. Males drop all caution and pretense and chase females with abandon. I have seen animals dash through a campsite without regard for human observers, leap to a boulder, and—misjudging the distance to the next rock—land upside down in a currant bush. These, recall, are the antics of males intent on becoming grandfathers. Somehow it works. Although not documented, gestation probably lasts about thirty days. A typical litter comprises four or five offspring. The young are weaned and are foraging on their own in mid-July or August.

Selected References—Telleen (1978); White (1953).

Yellow-bellied Marmot
Marmota flaviventris

Description—The yellow-bellied marmot is the largest and stockiest of local squirrels and has the relatively shortest tail. Adults range in total length from about 600 to 680 mm, of which the tail comprises less than one-third, 175 to 205 mm. Weights range from 2.5 to 5 kilograms or more, with heaviest weights in late summer when the animals have fattened for hibernation. As is typical of polygynous mammals, males average larger than females. Marmots (also called "woodchucks," "rockchucks," "whistle pigs," or "groundhogs") are quite variable in dorsal color, the abundant pelage ranging from yellowish brown through reddish brown nearly to black. The underfur is soft, dense, and grayish brown in color. The tail is colored like the back. The face, like the feet, is covered with short hairs, usually black in color, with irregular white markings about the mouth and chin. The underparts are rather thinly covered with yellowish (to reddish brown) hairs, hence the preferred common name. *Field Recognition*—Large size, short tail; habitat about boulders; whistling call.

Distribution and Habitat—The yellow-bellied marmot is an inhabitant of mountainous parts of western North America, from southern British Columbia to California and New Mexico eastward to the Black Hills of South Dakota. Several closely related species, including the hoary marmot and the woodchuck, complement this range so that species of *Marmota* occupy much

Yellow-bellied Marmot *(Gene Putney)*

of North America north of Mexico. In Colorado, the marmot occurs widely in the western three-fifths of the state and throughout Rocky Mountain National Park.

For marmots, suitable habitat has two requisites: boulders (or a reasonable substitute) for cover and lush herbage for food. They are probably most abundant in the rock piles about subalpine meadows, but they range from the foothills to well above timberline, mostly in open situations. They may burrow beneath woodpiles or cabins, and sometimes they live in dry culverts, road fill, or other man-made shelters.

Natural History—The yellow-bellied marmot is a familiar animal in the park and it is readily observed. The daily round of activity is rather stereotyped. Up with the sun, the marmot forages along well-worn paths for the green vegetation that makes up nearly all of its diet (although seeds are also eaten when available). Midmorning is a time for basking in the sun. About noon, the animals retire to the burrow. After the usual brief afternoon rain shower, the marmot reappears to bask again atop a boulder or other prominence. In late afternoon, foraging begins again in earnest. Within a few minutes after sundown, all will have retired to their burrows for the night. Basically, the program is that of tourists on well-earned vacation: marmots are gourmands and heliophiles—they eat and they sunbathe, and then they sleep.

Close watch of a colony of marmots reveals other sorts of behavior. Burrowing occupies a good part of the time. Burrows usually begin beneath a boulder and they may be extensive. Typically they are on a hillside, which prevents flooding. The burrow is the center of activity. The young are reared in the burrow, and it is there that the animals spend the midday period, the night, and the long winter. The burrow also provides protection from enemies and from inclement summer weather. In the main chamber, a nest is built of grasses and other fibrous materials.

A resting marmot may seem complacent, but be assured that it is alert. The colony has no single sentry. Any animal sensing danger whistles and stands on the alert. Others nearby immediately become alert as well. If danger is imminent, the animals retreat to the burrow, either quietly or with a "scream" or squeal. In addition to the squeal, six different whistles have been identified. A given whistle seems to have no specific meaning; rather, "alert" or "alarm" are communicated by a whistle accompanied by visual cues. There is no "all-clear" signal; resumption of activity indicates that danger has passed. Much marmot communication seems to serve a defensive function. Also, agonistic communication helps to maintain spacing between colonies.

The marmot colony consists of a single adult male, a harem of variable size, yearlings, and young of the year. Marmots meeting each other along a path may "greet each other, sniffing about the cheeks. Spacing is maintained by mutual avoidance and "threat," which may be communicated by a peculiar whistle or by a loud chattering of the incisors. A dominance hierarchy exists within the colony, with priorities maintained by threats and submissive gestures. Yearlings are the most frequent objects of threatening behavior. After repeated harassment, the yearlings tend to move from the colony, sometimes for distances of two kilometers. Dispersal—movement from place of birth to place of reproduction—is an important feature of animal behavior. Dispersal removes offspring from potential competition with the parents.

The dispersing marmot is without the social protection afforded individuals in established colonies. The disperser has but two eyes to look for danger; colonial animals have the protection of many eyes. It is hardly surprising that dispersing marmots are especially susceptible to predation. These are not fast-moving animals, and coyotes and foxes have no trouble catching them. Colonial marmots are subject to predation by actively burrowing predators (especially badgers), and coyotes excavate a few. Weasels prey on the young in their nests. Outside the protective refuge of the national park, marmots are subject to much wanton molestation by humans.

Marmots are hibernators. In late summer and early autumn they store large amounts of fat. After the annual molt is completed, they enter the burrow for the winter in September or early October to emerge in spring in April or May. The length of the hibernation period varies widely with elevation.

Breeding occurs in spring soon after emergence from hibernation. Gestation takes four to five weeks, and a typical litter comprises three to eight (average four or five) young. Apparently there is some variation in the timing of the breeding season, because small individuals sometimes are seen in spring, suggesting that they are young of litters born late the previous season. The young are altricial and do not appear above ground for about a month. Once above ground, their growth is rapid; young of the year enter hibernation nearly as large as adults. The animals disperse as yearlings; all males and many females move from the natal colony.

Selected References—Armitage (1991, 2003); Frase and Hoffmann (1980).

Wyoming Ground Squirrel
Spermophilus elegans

Description—This is a medium-sized ground squirrel. Adults range from 250 to 340 mm in total length, of which the tail comprises 60 to 100 mm. The ear is quite small, as is typical of burrowing rodents. Weights in early summer average about 325 g for males and somewhat less for females. The color generally is brownish gray, but close examination reveals a dappled pattern obvious difference is that the ground squirrel has no stripes on the head. Also, the tail is relatively shorter. The ground color of the upper parts is golden to reddish buff, grading to whitish beneath. On the shoulders and neck is a russet to golden "mantle," the basis for the common name. *Field Recognition*—Dorsal stripes not continuing onto head; size large for ground-dwelling striped squirrel.

Distribution and Habitat—The golden-mantled ground squirrel ranges through the Mountain West, from central British Columbia and Alberta southward to Arizona and New Mexico and from California eastward to Colorado and Wyoming. A closely related relict population occurs in Chihuahua, Mexico. The golden-mantled ground squirrel occurs in suitable situations throughout Rocky Mountain National Park, from lowest elevations on either side of the Continental Divide to well above timberline. The animals occur in a variety of situations that are exposed to direct sun at some time during the day. In the park they are found most commonly about rocks near the edge of forest or woodland. Rocky fill along roadsides shelters high populations, especially where a source of food is nearby. In southern Colorado and elsewhere, the animals also utilize mountain meadows extensively, but this is seldom so in the park. Perhaps this is due to the presence of the Wyoming ground squirrel, which seems to displace its golden-mantled cousin where the two species come into contact.

Natural History—The golden-mantled ground squirrel may be the most familiar small mammal in Rocky Mountain National Park. Certainly it is among the most beloved—its role as brazen pirate, mendicant, and park-jester is well rehearsed. No campsite, picnic ground, or scenic overlook is without its resident troupe, begging peanuts and other morsels from visitors' larders. With their reliance on summer stock and the tourist trade, one might question whether the animals have a "natural" history at all.

Away from tourist centers, these ground squirrels feed mostly on plant material, with morning being the most active period of feeding. Sharing their habitat with other squirrels (especially chipmunks), they feed on the stems and leaves of herbs, but seeds, berries, and fungi are eaten in quantity. As with other squirrels, they also eat some insects and carrion. On occasion they will eat eggs and young birds. When two individuals converge on the same food item, a dominance hierarchy decides which will feed, precluding undue bickering.

In late summer, heavy deposits of fat are stored on the back and sides, about the neck and shoulders, and over the lower abdomen. By mid-September they are set for the long winter, and in most parts of the park they do not have long to wait. With the first snow and cold they enter a long period of deep winter sleep. The torpid ground squirrel rolls into a tight ball, exposing as little radiative surface as possible. During hibernation, metabolism is regulated to a minimum. Stored fat fuels a sort of metabolic "pilot light" that results in a loss in body weight of about 0.2 percent per day. During warm spells, individuals at lower elevations may arouse for brief periods of activity above ground, but this rousing does not usually happen in the park, and few animals are seen in winter. After all, winter is far more hostile above the snow than beneath it. In spring, the squirrels emerge—sometimes burrowing through late-lying snowdrifts—to begin active foraging and to reproduce.

As with other hibernators, starvation is a common cause of mortality. Weasels take both adults and young, and hawks capture foraging animals. Rocky habitat protects these animals from badgers and diurnal activity precludes serious predation by nocturnal carnivores, such as foxes and owls.

The burrow is similar to that of a chipmunk. The main entrance (there may be others) is hidden beneath a boulder or shrub, and usually it is not marked by excavated debris. A steep entrance tunnel leads to a more or less complex maze of tunnels 5 to 10 cm in diameter and about 30 cm beneath the surface. At the end of the tunnel is the nest chamber. The nest is built of dry grasses and other soft materials, including suitable items salvaged from negligent visitors—string, paper, and bits of cloth and plastic. Generally there is some fecal material in the nest along with the cortege of parasitic and free-living insects and mites typical of burrowing animals.

Upon emergence in spring, male ground squirrels are in breeding condition. Females come into estrus and mate about two weeks later. Gestation takes about four weeks, after which about five (range, two to eight) altricial young are born. A single litter is produced each year, and the animals first breed as yearlings. Neonates are naked (save for facial vibrissae and a patch of hairs on the head) and pinkish in color, and they weigh about 5 g. At four days of age the lateral stripes are evident and the claws and external ears have begun to develop. At fifteen days, the upper parts are well-haired and the front toes have separated; hind toes separate three days later. The eyes do not open until the young are over four weeks old. On a diet of milk, newborns gain about 1.2 g per day; after weaning, they gain about 3.7 g per day until nearly full grown.

Selected References—Bartels and Thompson (1993); W. Carleton (1966); Hatt (1927); McKeever (1964); Yensen and Sherman (2003). Some older literature places this species in the genus *Callospermophilus*; that taxon is now considered a subgenus.

Rock Squirrel *(Jim Osterberg)*

Rock Squirrel
Spermophilus variegatus

Description—The rock squirrel is the largest of the true ground squirrels in our area. In fact, one might mistake it at first glance for a tree squirrel, but no tree squirrel here shares its pale color or its rocky habitat. The animals are 450 to 500 mm in total length and the tail is 185 to 210 mm long. Adults may weigh more than a kilogram. The upper parts are a mottled blend of black, buff, and white, and the animals are reddish buff beneath. Prominent black cheek patches and a white eye-ring mark the face. The feet are buffy to reddish. The tail is full and flattened, black and buff edged with white. *Field Recognition*—Large size, long flat tail, pale color; habitat in rocky, shrub-clad terrain.

Distribution and Habitat—Rock squirrels are mammals of southern affinities that reach their northernmost limits in Colorado and Utah and range southward to the Mexican states of Puebla and Michoacán. They are restricted in our area to the narrow band of foothills along the Front Range, as are some other species, including the Colorado chipmunk, the Mexican woodrat, and the rock mouse.

Rock squirrels have not been documented in the park, although their presence at the lowest elevations on the eastern boundary would come as no surprise. These large squirrels do occur sparingly in the canyons leading to the park from the east, and the observant traveler coming from Lyons or Loveland might expect to see them.

The rock squirrel—as the vernacular name suggests—is an inhabitant of rocky country, where it burrows extensively beneath boulders and shrubs. In settled areas, they frequently occupy the coarse fill along canyon roads. Quarries and streamside thickets are also utilized as cover. In our area, they occur to about 2,290 m (7,500 feet) in suitable habitat.

Natural History—The rock squirrel is a bona fide ground squirrel but it does not hesitate to climb shrubs or low trees to reach preferred food—nuts, berries, and other fruit. They also eat seeds of herbaceous plants, foliage, and small quantities of insects. Food is cached in the burrow. Hibernation or winter dormancy doubtless occurs, but details are unavailable.

Remarkably little is known about the biology of this animal, perhaps because it is of little economic importance (although rock squirrels can become pests in orchards). A closely related species, the California ground squirrel (*Spermophilus beecheyi*) is an important agricultural pest on the West Coast and it has been the subject of extensive study.

Rock squirrels breed once a year, in spring. Probably six or seven young are the mode, with eight being the maximum. Neonates are highly altricial and do not come above ground until nearly two months old.

Selected References—K. Johnson (1981); Oaks et al. (1987); Yensen and Sherman (2003).

Abert's Squirrel
Sciurus aberti

Description—Abert's squirrel is a large, heavy-bodied rodent, of striking appearance because of its conspicuous ear tufts and long, full tail. Adults are 525 to 575 mm in total length, and the tail is 240 to 300 mm long. Weights range around 700 g. The local race of Abert's squirrel (*S. a. ferreus*—with type locality west of Loveland) occurs in three distinctive color phases. In the park, a majority of individuals are dark gray dorsally, the banding of the hairs lend-

Abert's Squirrels *(Fi Rust)*

ing a salt-and-pepper pattern on close examination. There is a distinct, black lateral line and the belly is white. There may be a middorsal patch of brick-red hairs, but this is less common locally than in southwestern Colorado and adjacent parts of the Colorado Plateau. The grayish tail is prominently fringed with white hairs. Many animals in the park have pure black pelage. Occasional dark brown individuals are found. *Field Recognition*—Large size, tufted ears; gray, black, or brown color.

Distribution and Habitat—Abert's squirrel reaches its present-day northern limits in extreme southern Wyoming and is distributed southward in the
foothills and lower mountains to New Mexico and Arizona, with relict, outly-
ing populations in Chihuahua and Durango, Mexico. This beautiful mammal
occurs along the eastern margin of Rocky Mountain National Park at elevations to about 2,600 m (8,500 feet). The principal habitat of Abert's squirrel
is ponderosa pine woodlands, but the animals may range locally into other
forest types.

Natural History—Abert's squirrel is both larger and less boisterous than
its contentious cousin, the pine squirrel, or chickaree. The visitor who chan-
ces to see an Abert's squirrel ought to consider the day well spent. These are
beautiful squirrels but sporadic in distribution and given to fluctuations in
abundance.

Much of their diet is provided by the ponderosa pine—seeds, buds, inner
bark, and young male cones. Feeding trees are selected on the basis of low
levels of particular monoterpenes, the volatile chemicals that give pine trees
their turpentine aroma. In addition, the squirrels feed on berries and other
fruit, fungi, and some carrion as available. As other rodents, they gnaw bones
and antlers, presumably for their mineral content, sometimes carrying them
to the nest. Food is not stored in appreciable amounts.

Nests are built of twigs in the crotch of a branch or in a "witch's broom"
(a dense, pathologic growth of small branches perhaps stimulated by mistle-
toe infestation). In our area, most nests are at least 5 to 7 m above ground
in ponderosa pines of moderate size, trees averaging about a half meter in
diameter. The nest chamber is about 15 cm in diameter, carpeted with soft
plant materials or debris cast off by people. The animals retire to the nest at
night and during harsh winter weather.

Abert's squirrels are not known to defend territories. The home range
is rather large, averaging nearly 8 hectares (20 acres), some ten times that
of a pine squirrel (but recall that Abert's squirrel is a larger animal and that
its resources are less concentrated). Intraspecific fighting is most common
among males during the breeding season, and mating chases often are quite
vigorous and vocal.

Perhaps hawks (especially goshawks) are the most important predator of
Abert's squirrels. Terrestrial carnivores have difficulty preying on so arboreal
a rodent to any significant extent, and martens usually do not range down
into the open woodland frequented by the squirrels. The most important factors regulating populations (and their fluctuations) may be the availability of
food. When cones are scarce, Abert's squirrels have been reported to take
nearly three-quarters of the crop. Habitat has been influenced over much
of the squirrel's range by the intervention of people in the ponderosa pine

woodland. Also, the seed crop of the ponderosa pine is highly variable and could contribute to a pattern of cyclic abundance.

Abert's squirrels breed in spring—late March to May—and a litter of two to five (average about 3.5) young is born after a gestation period of approximately seven weeks. The newborn young are naked and blind, and the ears are unopen. They are about 60 mm in length and weigh some 12 g. At about seven weeks of age they are fully haired and venture from the nest for short periods of time. They are weaned at about nineteen weeks of age and reach full adult size some six weeks later. There are two periods of molt each year, in spring and fall. Summer pelage is brighter and has more white hairs than does winter pelage.

Selected References—Farentinos (1972); Hoffmeister and Diersing (1978); Keith (1965); Nash and Seaman (1977); Snyder (1992, 1998).

Eastern Fox Squirrel
Sciurus niger

The eastern fox squirrel is a tree squirrel about the same size as Abert's squirrel but grayish brown above, reddish brown on the sides, and reddish to buff on the belly. The ears are not tufted. The animals are 450 to 600 mm in total length, and the tail is 170 to 300 mm long. Weights range up to a kilogram, especially when individuals have fattened in preparation for winter.

This is a species of deciduous forests and woodlands. Fox squirrels have come to occur in Colorado only within the past century. Earliest populations were introduced deliberately to enliven Colorado's newy established urban woodlands. By the mid-twentieth century, fox squirrels were present along the full extent of the South Platte corridor across northeastern Colorado. Control of flooding and prairie fires apparently allowed establishment of continuous riparian woodland habitat that was not present prior to permanent Euroamerican settlement in eastern Colorado.

Fox squirrels are abundant and conspicuous urban wildlife, feeding on fruit and seeds of onamental plantings and shade trees. Occasionally they are deliberately fed by humans and they also exploit feeders intended for songbirds and eat orchard fruit and garden produce. As urban, suburban, and ex-urban has expanded into the mountains in recent decades, fox squirrels have followed the expansion, often moving beyond residential areas into native riparian woodlands along the major streams of the Eastern Slope, such as the Saint Vrain, Cache la Poudre, and Big Thompson Rivers. Given this tendency, it was only a matter of time before the animals reached Rocky Mountain National Park. In recent years the animals have been observed along Beaver Brook, south of the Beaver Meadows Entrance to the national park.

Fox squirrels are aggressive and appear to dominate the native Abert's squirrel at both artificial and natural food sources. On the Boulder Mountain Parks, expanding populations of fox squirrels appear to have depressed or displaced populations of Abert's squirrels.

Fox squirrels are interesting and even entertaining animals in their place. But their native range does not include Rocky Mountain National Park, and they almost certainly would not occur here without human assistance, deliberate or inadvertent. Park Service personnel will want to monitor fox squirrels to assess negative impacts on native tree squirrels, both Abert's squirrels and pine squirrels.

Selected References—Edwards et al. (2003); Fitzgerald et al. (1994); Koprowski (1994).

Pine Squirrel, Chickaree, or Red Squirrel
Tamiasciurus hudsonicus

Description—The chickaree—often called "pine squirrel" locally—is the smallest of local tree squirrels. Total length ranges from 300 to 350 mm, and the bushy tail is 115 to 135 mm long. Adults weigh 195 to 200 g. The ears are conspicuous but only slightly tufted. The textbook name for the animals— "red squirrel"—is inappropriate in our area (although descriptive over some parts of their broad range), because our animals are dark grayish brown in color, sometimes becoming slightly more reddish in summer pelage. In summer, the venter is nearly white and there is a distinctive black lateral line; in winter, underparts are grayish white and the black line is obscure. The tail is generally blackish brown, bordered with a conspicuous fringe of white-tipped hairs. *Field Recognition*—Small size, ears without tassels; chattering alarm call; habitat mostly in dense forests of middle elevations; conspicuous middens of cone scales and cores.

Distribution and Habitat—The pine squirrel is a boreal mammal, occurring from Alaska to Labrador and southward through the United States (at increasingly high elevations) to South Carolina, New Mexico, and Arizona. The chickaree does not occur in the Sierra Nevada and other far western mountain ranges, being replaced there by a closely related species, Douglas' squirrel (*Tamiasciurus douglasii*). Chickarees occur in the heavy forests of middle elevation, preferring the cover of spruce-fir, Douglas-fir, or lodgepole pine stands to that of ponderosa pine woodland. Criteria for suitable habitat include conifers to provide cones for food and sites suitably damp and cool for cone storage.

Natural History—The scolding call of the chickaree is familiar to anyone who has wandered by day along the forest trails of the park. There is some-

Pine Squirrel, Chickaree, or Red Squirrel *(Gene Putney)*

thing ventriloquial about the chickaree's voice, and it may take some patience to locate the source of the mechanical chattering sound. But these are persistent alarmists and the din will continue until the intruder moves on. Listening closely for the raspy crackle of claws against spruce bark, one should be rewarded by the sight of this bold and handsome defender of territorial rights. Chickarees reveal their presence not only by calls but by leaving a copious and characteristic sign—a midden of scales and cores of conifer cones.

Chickarees are highly territorial mammals. A repertoire of distinctive calls warns the intruder against trespass and challenges him to leave the vicinity. An additional call by the trespasser asks momentary peace of the trespassee. The territory ranges in size from about 0.4 to 1.2 hectares (1 to 3 acres), depending on the density of food resources. Territories may be defended by vigorous physical combat if ritual vocalization fails. Males and females defend individual territories throughout the year, except when the female is in estrus. Only then does a female drop her defense, and males converge on her territory, calling and chasing each other and jousting for dominance and mating rights.

The chickaree midden is an obvious feature of the forest scene. The pile of litter may be 6 to 10 m across and 30 cm or more deep, containing several cubic meters of debris. The largest middens represent the leavings of successive generations of squirrels over decades. Often middens are between felled logs or alongside windthrown trees. The surface layer consists of a dry mulch but lower levels are in various stages of decay, leading to a rich humus. Abandoned middens are slowly succeeded by mosses, kinnikinnik, and other acid-loving plants, but active middens usually are devoid of vegetation. Most frequently, the midden is in a permanently moist, shady location. The dense cover of spruce forest is ideal because lower branches tend to lie at or near the ground, shielding the midden from drying. Cones are stashed up to 30 cm deep in pits dug in the midden. Several cones are deposited in each pit and then the cache is covered with litter. Cones also may be cached in bogs, pools, and springs. Cones of lodgepole pine, which remain closed even when dry, may be buried less deeply or simply stockpiled above ground.

In winter and spring the squirrels dig up cones—often burrowing through the snow to locate them—and carry them to a branch, rock, or other vantage point, which serves as a feeding station. The seeds are removed and the inedible debris accrues to the midden. The principle is that of a person who builds a pantry and dining room out of cast-off jars and tin cans, but the overall effect is rather more pleasant.

In summer, the diet is somewhat varied, including buds, fungi, berries, and other fruits, but the mainstay remains conifer seeds. Bark sometimes is stripped from small branches and eaten. The result of this activity looks like porcupine sign on a modest scale. As cones begin to mature, the early "milk" seeds are eaten. In August, seeds reach the "dough" stage and cone storage begins, continuing in earnest through October. On a productive tree, the chickaree is a veritable cone-cutting machine, lopping off a green cone every two or three seconds. Cones of spruces are preferred, perhaps because of their large size and the fact that good cone crops occur two out of three seasons. Douglas-fir is a less reliable cone source, producing a large crop only one year in five. Lodgepole pine often is a staple because cones remain on the branches unopened and production is rather consistent from one year to the next.

Chickarees are active by day, especially in early morning. At night and during severe weather they retire to the nest, an informal globular affair 30 cm or more in diameter built of grasses and conifer needles and situated in a crotch 6 to 12 m above ground. The nest chamber is 10 to 12 cm around and lined with mosses and shredded grass. Chickarees may also nest in tree holes or hollow logs, and occasionally they nest in holes at ground level.

Chickarees spend a good deal of time on the ground, where they are preyed upon by weasels, foxes, and coyotes. The classic enemy of the pine squirrel is the American marten, a weasel-like arboreal carnivore. To escape danger in the trees, chickarees may jump six meters to the ground.

Chickarees mate once a year, usually in April. After a gestation period of about forty days, one to six (average, four) young are born. The young are blind and hairless but rather robust, with disproportionately large heads (as is typical of newborn mammals). Young squirrels are nursed until mid-July and do not leave the nest until one-third grown. If the nest is disturbed, the mother may carry the young one-by-one in her mouth to an alternate nest. After a period of training in the art of being a chickaree, the young leave the maternal territory to establish their own domains.

Selected References—Finley (1969); Hatt (1943); C. Smith (1968); Steele (1998); Yahner (2003).

FAMILY GEOMYIDAE—POCKET GOPHERS

Pocket gophers are unique North American rodents, strongly specialized for subterranean life. There are six living genera, with about forty species. Three genera (including four species) occur in Colorado, but only one species lives in Rocky Mountain National Park.

Northern Pocket Gopher
Thomomys talpoides

Description—The northern pocket gopher is a rather small, stocky animal, its architecture suiting its ecological role as a biological excavation service. Total length is 200 to 230 mm, and the sparsely haired tail is 50 to 70 mm long. Adults weigh about 120 to 150 g. Males are somewhat larger than females, especially in cranial dimensions. In our area, northern pocket gophers are brownish in color, grayish to medium brown on the Eastern Slope, and darker brown to nearly black west of the Continental Divide. The underparts and tail are paler in color and more sparsely furred. Probably the most obvious feature of the animals is their large yellowish-orange incisors, always in view because the lips close behind them. The ears are tiny. The large cheek pouches open externally rather than into the mouth cavity, and they are lined with fur. The limbs are short and powerful and the forelimbs are strongly clawed. *Field Recognition*—Moderate size, short tail; exposed incisors; shallow burrows; mounds conspicuous but with no obvious entrance.

Distribution and Habitat—The northern pocket gopher is a mammal of the Mountain West and the Northern Great Plains. In Colorado, this is mostly an animal of the mountains; other species of pocket gophers inhabit western valleys and the eastern plains. Northern pocket gophers occur throughout Rocky Mountain National Park in open situations with well-drained soils. Pocket gophers inhabit all open habitat types in the park but reach greatest abundance in meadows, where perennial forbs provide a rich food supply. In ranchlands adjacent to the park, hayfields are favored habitat. Pocket gophers also occur in grassy parks and above timberline. Their burrows are conspicuous in the alpine tundra along Trail Ridge Road.

Natural History—Northern pocket gophers, known simply as "gophers" or sometimes as "moles" (quite incorrectly, because moles are soricomorphs and do not occur in the mountains of Colorado), are the most specialized burrowers in the local fauna. Only rarely are they seen above ground. The external ears and the eyes are greatly reduced, further adaptations to their digging behavior. Seemingly, no soil is too rocky, hard, or shallow for them. I have seen evidence of gophers burrowing beneath the thin alpine sod covering a large, flat rock. The soil—probably trapped from the wind by pioneer plants—was less than three centimeters deep. The gopher simply pushed its way along between rock and sod, leaving an arch of turf overhead. As satisfactory a burrow might have been built between a living room floor and a carpet; the effect was much the same. The lips close behind the incisors, so the mouth can be closed while rocks and soil are carried with the teeth. The burrow system may be over 150 m in length, usually from 10 to 45 cm below the surface. This represents the excavation of nearly three tons of soil. Side tunnels and chambers are filled with food or feces or are used for nesting. Excess soil is thrown out in characteristic loose mounds. Gopher mounds (unlike mounds built by Wyoming ground squirrels) do not have an entrance

Pocket gopher "eskers" beneath melting snowbank *(David Armstrong)*

hole. Waste soil is pushed out on the surface and then the tunnel is plugged. Abandoned burrows are preempted by a variety of animals, including other rodents, salamanders, toads, snakes, and insects.

The diet consists exclusively of plant material. During spring and summer, foliage and stems are eaten, forbs more than grasses. Vegetation is clipped at night from around the mound, and it may be stored in subterranean chambers. During the winter, the animals subsist largely on roots, bulbs, and tubers. Some foraging occurs above ground in snow tunnels, either on the surface of the soil or in the snowpack itself. In spring, nest chambers may be built high in the snowpack, because tunnels in the ground are saturated with meltwater. Tunnels in the snow are packed with soil brought up from below ground. After snowmelt in spring, these sinuous winter casts—ridges 5 to 10 cm across and often several meters in length (sometimes called "gopher garlands" or "eskers")—are conspicuous features of the mountain landscape. Their presence suppresses the growth of some plant species and thus influences plant succession.

Badgers and coyotes excavate pocket gophers and prey on them. Weasels also capture some and owls take a toll, especially dispersing young, which tend to move above ground. Ticks, mites, lice, and fleas affect pocket gophers as they do most mammals. Endoparasites include both roundworms and flatworms.

Under favorable conditions, populations may reach densities of fifty or more individuals per hectare (twenty per acre). The soil in such situations may be so completely undermined that it gives away underfoot. Often it is impossible to say where one burrow system stops and the next begins, although underground there is little or no overlap between adjacent gophers. Mounds may cover vegetation, lowering production and driving ecological succession. On rangelands and in cultivated areas, especially where natural predators have been limited by humans, pocket gophers may become significant pests. Their mounds damage mowing equipment and sometimes gophers burrow through ditch banks, giving the rancher unsolicited assistance with the irrigation program. However, pocket gophers are important agents in the soil-building process, aerating the soil and mixing materials between soil horizons. Fortunately, pocket gophers (and all other wildlife) have free rein in the national park to perform their unique roles in the continual evolution of ecosystems.

Adult pocket gophers breed in the spring, beginning as yearlings. Mating occurs in April or May and three to ten (average, four to six) young are born in April or June. A single litter is produced each year. The young mature rapidly and are above ground as early as late June. From July to September the young leave the maternal burrow to establish residence on their own.

Selected References—R. Baker, Bradley, and McAliley (2003); Hansen (1960); Hansen and Ward (1966); Verts and Carraway (1999).

FAMILY CASTORIDAE—BEAVERS

There are two living species of beavers, which make up a single Holarctic genus (*Castor*). The family is less diverse today than it once was; fourteen extinct genera are known as fossils.

American Beaver
Castor canadensis

Description—The beaver is the largest rodent in Rocky Mountain National Park, indeed, the largest in North America north of Panama. Adults are about a meter long, of which the broad, flat tail comprises about one-third of the total length. Large old males may weigh over 25 kg. The animals are a rich brownish color above, paling somewhat to golden brown beneath. The dense underfur is grayish brown. The scaly, nearly naked tail and feet are black. *Field Recognition*—Large size, flat tail; signs: dams, lodges, waterways, gnawed tree stumps.

Distribution and Habitat—The American beaver ranges throughout most of North America north of Mexico, except for parts of the Arctic Slope,

American Beaver *(Fi Rust)*

the Desert Southwest, and peninsular Florida. This is a familiar mammal throughout Rocky Mountain National Park wherever permanent streams of moderate grade provide suitable habitat.

Natural History—Certainly the beaver is among our most familiar and fascinating native mammals. The fur trade, with the beaver as a mainstay, was responsible for the early exploration of much of North America. Beavers have had an important role in ecological as well as social history. They have a more profound and conspicuous effect on their immediate environment than any mammal other than humans. Major features of the landscape in the national park (Beaver Meadows and Horseshoe Park, for example) owe their existence to the persistent work of innumerable generations of beavers over thousands of years.

The most far-reaching ecological effects are produced by the construction of dams. Barriers of logs, sticks, rocks, and mud are built across shallow streams. The dam may be two meters high and several hundred meters long (the record is 4.2 m high and 1,000 m long). The pond impounded by the beaver dam protects the lodge from predators and assures a swimming area beneath the winter ice. As the catchment basin behind the dam fills, the surrounding soil becomes waterlogged. Many kinds of plants cannot survive in the saturated, oxygen-poor soils. They die and their demise allows the invasion of species adapted to permanently moist soil: alder, willows, cottonwood, aspen. The bark and twigs of these species are the staple foods of beavers. Thus, a beaver pond not only serves as an all-weather transportation route and a protective moat but also favors a plant community dominated by preferred food species. Beavers are not just builders, they are farmers as well. And they also are innkeepers, for the pond provides still-water habitat for a variety of other wildlife—muskrats, fish, mink, ducks, and shorebirds—that might not occupy the swiftly flowing waters of an unmodified mountain stream.

A stream not only carries water but it also carries a load of silt and organic debris. As stream flow is slowed, its load-bearing capacity diminishes. Silt falls to the bottom of the pond. The long-term fate of the beaver dam is no different than the fate of a man-made dam. Eventually (unless carried away by flood), the dam becomes a retaining wall at the lower end of a rich deposit of silt and organic detritus. The pond becomes a meadow and one day the meadow may become a forest. Beavers fascinate us with their industry. They can also help us to put our most colossal works in proper perspective, as they show that we are powerless against the obstinate and inexorable forces of ecological succession and that our creations are ephemeral in the immensity of geological time.

Beavers build "houses" of various kinds. Dens, simple burrows or surface dens walled with sticks and mud and accessible by an underwater tunnel, may be built along streambanks. Lodges are familiar and common. Unlike the bank den, a lodge is built in the open water of the pond. It may be 2 m or more in height and up to 5 m in diameter. The lodge is built in water 2 to 3 m deep. The foundation has a doorway, and the entire structure is hollow. Logs, limbs, and sod form the walls, which narrow to enclose the top. Most of the house is plastered with mud and sod, although some open areas aid in ventilation. Inside, a floor is built a few centimeters above the high-water line. Here a nest chamber is built, lined with grass and shredded bark.

Systems of canals may be built to float logs and food materials to the pond, and the water level in canals may be maintained with a system of dams. The "engineering" ability of beavers is remarkable and has earned them a place in folklore and a reputation larger than life. We are inclined to ascribe their feats to superior intelligence, but in fact their "ingenuity" stems mostly from a highly evolved program of innate behavior. One frequently hears, for example, that a beaver can fell a tree in any desired direction, such as toward the water. Actually, cut trees fall toward the water because trees grow toward the open space above the stream or pond where light is more intense. Thus, competition for light inclines trees in a fortuitous direction. Reports of beavers pinned beneath falling trees are common enough to dispel some of the legends concerning their alleged great skill and intelligence.

The diet consists exclusively of vegetable matter and varies in composition with the season. Grass and other herbage are eaten during the summer, and the consumption of bark during the growing season is largely incidental to preparing building material. Branches of conifers may be cut for construction material but they are rarely eaten. Reingestion of soft feces has been reported.

Aquatic habits protect beavers from serious predation. Mink can enter the den to prey on the kits. Although wonderfully graceful in the water, beavers are rather clumsy and slow on dry land. When dispersing overland or attending to their needs for food and building materials, they may be surprised and killed by coyotes, bobcats, or mountain lions. When near the water, of course, they escape quickly from terrestrial predators, a quick slap of the tail warning the rest of the colony of danger. Tularemia and parasites exact a toll on the beaver population each year. Flood and drought probably were the most effective controls on populations before the arrival of European settlers. Over-trapping pushed the beaver to the verge of extinction in many areas, but now habitat modification by humans may be a more important factor in population control over most of the beaver's wide range.

Beavers are highly modified for aquatic life. The hindfeet are webbed. The eyes are small and have a clear inner "lid" that allows the eyes to remain open underwater. The ears are short and valvular—capable of being closed when the animal submerges. The nostrils also are valvular. The pelage is dense and heavy, with a sleek, waterproof coat of coarse guard hairs and a fine, dense underfur. The body is very streamlined. The urogenital and digestive tracts empty into a single chamber, the cloaca, and hence have a common opening. (This feature makes the sexes virtually indistinguishable externally.) Due to special controls on heartrate and breathing, the animals routinely remain submerged for four to five minutes, with maximal dives of fifteen minutes.

There is a single molt annually. The two inner toes of each hindfoot are cleft and are used in grooming to maintain the pelage. Paired anal scent glands called "castors" are present in both sexes but are better developed in the male. Their secretions may function in courtship or territorial marking.

The social life of the beaver is based on a nuclear family—a pair of adults, the yearlings, and the kits. A large colony may consist of several families. When crowded, individuals disperse along streams or overland to found a new colony. In prime habitat in the national park there may be a beaver colony every 3 or 4 km of stream.

Beavers breed in January or February, and four or five (range one to nine) young are born in April or May after a gestation period of some 120 days. Females produce a single litter of young per year. Newborn beavers are small but are fully furred and have the eyes open. Females breed at two years of age, but full growth may not be achieved for several years. The young remain in the parental den as yearlings and then disperse. Beavers are long-lived rodents, the record being nineteen years.

Selected References—B. Baker and Hill (2003); E. Hill (1982); Jenkins and Busher (1979); Neff (1959); Rue (1964b).

FAMILY CRICETIDAE—NATIVE MICE, RATS, AND VOLES

The cricetids comprise a diverse assemblage of rodents, including at least nine species in six genera locally. Some twenty-five species of cricetids occur in Colorado. Two common household pets, the hamster (*Cricetus*) and the gerbil (or jird—*Meriones*), are Old World representatives of this family, which includes nearly 700 species in some 130 genera. There is no real consensus on the classification of these mammals. Many zoologists contend that the cricetids ought to be considered part of the family Muridae, the great group of Old World mice (the family of the all-too-familiar house mouse, *Mus musculus,* and the black and Norway rats, *Rattus*).

Two distinctive subfamilies of the Cricetidae occur in Rocky Mountain National Park—the cricetines (mice and woodrats) and the arvicolines (voles and muskrat). The smaller members of these two groups are distinguished by many people as "field mice" and "meadow mice," respectively.

Deer Mouse
Peromyscus maniculatus

Description—The deer mouse is highly variable in color and size in our area, because the foothills of the Colorado Front Range represent a zone of intergradation between a larger, darker mountain race and a smaller, paler plains subspecies. Total length ranges from 145 to 180 mm, and the tail is 55 to 75 mm long. Weights range from about 18 to 30 g. The grayish ears are conspicuous but obviously shorter than those of the rock mouse. The color of the back varies from grayish tan to rich reddish brown. The belly and feet are white, although they sometimes appear grayish as the bases of the hairs sometimes show. The tail is black above, whitish below. The rock mouse is the only local species with which the deer mouse might be confused. The deer mouse is smaller in size than the rock mouse and has markedly shorter ears and tail, and adults are predominantly brownish in color rather than grayish.

Deer Mouse *(Gene Putney)*

Field Recognition—Small size, brownish color with white underparts; tail shorter than head and body and markedly bicolored.

Distribution and Habitat—The deer mouse occurs from northern Canada to southern Mexico and from coast to coast in the United States (including many offshore islands), except in the Southeast. Virtually every terrestrial habitat in Rocky Mountain National Park supports a population of these ubiquitous little mice, although the animals are more common in upland habitats than in meadows and shoreline communities. Forest edge situations and broken, shrubby terrain probably afford the best conditions and support highest populations. Areas disturbed by fire, mining, or settlement and overgrown by weedy vegetation support large numbers of deer mice. Weeds, by nature, are invasive, usually annual plants that produce copious amounts of seed, thus providing abundant food for seed-eating rodents. Weedy plants are opportunistic invaders of ephemeral habitats. In a certain sense, so are deer mice, and it is rather useful to think of them as "animal weeds." It came as no surprise to learn that deer mice were the first small mammals to take up residence on the debris fan left by the Lawn Lake Flood of 1982. Deer mice comprised nearly 80 percent of small mammal biomass on and near the alluvial fan. The elevational range is from the foothills to the tops of the highest peaks.

Natural History—The deer mouse is our most common native mammal. Being nocturnal, they seldom are seen, and only an occasional nest or a trail of tiny, elongate droppings reveals their presence, but they are surely there. This is the local mouse, and it is unfortunate that they are so secretive for they are beautiful little mammals. Were they more widely known, some of the popular misconceptions about mice might be dispelled, or at least momentarily forgotten. True, they can be pests, particularly if allowed the run of a pantry. They feed on virtually any vegetable matter and humankind's provisions are an irresistible lure. It is also true that they may set up housekeeping (including a very active nursery) among clothes in a neglected trunk, leaving a tattered shambles at the end of the season. But the motive is hunger, cold, or curiosity—never malice.

Away from human settlement, deer mice live in nests of soft grasses beneath shrubs, rocks, logs, or debris or in burrows abandoned by other animals, especially pocket gophers. Unlike voles, they do not make runways, but when foraging they do make use of those of other species. They are fairly agile climbers, foraging readily in low shrubbery, but they are far less arboreal than their long-tailed cousin the rock mouse. The diet consists of seeds, fungi, berries, and other fruits, with lesser amounts of green herbage. Insects are eaten when available and may make up the bulk of the diet for some individuals in season. Food habits change with local and seasonal availability. In diet as in habitat selection, opportunism is the rule. Adaptability, coupled with a remarkable reproductive potential, is probably the key to their obvious success over a wide geographic and ecological range.

Home ranges seem to vary among individuals. Some mice are rather sedentary whereas others range over a quarter hectare or more. Generally, immature individuals seem to range more widely than do adults, and males wander farther than females do. Juvenile males were the most abundant mice on the alluvial fan left by the Lawn Lake Flood. There is no well-defined territory, although mutual avoidance may promote spacing. Unlike many rodents, deer mice can be crowded—even on short rations—and show no particular evidence of stress. A male may share a nest with a pregnant female, and a mother will tolerate the presence of weaned juveniles while she is nursing their younger siblings. Such tolerance is rather uncommon among small mammals.

In many situations, deer mice are the most abundant mammalian consumers. As a consequence they form an important link in the food web, providing the energetic link between plants and flesh-eating animals. Coyotes, foxes, bobcats, weasels, skunks, owls, and snakes all feed on them. When pursued, the deer mouse follows an erratic zigzag course to the nearest cover and then becomes motionless. So stereotyped is this behavior that a mouse may hide its head and freeze, leaving the posterior wholly exposed to view. Like many other aspects of animal behavior, this pattern seems to leave room for improvement. But over the long run, their behavior must work. These are successful animals by any criterion. The mice host a wide variety of external and internal parasites. Predation, parasites, a harsh environment, and the stress of almost continual reproduction contribute to a short life expectancy. A year-old mouse is old indeed; few survive a second winter.

Female deer mice are polyestrous and exhibit postpartum estrus. The average female stays pregnant almost continually throughout the warmer months of the year. In more hospitable climates, these animals breed year-around, but in the Southern Rockies, the reproductive season is from about April to September. The gestation period varies from about twenty-three days to over four weeks, the longer extreme being more characteristic of lactating females.

The mother gives birth in the daytime (as is typical of nocturnal mammals). There are only six mammae, but litters of one to nine are known to have been reared successfully. Females at higher elevations tend to have fewer, larger litters than do those at lower elevations, perhaps because the breeding season is shorter.

The pinkish newborns are naked (except for facial vibrissae) and blind. The ears are closed, and the toes, although clawed, are not yet separated. Newborn young are about 45 mm long and weigh about 1.5 g. The gray juvenal pelage develops the first week and the eyes open at the end of the second. The young are weaned abruptly at about 3½ weeks, when the mother gives birth to a new litter. By that time the young are quite agile and forage on their own. They molt to a grayish brown subadult pelage at about six weeks of age. By this time, or soon after, both males and females are reproductively mature (although only about half their eventual body weight), and—unless bad weather intervenes—they may breed, although full size and adult pelage are several weeks away.

In the Rocky Mountain region, deer mice appear to be a natural reservoir of hantavirus, the causative agent of an acute pulmonary syndrome that was first recognized in the Four Corners area of the American Southwest but now is reported rather widely in both North and South America. Persons who need to enter seasonal cabins, livestock barns, outhouses, rock shelters, or other closed, dark spaces where rodent dung and dust can accumulate need to take precautions against hantavirus infection. A prudent first step is to consult the Worldwide Web page of the Centers for Disease Control.

Selected References—Armstrong (1977, 1993); Callisher et al. (2003); Douglas (1969); J. King (1968); Merritt and Merritt (1980).

Northern Rock Mouse
Peromyscus nasutus

Description—This is a relatively large, long-tailed mouse. Adults are 170 to 200 mm in total length, and the tail is 80 to 100 mm long. Weights range around 28 to 30 g. Adults are grayish above, buffy on the sides, and dirty white beneath. The tail is bicolored (although sometimes obscurely so). Only the deer mouse could be confused with the rock mouse, and once one actually has seen a rock mouse, with its remarkably long (22 to 24 mm) ears, there can be no question about the distinction. *Field Recognition*—Grayish color, large size, relatively long ears, and tail as long as body.

Distribution and Habitat—The rock mouse is mostly a mammal of the foothills, mesas, and lower mountains of the Southwest, ranging from Arizona, New Mexico, and Texas and then northward in a narrow band along the foothills of the Colorado Rockies nearly to the Wyoming boundary. This linear, "peninsular" distribution is shown also by the Mexican woodrat, the Colorado chipmunk, and the rock squirrel. The common name "rock mouse" is an appropriate one, for this is a species of broken foothills habitats. In our area the animals most often are associated with stands of mountain mahogany and bitterbrush, shrubs typical of rocky sites. Stands of ponderosa pine and Rocky Mountain juniper are also occupied. The elevational range of

Northern Rock Mouse *(R. B. Forbes/ASM Mammal Images Library)*

the species is rather narrow, from about 1,675 to 2,560 m (5,500 to 8,400 feet), depending on local exposure and topography, and reaching highest elevations on south-facing canyon walls.

This mouse first was discovered in Estes Park. For many years the species was considered a subspecies of a mostly Mexican species, *Peromyscus difficilis,* but it is now recognized as a distinctive species. The animals occur in Rocky Mountain National Park only along the extreme eastern boundary, the western margin of Estes Park.

Natural History—The rock mouse makes its home in rough, rocky terrain, and little is known of its habits. Like other species of the genus, it is largely a seedeater, feeding on seeds and fruits of a variety of plants but taking insects as opportunity allows. The habitat is shared with the smaller, shorter-tailed deer mouse, and no study has been made of the means by which the species, both nocturnal, divide resources between themselves. One might suppose that, with its longer tail for balance, the rock mouse would be the more agile climber, better suited to clamber about shrubs and rocks in its foraging rounds.

Male rock mice are in breeding condition from about March or April through August. Females are polyestrous, with breeding beginning in April and continuing through July with the last young born in August. Two to six young are born after a gestation period of three to four weeks. Quite probably females born early in the season breed their first summer, but the extent to which this happens is unknown.

Selected References—Armstrong (1996); M. Carleton (1989); Cinq-Mars and Brown (1969); J. King (1968).

Bushy-tailed Woodrat
Neotoma cinerea

Description—Bushy-tailed woodrats are the largest of Coloradan woodrats. Adults range from 375 to 420 mm in total length, and the tail is 150 to 190 mm long; males are on average about 15 percent larger than females. Males weigh about 350 g, females about 300. The pelage is long, dense, and remarkably soft. The upper parts are golden to orangish buff, becoming grayish when the pelage is worn, and the hairs of the underparts are white with

Bushy-tailed Woodrat *(R. B. Forbes / ASM Mammal Images Library)*

grayish bases. As the common name suggests, the tail is bushy (especially pronounced in adult males), quite distinctive among Coloradan woodrats. The tail is pale gray above and white below.

Distribution and Habitat—The bushy-tailed woodrat is a mammal of the Mountain West, ranging from Alaska southward to New Mexico and from the Pacific Coast to the badlands and escarpments of the western Dakotas and Nebraska. In Colorado, the animals occur through mountainous parts of the state and in the rough country along the rim of the High Plains in the northeast. They occur throughout Rocky Mountain National Park to elevations above timberline and are especially abundant in talus slides and fractured cliff faces.

Natural History—This is a packrat's packrat. Few local rodents are the subject of more—or more amusing—folktales and, interestingly enough, most of the legends are true. There is a common misconception, however, that this is a thief with a conscience, that packrats—or "trade rats"—will not steal an object without leaving another in exchange. In fact, such "trades" do occur, but they stem from limited cargo capacity and not from some innate sense of fair play. The collecting instinct is so strong that one object is dropped to allow another to be picked up. To give an idea of the range of the animal's tastes, here is a partial catalog of the contents of some dens in Colorado: tar paper, nails, rattlesnake carcass, peach pit, snakeskin, rope, leather glove, shotgun shell, coal, bolt (and spare nut), hacksaw blade, wire, porcelain insulator, sticks, stones, and dung. Bones are common in dens; they are used for construction material and gnawed for their mineral content.

Collected materials add to the bulk of the den, which protects the animals from perils both physical and biological. The den is built mostly of sticks from nearby trees and shrubs. It is usually situated in a vertical crack or on a shelf in a cave or building. Within the house, a cup-shaped nest is built of fibrous plant materials. A given den may contain more than one nest.

The diet of bushy-tailed woodrats is catholic. There is a predilection for foliage over other parts of plants, but virtually any plant species is suitable. Food may be eaten on the spot during the nocturnal foraging expedition or it may be stored. Large quantities of leaves are stored in crevices in the rocks for winter use.

Like other mammals, these rats host a variety of parasites. Their predators include coyotes, bobcats, and raptorial birds (especially owls). Snakes and weasels take the young. In general, however, inaccessible habitat probably protects them from most predators.

The bushy-tailed woodrat typically has a single litter of young per year, but postpartum estrus does occur, and females pregnant while lactating have been reported. Females attain sexual maturity during their first winter and breed as yearlings. After a gestation period of about four weeks, one to six (mode, four) young are born.

    Selected References—Finley (1958); Monty and Emerson (2003); F. Smith (1997).

Mexican Woodrat
Neotoma mexicana

    Description—This is the smaller of our two local woodrats. Adults range in total length from 300 to 360 mm, of which the tail comprises 130 to 170 mm. As with woodrats generally, males are larger than females. In color, the upper parts are grayish brown, with a heavy sprinkling of blackish guard hairs and a dirty yellow wash, especially noticeable on the sides. Beneath, the hairs are gray-based and white-tipped. The tail is covered with short hairs and markedly bicolored, with a black middorsal stripe. *Field Recognition*—Moderate size, short-haired tail; habitat in horizontal rock formations of foothills.

    Distribution and Habitat—The Mexican woodrat is a mammal of the southwestern United States and western Mexico. The northern limits of the range are along the Front Range in northern Colorado, and the species ranges southward to Honduras and El Salvador. In Colorado, the foothills provide

Mexican Woodrat *(R. B. Forbes / ASM Mammal Images Library)*

the Mexican woodrat with ideal habitat. Broken exposures of sedimentary rock provide an abundance of horizontal cracks and overhangs, the preferred denning sites. Typical vegetation on such outcrops consists of stands of shrubs with scattered junipers and ponderosa pines. Structures, such as mines, cabins, and outbuildings, may be occupied. In the vicinity of Rocky Mountain National Park, Mexican woodrats may occur at elevations in excess of 2,440 m (8,000 feet), but they are more common somewhat lower in the foothills.

Natural History—The den of a Mexican woodrat is mostly a deep rock shelter. A few sticks may mark the entrance, but most of the plant material present will have been gathered as food. The large piles of debris accumulated by bushy-tailed woodrats are not typical of the Mexican woodrat; the collecting instinct seems to be much weaker. The nest is cup-shaped, with or without a roof, and built of matted fibers and bark.

The diet consists largely of foliage from shrubs and forbs. Dry twigs of shrubs from which the leaves have been eaten compose the bulk of the house. Other parts of flowering plants—flowers, fruits, stems—are also eaten, and conifer needles are important in the diet locally. The composition of the diet depends more on availability than on preference for one species over another. Large quantities of food are stored in autumn for winter use. The animals are nocturnal and active throughout the year.

Mexican woodrats begin to breed in March. After a gestation period of about four weeks, two to five (mode, three) young are born in April. There apparently is a postpartum estrus in at least some individuals. At any rate, most females bear two litters of young in a summer. Some females born early in the year reproduce their first summer, but males do not enter the reproductive population until they are yearlings.

Selected References—Brown (1969); Cornely and Baker (1986); Finley (1958).

Southern Red-backed Vole
Myodes gapperi

Description—This is a beautiful little animal, 125 to 150 mm in total length, with a tail 33 to 44 mm long. Adults weigh 20 to 30 g. A broad patch of rich reddish hairs extends from head to tail, contrasting rather strongly (unless badly worn) with the buffy sides. The belly is silvery white to buffy.

Field Recognition—Small size, fairly short tail; reddish back contrasting with buffy sides.

Distribution and Habitat—The southern red-backed vole is actually a northern mammal, ranging from central Canada southward along mountain ranges to California, Arizona, and New Mexico and North Carolina. The animal is "southern" only by comparison with a closely related mouse, the Holarctic red-backed vole (*Myodes rutilus*), which occurs in Alaska and northern Canada and ranges across boreal Eurasia. In Colorado, the southern red-backed vole ranges in the mountainous central part of the state, throughout forested parts of Rocky Mountain National Park. Spruce-fir and lodgepole pine forests at middle elevations present optimal habitat, but the animals also live in elfin woodland near timberline. Although frequenting moist areas in forests, red-backed voles are seldom found in wetlands. This and other voles make up a distinctive subfamily of cricetid rodents, known either as Microtinae or Arvicolinae. The colloquial terms "microtines" or "arvicolines" are interchangeable.

Natural History—Red-backed voles burrow to nest beneath logs or rocks and tunnel beneath the duff that litters the forest floor. They are active throughout the year. Chickaree middens are a common habitat. The voles take some stored conifer seeds but probably make greater use of the fungi that grow in the moist litter of cone scales deep in the midden. They also eat

Southern Red-backed Vole *(Joseph F. Merritt)*

some herbage, berries, bark, and occasional insects. Unlike molars of evolutionarily more derived voles, the cheekteeth are not ever-growing and thus are poorly adapted to a steady diet of abrasive grasses. The animals may be active at any time but are most active at night. Populations to fifty animals per hectare have been reported.

As with other small rodents, red-backed voles are preyed upon by a variety of carnivorous birds and mammals. In their forested habitat, perhaps weasels are the most important predators. Maximal longevity is about twenty months.

Breeding begins in March beneath the snowpack, continuing throughout the warmer months until October or November. An average of six (range, two to eight) altricial young are born after a gestation period of about eighteen days. Females show postpartum estrus. Eyes open at about two weeks, and weaning is completed about day eighteen. The natal nest is a simple, orange-sized globe of plant fibers.

Selected References—Merritt (1981); Merritt and Merritt (1978a, 1978b). This species formerly was placed in the genus *Clethrionomys*.

Western Heather Vole
Phenacomys intermedius

Description—This is a small vole, ranging from about 135 to 145 mm in total length and from about 25 to 35 mm in length of tail. Weights are from 30 to 40 g. Externally, this is a rather nondescript species, grayish brown above, pale gray to white (or even slightly buffy) below. The fur is fluffy and soft. The tail is pale below, darker above, usually with enough white hairs to lend a salt-and-pepper appearance. Only by examining the teeth can one be absolutely certain of the identity of this mouse. Unlike other local voles, the inner angles of the lower molars (as viewed from above) are deeper than the outer angles. The species most readily confused with the heather vole is the larger montane vole, which is mostly a species of the wetlands and an obligate runway builder. *Field Recognition*—Small size, grayish color, with short, white-speckled tail.

Distribution and Habitat—The western heather vole is mostly a species of the western mountains, from southern Yukon southward to California and New Mexico. The species occurs—at least locally—throughout mountainous parts of Colorado and is known from a number of places in Rocky Mountain National Park. Favored habitat may be lodgepole pine forests, with their frequent understory of heaths, like broomstick huckleberry. However, the animals have been reported from a variety of situations, from open pine woodlands to dense subalpine forest and from shrubby burns to tundra margins. The heather vole probably occurs throughout the park except at highest elevations.

Natural History—The heather vole is probably the least-known rodent in Rocky Mountain National Park. This dubious distinction stems from its apparent scarcity here (and elsewhere in Colorado); of course this "scarcity" may be merely an artifact of our crude techniques for studying small, secretive mammals. Heather voles nest in burrows in summer and at or near ground level in winter. They forage along the surface in well-concealed runways, best developed in the immediate vicinity of the nest. The animals are active throughout the year and (in summer at any rate) are mostly crepuscular and nocturnal.

The cheekteeth of heather voles are rooted, precluding a strict diet of grasses (which are abrasive and wear the dentition rapidly). Rather, a variety of plant foods (including herbage of forbs, berries, seeds, and fungi) is eaten. Bark is an important food item, especially in winter. Food is piled in caches near the nest throughout the year.

Predation on heather voles has not been studied in our area, but surely these animals—like other small rodents—figure in the food web from plant to carnivore and eventually to microbe, their importance limited only by their seemingly meager numbers.

The heather vole is polyestrous and undergoes postpartum heat. The animals breed throughout the warmer months, from June to August. Two to eight (average about five) young are born after a gestation period of about three weeks. Development is rapid and females of early litters mature sexually and breed their first summer. Males, however, apparently do not.

Selected References—Armstrong (1977); McAllister and Hoffmann (1988); Williams (1952).

Long-tailed Vole
Microtus longicaudus

Description—The long-tailed vole (as both common and Latin names imply) has a relatively long tail; at 55 to 65 mm, one-third the total length of 175 to 195 mm. Weights range from 40 to 55 g. The color is the same as the montane vole, grayish to grayish brown above and paler beneath, but the tail is distinctly bicolored and the upper parts may show a slight reddish tinge.

Field Recognition—Relatively long tail, runways poorly developed.

Distribution and Habitat—The long-tailed vole is a mammal of the Mountain West, ranging from southern Alaska to southern Arizona and eastward to the Black Hills of Wyoming and South Dakota. The western three-fifths of Colorado is occupied, a range encompassing all of Rocky Mountain

Long-tailed Vole *(R. B. Forbes / ASM Mammal Images Library)*

National Park. Long-tailed voles utilize a wide variety of habitats, tolerating a broader spectrum of conditions than do our other voles. They are found in moist situations, such as streamside woodlands, aspen groves, and spruce-fir forest, and also in drier situations, including upland meadows, ponderosa pine woodland, and Krummholz stands at treeline.

Natural History—Runway building is less prevalent in long-tailed voles than in other local microtines. Hence, the animals range through habitats with little ground cover. Shallow burrows are excavated among roots or beneath litter, and the nest is at or near ground level.

As with the montane vole, the cheekteeth are ever-growing. This is an adaptation to a diet of grasses, which contain an abundance of abrasive silica. As the teeth are worn off, they are replaced continually from below. Bark, fungi, berries, and some seeds add variety to the diet. As herbivores, long-tailed voles are, in turn, food for carnivores and thus are an integral part of the food web in local biotic communities.

The older literature refers to this species as *Microtus mordax,* the "cantankerous vole," in reference to its reputed foul temper. I cannot say that these are actually less congenial than other voles, however. None of the voles is particularly tolerant of human intruders or other mice of the same species. Wounding by bites from other voles is common, and rates of wounding often increase as populations grow denser.

Like most other voles, this is a polyestrous species with a high rate of reproduction. The animals breed throughout the warmer months of the year and produce several litters of one to seven (average about four) young at approximately twenty-one-day intervals. As is true of other mammals with short periods of gestation, the young are altricial. Growth is sufficiently rapid that females may reach reproductive maturity their first summer.

Selected References—Pugh et al. (2003); Smolen and Keller (1987); Stinson (1978).

Montane Vole
Microtus montanus

Description—The montane vole is about 155 to 180 mm in total length, and the tail is usually less than one-third that long, 40 to 60 mm. Weights range from 35 to 55 g. Above, the color is grayish to grayish brown, sometimes with a hint of a yellowish wash; the underparts are silvery gray. The tail is indistinctly bicolored. The montane vole is superficially similar to some other local microtine rodents. It differs from the long-tailed vole in its relatively shorter and less distinctly bicolored tail. It differs from the heather vole in its somewhat larger size and heavier body. At a quick glance (except for the red-backed vole), "a vole is a vole." Positive identification often depends on details of teeth and skull. To some extent, habitat differences separate the several species. *Field Recognition*—Habitat mostly in wetlands, especially wet meadows; grass-roofed runways conspicuous.

Distribution and Habitat—As its name implies, the montane vole is largely a mountain mammal. Ranging from southern British Columbia to Arizona and New Mexico, it occurs along the Sierra Cascade and Rocky Mountain systems and on lesser ranges of the Great Basin between them. This mouse occupies higher parts of central and western Colorado, occurring throughout Rocky Mountain National Park in suitable habitat. Montane voles are especially abundant in moist meadows and bogs and in aspen woodlands. They may occur also in drier meadows and in sagebrush stands with a grassy understory, but generally they are not found in unbroken coniferous forest. These mice seem to be obligatory runway-builders, so they need a dense cover of grasses.

Natural History—The montane vole has a well-developed runway-building instinct. In a moist meadow, remove the thatch from the surface of the ground

Montane Vole *(James F. Parnell)*

and you will likely uncover a segment of a runway, a well-worn path about 3 cm wide. When populations of voles are high, such runways form an intricate network obvious to the most casual observer. The runway is a foraging path, and active runways are littered with short (3 to 10 cm), neatly clipped bits of grass. Ball-shaped nests of grass fibers are built along the runway. The superficial root systems of aspens also provide an abundance of nesting holes. The montane vole is mostly nocturnal but may be active by day as well, especially when populations are high. Hidden in a "subway tunnel" beneath the litter, however, they are seldom seen. The animals do not hibernate but are active throughout the year.

The diet consists mostly of grasses. As with the long-tailed vole, the montane vole has ever-growing cheekteeth suitable for eating abrasive foliage. As the molars are worn off at their crowns, they are replaced from the roots. A variety of other plant foods supplements the diet. Montane voles are preyed upon by virtually all local vertebrate carnivores—mammals, raptorial birds, and garter snakes.

Like a number of other arvicolines, montane voles exhibit cycles of abundance. Local voles do not show the dramatic population explosions and crashes of their northern relatives, the lemmings, but there is nonetheless an obvious cycle of "boom and bust." Cycles have not been detailed in Colorado, but they do exist. Some years, voles are virtually impossible to capture and other years they are so abundant that they are active by day and seldom out of sight. As in all populations, numbers increase if the birth rate exceeds the death rate, and because generations overlap, excessive births mean more reproductive individuals in each successive generation, so populations tend to increase in an exponential ("geometric" or "Malthusian") fashion.

A particular tract of habitat has only so much carrying capacity for a particular species. When that carrying capacity is reached or exceeded, something has to give—either recruitment (birth and/or immigration) must be reduced or loss (death and/or emigration) must be increased. A species may solve this population challenge by changing any of these variables. Lemmings rely on emigration (which ultimately increases the death rate as individuals move into unsuitable habitat). Montane voles decrease the birth rate somewhat as populations increase. Also, the incidence of fetal and nestling mortality increases markedly. The population of montane voles in spring is about constant from one year to the next, but differences in survivorship result in a peak population every three or four years.

Montane voles are polyestrous and breed throughout the warmer months of the year. Breeding begins in early spring and the first litter may be produced under the snowpack. A litter of two to ten (average, five or six) young is born after a gestation period of about three weeks. There is a postpartum estrus. The young are altricial, but development is rapid and females born early in the season may breed their first summer.

Selected References—Armstrong (1977); Sera and Early (2003); Vaughan (1969, 1974).

Sagebrush Vole
Lemmiscus curtatus

The sagebrush vole is a relatively small, short-tailed vole, generally gray in color. Sagebrush voles formerly were placed in a genus *Lagurus*. A species of bunch-grass steppe and sagebrush, it occurs mostly in the Great Basin. It is a runway builder and appears to require a grassy understory beneath shrub cover. It frequently has been found in association with Merriam's shrew. Sagebrush voles occur north of Fort Collins, in the Laramie River Valley, and in North and Middle Parks, and thence northwestward to Washington state. The locality of record nearest Rocky Mountain National Park is Hot Sulphur Springs, in Grand County. The animals may eventually be found in drier situations in and near Arapaho National Recreation Area.

Selected References—Carroll and Genoways (1980).

can jump up to two meters. In keeping with this jumping habit, the hindfeet are huge and the tail—of obvious use in balancing and steering when airborne—is elongate. Although mostly nocturnal, they are seen by day if the nest is disturbed. The summer nest is in tall grass. Teeth are adapted to a diet of seeds, but some foliage is eaten as are occasional insects.

In July and August, the animals store fat to provide energy for maintenance during the long period of hibernation. Individuals that store too little fat do not survive until spring. In September, the animals enter the hibernaculum, which is a hole beneath a stump, log, or clump of willows, as much as a meter deep. The winter nest—a sphere of grasses lined with soft plant fibers—must be below the frost line and will be insulated with snow. Jumping mice emerge from hibernation in May or June—females about ten days later than males—having lost about one-fifth of their body weight over the winter. Temperatures of about 10 degrees Celsius (50 degrees Fahrenheit) seem to trigger arousal.

Western jumping mice are seldom found far from water. A study in southeastern Wyoming indicated that home ranges are linear areas 15 to 50 m wide and 50 to 350 m long, usually paralleling a stream. Females have smaller home ranges than males and tend to be more sedentary, cruising the same home range in successive seasons.

As mice go, western jumping mice are notably long-lived, some surviving four years or longer. Deer mice, by contrast, almost never survive two winters. Perhaps the hibernating habit of jumping mice has something to do with this relative longevity. An animal that hibernates for eight or nine months of the year actually "lives" only about one-fourth to one-third of its life and "coasts" through the rest. Recall that our bats—which not only hibernate but also drop their body temperature while at rest during the day—are among the longest-lived of small mammals. During hibernation, the jumping mouse is also safe from most of the myriad predators that find it a worthy meal, although the stress of arousal from hibernation may be the most forceful check on populations. During summer, the animals fall prey to foxes, coyotes, bobcats, weasels, garter snakes, and owls.

Males come into breeding condition soon after coming out of hibernation. Females breed their first week above ground. Gestation takes about eighteen days and five young (range, four to eight) compose a typical litter. The young are weaned at about one month of age. A single litter per year is the general rule. Additional litters of young (and their mothers) could hardly fatten for winter during the short season remaining above ground.

Selected References—Armstrong (1993); Brown (1967b, 1970); Hart et al. (2004).

FAMILY ERETHIZONTIDAE—NEW WORLD PORCUPINES

The five genera (sixteen species) of erethizontids occur only in the New World. A single species occurs in the United States and Canada and another, the co-endou, ranges northward to Mexico; all other species are South American. Old World porcupines (family Hystricidae) resemble New World porcupines in many ways, but there is as yet no strong consensus among mammalogists about their evolutionary relationship.

North American Porcupine
Erethizon dorsatum

Description—Among local rodents, porcupines are second in size only to the beaver. Adults range from 700 to 850 mm in total length, and the tail is 200 to 280 mm long. A large adult may weigh over 15 kg. The animals appear even larger and heavier than they actually are because of the abundant pelage. Three kinds of hairs are present. The underfur is soft, thick, and dark in color, blackish to grayish brown. Over the back, tail, and limbs, long (to 10 cm), coarse guard hairs are present. These are mostly yellow in local animals. On the belly, the guard hairs are much shorter and brownish in color. Between the guard hairs and the underfur are the infamous quills, actually highly specialized hairs. The quills are hollow and may be 6 to 8 cm in length. The barbed tips are black and the waxy shaft is white to yellowish.

The overall color of a porcupine varies with the animal's attitude and the observer's vantage point. Resting calmly, porcupines viewed from the front appear to be black, with a yellowish cast lent by the guard hairs. More common, however, is a posterior view of an irate porcupine. With quills erect, the color scheme is much paler, the shade of the exposed shafts of the quills. *Field Recognition*—Large size; waddling gait with swaying of quills and coarse guard hairs.

Distribution and Habitat—The North American porcupine occurs from Alaska and Canada southward to northern Mexico. In the United States, the animals are present in all forested regions except the Southeast. The species is present in the mountains of Colorado and occurs in suitable habitat throughout the state. Porcupines probably are most abundant in the open ponderosa pine woodland of moderate elevations in the foothills and mountains. Along streams, they range into the broad-leafed riparian woodlands of the plains, and willow thickets provide shelter and food in the alpine zone. Visitors may expect to see porcupines at least occasionally in nearly all terrestrial habitat types in Rocky Mountain National Park.

Natural History—Porcupines are called by a variety of vernacular names, including "porky," "quillpig," and (quite erroneously) "hedgehog" (actually

10

ORDER CARNIVORA
Carnivores

Carnivores are native to all continents but Australia, and there they were introduced (in the form of the dingo) by early humans. The order Carnivora includes both terrestrial representatives and an impressive array of marine species (the seals, sea lions, and walruses). There are about 285 species of carnivores in some 125 genera. A broad spectrum of the extant diversity of terrestrial carnivores occurs in Rocky Mountain National Park, where these mammals participate in the "top layer" of the food web in most biotic communities. The list of carnivores in Rocky Mountain National Park is dynamic, "a work in progress." Two carnivores—the gray wolf and the grizzly bear—were extirpated from the area in the early twentieth century. Wolves may eventually restore themselves to the park. River otters disappeared a century or more ago but are being restored. If the black-footed ferret ever occurred here, it is gone now. The status of the wolverine here and elsewhere in Colorado is poorly known. The Canada lynx has been rare or absent through the last century but is being restored in Colorado and eventually may re-inhabit Rocky Mountain National Park. The raccoon has come to occur in the park in rather recent years, and the ringtail is of possible occurrence. Hence, as many as twenty species of carnivores representing six families may have occurred in Rocky Mountain National Park in the past century.

FAMILY CANIDAE—DOGS AND ALLIES

The dog family is successful and widespread, with a range on land nearly as great as the entire order Carnivora. There are thirty-five species of canids, arrayed in about a dozen genera. Four of the six canid species that have lived in Colorado within historical times are known from Rocky Mountain National Park.

Coyote
Canis latrans

Description—The coyote is about as large as a medium-sized shepherd dog; total length is 100 to 120 cm, and the full tail is 30 to 40 cm long. Males average larger than females. Adult males average about 11 kg in weight, females a kilogram lighter, but individuals in excess of 20 kg have been reported. The general color is buffy to reddish gray above, paling to nearly white below. The head, ears, and limbs are prominently marked with reddish hairs, and the full tail may be marked with black-tipped hairs. Both albinism and melanism have been reported, but neither condition is common. *Field Recognition*—Tail black-tipped, "tucked," and directed downward when running.

Distribution and Habitat—The coyote ranges from the Arctic Slope of Alaska southward to northern Costa Rica and from the Pacific Coast eastward to New England and Maritime Canada. In recent years the animals' geographic range has expanded in the United States, both in the Northeast (into the former range of the gray wolf) and Southeast (into the former range of the red wolf). The animals occur statewide in Colorado and throughout Rocky Mountain National Park. Coyotes are highly adaptable animals and range through a wide variety of habitats in search of food and cover. They are more common in open, park-like situations, woodland, and rough, brushy country than in closed forests.

Natural History—The coyote—whose name is a corruption of their Aztec name, *coyotl*—is certainly the most frequently encountered of local canids. Unlike its larger cousin, the gray wolf, the coyote has thrived over most of

Coyote *(Gene Putney)*

its range despite concerted human efforts to eradicate it. Indeed, the animals actually have expanded their range in the past few decades. Even those who fear economic impact from the coyote's alleged depredations on their livestock often admit a certain grudging respect for their persistent adversary.

Part of the coyote's versatility is attributable to a catholic diet. Studies of scat from Moraine Park indicated that carrion of deer and elk was the principal food. In many areas, rabbits and hares are staples, especially during the warmer months. Mice, voles, woodrats, ground squirrels, beaver, porcupines, marmots, pocket gophers—in short, virtually all rodents—are eaten. Some birds, especially ground-nesters, are taken. Even other carnivorous vertebrates—such as weasels, shrews, snakes, and even skunks—are eaten, despite their usually strong odors. Larger prey, such as deer, is taken on occasion, especially when snow or ice makes travel difficult for ungulates. Plant material may make up 10 to 20 percent of the diet.

Coyotes frequently hunt in pairs, sometimes displaying intricate patterns of teamwork. Unlike wolves and some feral dogs, however, they do not typically hunt as packs. A habitual hunting trail is followed, often as much as 15 km in length. The runway makes use of game or stock paths as well as roads and other man-made trails. The animals are not averse to swimming. A single hunting trail may be used by a coyote throughout its life (to ten years or more), as long as food remains available. Like many breeds of domestic dogs, coyotes follow a scent quickly until potential prey is sighted and then they freeze momentarily before pouncing on the quarry. Excess food is sometimes cached.

As is true of other canids, coyotes have anal scent glands. When individuals meet, mutual sniffing occurs. Scent varies with the individual and lends a distinctive odor to the urine, which is used to mark the boundaries of the animal's domain. The bark of the coyote—a series of "yips" or "yaps" and a trailing howl—is perhaps the most exciting vocal offering of our extant native fauna. The sound of this nocturnal serenade is a hopeful sign that at least part of the natural system remains intact. May it never vanish from the West.

Coyotes are susceptible to rabies and tularemia. Virtually any parasite found on domestic dogs also afflicts coyotes. Social tendencies help to foster a heavy load of ectoparasites, such as fleas, ticks, and mites, and the notoriously uninhibited diet assures a wide range of internal parasites as well.

Coyotes breed first as yearlings from January to March. The animals seem not to mate for life, although pairs may remain together for several years. Packs of three or four (and sometimes a dozen or more) individuals may run together before pairing begins. Females are monoestrous, becoming receptive in mid- to late winter. Gestation takes 60 to 63 days. Five to seven pups compose a typical litter. Occasionally two litters are found in a single den, suggesting that some males are polygynous. The young are born virtually hairless, and the eyes do not open for 9 to 14 days. The male forages to feed the nursing female. Hybridization between coyotes and domestic dogs is not uncommon.

The young are reared in a burrow, often the remodeled lair of a badger or other mammal. Dens are frequently found near water and they range from simple holes to extensive systems of tunnels with several entrances. The female may prepare a number of dens before whelping, moving the pups if disturbed. The male helps to provision the mother and their pups. The young emerge from the den at about three weeks of age. When pups are 8 to 10 weeks old, the den is abandoned and the family forages as a group until fall, at which time the family unit disbands. Longevity in the wild usually is less than ten years.

Selected References—Bekoff (1977, 1982); Bekoff and Gese (2003); Bekoff and Wells (1980, 1986); Young and Jackson (1951).

Gray Wolf
Canis lupus

The wolf is gone from Colorado, the last meager remnant of the population eradicated in the southern part of the state in the 1940s. In our area they were gone even sooner. In his 1911 *A Biological Survey of Colorado,* Merritt Cary noted that wolves were common in North Park and present but scarce in Middle Park. They were reported as abundant in the vicinity of Estes Park in 1894, but apparently they were gone before Rocky Mountain National Park was established in 1915. In the works of Enos Mills—pioneer naturalist and "poet laureate of Longs Peak"—I find no specific reports of wolves in the immediate area, although in *The Rocky Mountain Wonderland* (1915), he mentioned wolves in North Park and later noted that a "scattering of wolves" remained in the area of the nascent national park itself.

Wolves were trapped and poisoned because of transgressions (real and imagined) against stock growers, but human extirpation of the bison and decimation of wapiti by market-hunting may have been the ultimate reason for their demise. Wolves survive today in North America in parts of Alaska, Canada, and the Great Lakes states. The gray wolf is half again as large as a coyote, about the size of a large German shepherd, and the head is markedly broader and more massive. Running alone or in small packs, wolves hunt a circuitous route as much as 150 km (90 miles) in length (but more commonly 30 to 100 km long). Given the apparent success of gray wolf restoration in the Greater Yellowstone Ecosystem and in Idaho, it is possible that wolves will return eventually to the Southern Rockies. A majority of the general

public favors wolf restoration, but mostly because of concern by the livestock industry, the Colorado Division of Wildlife has no plans to restore wolves and the Colorado General Assembly has explicitly prohibited restoration. Nonetheless, in May 2005 the Wildlife Commission approved guidelines for the management of wolves that might disperse to Colorado. Wolves that arrive in the state will be considered as members of an endangered species and will be treated accordingly.

Unfortunately, the first wolf known to have arrived in Colorado from Yellowstone was a female killed in traffic in June 2004 on Interstate 70 near Idaho Springs. That animal may well have wandered near or through Rocky Mountain National Park on her way south. In February 2006, Division of Wildlife personnel captured video images of a wolf in North Park, roughly 40 miles (65 km) northwest of the national park.

There are about two dozen observational reports of wolves in the wildlife observation files at Park Headquarters, accumulated since the 1970s. Unfortunately, none of those reports appears to be substantiated with photographs, casts of tracks, or hair or scat samples, any of which might provide definitive proof of occurrence. Meanwhile, arrival of wolves in Rocky Mountain National Park is probably not a matter of whether, but a matter of when. Wolves that arrive in Rocky Mountain National Park will be welcomed as a natural component of ecosystems, a part that has been absent for a century or more. A carefully controlled release of wolves is one option in the ongoing effort to manage elk in the national park and to mitigate their impact on native vegetation.

Selected References—Armstrong and Amoroso (2002); Ballard and Gipson (2000); Lopez (1978); Mech (1974); Paquet and Carbyn (2003); Paradiso and Nowak (1982); Rocky Mountain National Park (2006); Sharpe et al. (2001); Young and Goldman (1944).

Red Fox
Vulpes vulpes

Description—Adult red foxes range from about 90 to 120 cm in total length, of which the long, full tail comprises about one-third, 30 to 40 cm. The abundant long pelage makes these slender animals appear larger and heavier than they really are; weights range from 3 to 6 kg, males averaging about one-quarter larger than females. In color, the red fox is unmistakably familiar—the upper parts are yellowish orange; the belly, chest, chin, and the tip of the tail are white; legs, muzzle, and backs of ears are black. Occasional individuals of black, "silver," or "cross" (brownish marked with black) phases occur with more typical litter mates. Foxes of non-red phases are not common in Colorado, and they have not been reported in the national park. *Field Recognition*—White-tipped tail; black feet.

Distribution and Habitat—The red fox is a Holarctic animal; it occurs across Eurasia and in North America, from Alaska southward through most of the United States except for the driest parts of the Great Plains and the Desert Southwest. Red foxes occur in suitable habitat throughout Colorado, and they are present in the park on both sides of the Continental Divide. These are mostly mammals of moist forest and wetlands, and in our area they are found most commonly in forest edge situations, about beaver ponds, and in early successional openings following fire, blowdown, and logging. Such situations provide an abundance of suitable rodent food. Red foxes are never found far from water.

Natural History—Red foxes are opportunistic feeders, although food habits have not been studied intensively in the West. In the East, however, cottontails are a staple, and mice and other rodents make up about half the diet. Birds, reptiles, insects, amphibians, eggs, and fruit are eaten as opportunity allows. Some carrion is eaten, and plant material, especially fruit, is taken as available.

The animals hunt by smell, "following their noses" for a few dozen meters or so and then pausing to look around, often leaping to the top of a log or other vantage point. A hunting trail is worn by an individual following the same route night after night. Mostly nocturnal, the animals may also hunt at dawn and dusk. Every brushpile and thicket is investigated thoroughly. Burrowing mammals may be dug out, but foxes seldom chase prey for any great distance, relying on surprise more than speed to gain the advantage of the quarry. When food is abundant, it may be cached against the prospect of lean times ahead. Adult red foxes need about 2.25 kg of prey per week—the equivalent of perhaps 100 average mice. During the breeding season, foxes hunt in pairs. The home range is typically 2 to 8 km in diameter, depending on the density of food resources. As is true of most carnivores, the red fox is active throughout the year.

Dens are used as shelter during severe weather and when the pups are being reared. Usually the den is a renovated hand-me-down from some other animal, such as a beaver, a marmot, or a badger. Dens may be in banks, beneath roots or downed timber, or even in abandoned buildings, usually near permanent water. There may be several entrances 15 to 30 cm in diameter.

Once the pair bond is formed, male and female are virtually inseparable, hunting and playing together. The same individuals may pair in successive seasons, but during the autumn all individuals are solitary. Foxes are monoestrous, breeding annually in winter. The gestation period is fifty-two days. Litters of one to eleven young have been reported, but four or five is the

Red Fox *(Gene Putney)*

usual number. Born blind, the young are balls of dark grayish brown fur with white-tipped tails. The eyes open at about one week of age, but the pups remain in the den until they are about five weeks old. Then they begin to spend increasing amounts of time playing outside the den with each other and with "toys"—bits of bone, fur, or other refuse. The young are weaned at two months and begin to hunt with the parents, putting to productive use the skills developed in earlier play. The deciduous milk teeth are lost at four months, and the glossy reddish subadult pelage is donned about two months later. In early autumn, the family disperses.

Enemies of the red fox include hawks, golden eagles, coyotes, and bobcats, all of which are known to prey on the pups. Fleas, ticks, roundworms, and tapeworms parasitize the animals. Some parasites are shared by red foxes and domestic dogs. Rabies is not uncommon. Humans—with their vehicles, firearms, and traps—are the major enemy of the red fox today.

Small, paired, anal scent glands lend the animals a pungent "foxy" odor, which allows humans (at close range) to identify foxes (or their dens) in general and presumably allows foxes to identify each other in particular. The bark is a short "yip," not unlike that of a terrier.

Selected References—Cypher (2003); Larivière and Pasitschniak-Arts (1996); Rue (1969); Samuel and Nelson (1982).

Gray Fox
Urocyon cinereoargenteus

Description—As in other foxes, the abundant pelage of the gray fox makes the animals appear larger than they actually are. Males range in total length from about 90 to 100 cm; females are slightly smaller. The tail is long—about the length of the body (30 to 35 cm)—and full. Weights range from about 3.5 kg for small females to over 4.5 kg for large males. The overall color is grayish, but the back is marked with a grizzled, black medial stripe that continues posteriorly as a mane of black bristles atop the black-tipped tail. The white underparts are separated from the grayish back by a prominent line of reddish hairs that extends from the backs of the ears, down the sides of the neck, along the sides, to the underside of the tail. The limbs are also reddish, and the short muzzle is black. *Field Recognition*—Black-tipped tail with dorsal mane of bristles; reddish lateral markings. The grayish-colored "cross fox"—a color phase of the red fox, *Vulpes vulpes*—has a white-tipped tail and lacks the dorsal mane of black hairs that distinguishes the gray fox.

Distribution and Habitat—The gray fox is a mammal of southern affinities, ranging northward through much of the United States (except for the highest parts of the Mountain West) to extreme southern Canada and south-

Gray Fox *(Mike Blair/Kansas Department of Wildlife & Parks)*

ward into northern South America. The animals are documented by museum specimens from Estes Park and northwest of Lyons. In wildlife observation files at Park Headquarters are a few reports of gray foxes from both sides of the Continental Divide.

In the West, gray foxes live in rough, broken country covered with woodland and shrubs. In Colorado, they are most common in the piñon-juniper country of the southern part of the state, but they do occur northward along the foothills in ponderosa pine woodlands.

Natural History—Gray foxes are less conspicuous than red foxes, even in areas where both species are abundant. Gray foxes are more secretive and less tolerant of civilization, more tolerant of dry conditions, and they seem to prefer denser overhead cover. Although mostly nocturnal, they may be active at any time, often feeding at dawn and dusk. The call is a hoarse, broken bark, and there is much olfactory communication, scents being deposited as urine and feces.

Like other foxes, the gray fox spends part of its time in a den, but it seemingly is not very particular about what that den is like. The retreat may be in a hollow log, beneath brushpiles or rubbish, under an abandoned building, or in a burrow excavated by some other animal. Sometimes—but apparently as a last resort—they may dig a burrow of their own. The den is usually within a kilometer of permanent water and it contains no formal nest. Reported home ranges vary widely, from about 100 to 1,000 hectares.

Gray foxes are agile climbers, remarkably arboreal for canids. Trees are used as refuges from danger and sometimes as a foraging ground. The diet includes small rodents and rabbits, insects, some birds, reptiles, and amphibians. Considerable quantities of fruits and berries are eaten as available, as is carrion. In short, gray foxes are opportunistic feeders and the diet varies widely with season and geographic location.

Fleas, ticks, and roundworms parasitize gray foxes. Rabies sometimes takes a toll, and the young may fall prey to large raptors. Otherwise, as is true of most large mammals, the greatest danger is persecution, exploitation, and habitat modification by humans.

Gray foxes apparently are monogamous and they mate about February or March. A litter of one to seven (average about four) 90-gram young is born after a gestation period of about nine weeks and reared in an unlined den. The male provisions the female when she is confined with nursing pups. The newborn young are blind but fully furred, development is rapid, and the juveniles forage with the parents by mid-summer. In autumn, the family unit disperses. Gray foxes generally breed first as yearlings. Maximum longevity is fourteen to fifteen years, but most animals in any population are less than two years old.

Selected References—Armstrong (1972); Cypher (2003); Fritzell and Haroldson (1982).

FAMILY URSIDAE—BEARS

Bears are closely related to dogs. They are mostly a northern group, although some species do occur in the Malayan Region, the Andes of South America, and the Atlas Mountains of North Africa. There are eight living species of bears, of which one occurs in Rocky Mountain National Park, and another occurred as recently as a half-century ago.

Black Bear
Ursus americanus

Description—Black bears are familiar to most people, if only from folk literature. A large male may be 175 cm long and weigh nearly 225 kg (about 500 pounds), although the average length is nearer 150 cm (including the stubby

Grizzly, or Brown, Bear *(Lee Kline)*

knew and the last reported from northern Colorado. The loss of the grizzly bear—like the loss of the gray wolf—leaves the wilderness ecosystems of the national park incomplete, ecologically and aesthetically and, many would argue, morally. However, given the grizzly's unpredictable habits and prodigious resource needs—both food and room to roam—its restoration in the park seems unwise, perhaps inhumane, and unlikely.

Selected References—Craighead and Mitchell (1982); Pasitschniak-Arts (1993); Pasitschniak-Arts and Messier (2000); Schoonmaker (1968); Schwartz et al. (2003).

FAMILY PROCYONIDAE—RACCOONS AND ALLIES

The procyonids are mostly an American group; the red panda of Asia is the sole exception. There are fourteen recent species in the family, including raccoons, ringtails, coatis, and the kinkajou. A single species, the northern raccoon, is documented in Rocky Mountain National Park, although a second species, the ringtail, is of possible occurrence.

Ringtail
Bassariscus astutus

Description—The ringtail—sometimes inappropriately called "ringtailed cat" or "civet cat"—is a distinctive animal. About the size of a house cat, it looks like an artist's composite, with the head of a fox, the lithe body of a squirrel, and a long, showy ringed tail an elegant step beyond the raccoon's.

The animals occur from Colorado, extreme southwestern Wyoming, and Oregon southward to Oaxaca, Mexico. In Colorado, the animals are present on both sides of the Continental Divide but seemingly are more common on the Western Slope. In 1954, a ringtail was reported from Grand County, south of Hot Sulphur Springs, signaling its possible occurrence in Arapaho National Recreation Area. More recently there have been intriguing reports of the animals from the foothills of Boulder County, southeast of the national park, and in northern Larimer County.

Ringtails inhabit rough, broken country with shrubby vegetation. They eat rodents, insects, berries, and some carrion. They are strictly nocturnal and are so secretive that they often are fairly abundant in areas where they remain unnoticed.

Selected References—Armstrong (1982); Neuwall-Poglayen and Toweill (1988).

Northern Raccoon
Procyon lotor

Description—The raccoon figures so prominently in American folklore that it is familiar to nearly everyone. Adult males are 800 to 950 mm in total length, and females range about 50 mm shorter. The full, ringed tail comprises about one-third of the total length. Weights range from 6 to 10 kg (15 to 25 pounds) or more. Local raccoons are rather pale in color, buffy to silvery gray beneath and grizzled grayish yellow above, heavily overlain with black. The guard hairs of the back are long and tipped with black, forming a prominent middorsal line. The face is marked with a conspicuous black mask. The tail is cylindrical (not at all flattened like the ringtail's), and the black rings are complete (although darker and wider above than below). The only local species that might possibly be confused with the raccoon is the smaller, more slender, and paler ringtail. *Field Recognition*—Black mask; completely ringed, bushy tail.

Distribution and Habitat—Raccoons range through most of temperate and tropical North America, from northern Alberta to Panama, except for the highest mountains and the driest desert basins. Raccoons apparently have become abundant in Rocky Mountain National Park only in rather recent years. They first were reported in the western part of the park in 1957; in 1958, a raccoon was observed crossing Trail Ridge Road at Tundra Curve, above 3,350 meters (11,500 feet). During the 1960s, the animals increased dramatically at lower elevations east of the Continental Divide. Raccoons inhabit moist situations, especially streambanks and shorelines, although they forage over a diversity of habitats. Observations of raccoons are concentrated near people: visitor centers, picnic areas, and campgrounds, perhaps partly because people are concentrated near the riparian habitats that raccoons favor and also because raccoons are attracted to the food resources provided by careless visitors, whether refuse or the contents of a poorly secured ice chest. Raccoons should not be invited to dinner; bears may crash the party.

Natural History—A great deal has been recorded about the habits of the raccoon, especially the animal as it occurs in the eastern part of the country—the source of much of our wildlife lore. True to legend (and true to their name—*lotor* means "washer" in Latin), the animals rinse their food, perhaps to aid the sense of smell. The animals are seldom found far from water, for they exploit the diverse food resources of streambanks and shorelines. Raccoons are omnivorous; availability is a far more important criterion of diet than is preference. In our area, small mammals, amphibians, fishes, various invertebrates, and native fruits probably constitute the bulk of the diet,

Northern Raccoon *(Gene Putney)*

which is supplemented by occasional birds, eggs, and carrion. Ranging here above the limit of vegetable gardens and cornfields, raccoons often turn to camp kitchens and bird feeders to levy their tithe from civilization.

Foraging raccoons may follow a circuit several kilometers long over several nights' activities. During the day they seek shelter beneath boulders or logs, in tree holes, or in bank dens, shifting from one shelter to another almost nightly. Raccoons swim well, with a strong "dogpaddle," buoyed high in the water by their abundant fur coat. They also climb with agility. The well-developed grasping "hand" allows dexterous manipulation of objects and a tenacious grip.

Raccoons do not hibernate, and they may be active during severe winter cold. When snow covers the foraging trail, however, they often retreat to cover and spend the unfavorable period asleep, living on stored fat. Dormant raccoons—like dormant bears and unlike hibernating ground squirrels and hibernating bats—arouse readily when sufficiently disturbed. Mature animals den singly.

The mating system is promiscuous. Females are monoestrous, coming into heat in February or March. Males exhibit no obvious reproductive cycle; timing of breeding depends on the receptivity of females. Males—reproductively active their second winter—wander widely, whereas females in estrus tend to be more sedentary. Females may breed as yearlings. The gestation period is about sixty-three days and up to seven (usually three or four) young are born in April or May, well-furred but with the familiar mask and tail rings indicated only as pigmented skin. Eyes and ears are closed until the third week. As in other promiscuous species, the mother alone cares for the young. Milk is the sole food until the young begin to forage for themselves at 8 to 12 weeks of age. They are weaned completely by early fall, but full growth takes about two years.

Adult raccoons are subject to few predators. They are not particularly fast, but they are agile and evasive. If all else fails, they stand and fight ably. Larger carnivores, like coyotes, take a toll on raccoons, but probably this predation is minimal on mature animals. Like other carnivores, raccoons support roundworms, tapeworms, ticks, and lice, but parasitic disease seldom is fatal. On adequate range, protected from hunting and trapping, a two-year-old raccoon will have avoided all major perils except the automobile and may expect a lifespan of three to five years, occasional animals living twice that long.

Selected References—Gehrt (2003); Kaufmann (1982); Lotze and Anderson (1979); Rue (1964a).

FAMILY MUSTELIDAE—WEASELS AND ALLIES

Of the eight kinds known from Colorado, at least six species of mustelids have lived in Rocky Mountain National Park over the past century. Altogether, the family includes some sixty species, most common in the Northern Hemisphere but occurring in South America, Africa, and Southeast Asia as well. Skunks (Mephitidae) are close relatives and formerly were included in this family.

American Marten
Martes americana

Description—Martens are medium-sized, arboreal carnivores, distinctly weasel-like in appearance and habits. Adult males average about 600 mm in total length, females about 550 mm. The full tail is 180 to 210 mm long. Weights range from about 650 g for small females to over 1,200 g for large males. Dorsally, the glossy fur is medium brown, the tail somewhat darker. The chin and belly are paler, ranging from buffy to almost orange. The ears are upright and rounded, sometimes marked with a buffy rim. As in other weasels, there are abdominal and anal scent glands. *Field Recognition*—Medium size; pale venter, dark, solid-colored tail; arboreal habitat.

Distribution and Habitat—The American marten—or "pine marten" as it is often called locally—is mostly a boreal mammal, ranging across Alaska and Canada to Newfoundland and southward at increasingly high elevations along mountain ranges to California and New Mexico. In the East, its former southern limits were in Illinois and Ohio. Martens are most typical of subalpine spruce-fir forest, but their range of habitats in Colorado is fairly broad, including tundra rock piles and talus slopes as well as montane woodland. The marten occurs in suitable habitat throughout Rocky Mountain National Park.

Natural History—Martens are the most arboreal of local mustelids, sometimes moving great distances from tree to tree without ever touching the ground. In the trees, martens prey on pine squirrels (especially in winter) and birds. They are also at home on the ground, where they hunt mice, chipmunks and ground squirrels, marmots, rabbits, and pikas. Insects and carrion may supplement the diet. Prey is killed by a bite to the neck or base of the skull. Martens usually take their prey to cover to eat it. Except for the largest prey items, the food is consumed completely. Thus, the feces contains an abundance of hair, feathers, and bits of bone. Martens are active throughout the year and are mostly nocturnal, showing peaks of activity just after dusk and just before dawn. Days—and the most severe winter weather—are passed in tree holes, abandoned nests of pine squirrels, and similar shelter. It

American Marten *(Chase Swift)*

should be mentioned that martens seem to tell time with their stomachs and not with their eyes; they are not averse to foraging by day if appetite dictates. Minimal home range for males is 2 to 3 square kilometers, more than twice that of females.

There is a single gradual molt annually in autumn, and the dense fur that insulates the feet in winter simply is worn away by summer. The animals have a charming tolerance of humans, often described as "curiosity," with good reason. Headlong retreat is the response to archenemies like goshawks and owls, but the reaction to other animals—including people—is to select a comfortable spot to observe the observer, often hissing or growling mild disapproval from a branch or fallen log. Martens sometimes follow hikers through the subalpine forest for several minutes, remaining barely out of sight in the timber. They can become quite tame, taking table scraps or entering occupied cabins periodically to rid the premises of mice.

A variety of larger carnivorous mammals and birds have been reported to eat martens, but arboreal habits and general scarcity protect them from becoming staple fare for any predator. A number of diseases and parasites have been reported. Habitat destruction and trapping are the greatest perils over most of their range.

Martens are monoestrous. They mate in summer, but implantation is delayed for 6 to 8 months, and the one to five altricial young are not born until April, following an active pregnancy of fewer than 30 days. The young are blind at birth and barely furred, but—as is typical of members of the weasel family—development is rapid. The young are weaned at two months and leave the nursery nest. They first breed their second autumn.

Selected References—Clark et al. (1987); Powell et al. (2003); Strickland et al. (1982).

Ermine, or Short-tailed Weasel
Mustela erminea

Description—The ermine is the smallest carnivore in the Southern Rockies and one of the smallest anywhere in the world. Adults are from 200 to 250 mm in total length, males averaging considerably larger than females. The tail is about one-third the length of the head and body, 50 to 65 mm long. Weights range from 30 to 55 g. In summer, the upper parts are brown, the belly and chin usually white. In winter, the animals are entirely white except for the tip of the tail, which remains black throughout the year. It is in this white pelage that short-tailed weasels most often are called (and marketed as) "ermine." Our local weasels are easily distinguished from each other if due attention is paid to size and relative length of tail. *Field Recognition*—White

Ermine, or Short-tailed Weasel *(William Ervin)*

venter and obviously small size distinguish the ermine from other local mustelids; short tail, about one-third length of head and body.

Distribution and Habitat—The ermine has a Holarctic distribution, occurring in both Eurasia and North America. On the latter continent, it ranges from the Arctic Islands, coastal Greenland, and Alaska southward through the boreal forest of Canada, the forested mountains of the western United States, and the eastern deciduous forest to Iowa and Maryland. The animals occur throughout Rocky Mountain National Park. In Colorado, typical habitat includes aspen woodland, subalpine forest, and talus slides.

Natural History—As with its larger cousin, the long-tailed weasel, the ermine is a rather strict carnivore, feeding on mice, shrews, chipmunks, small woodrats, young rabbits, and pikas. Some birds are taken, as are occasional invertebrates. The prey may be much larger than the agile predator, which typically kills by a quick bite to the base of the skull. Populations never have been studied in Colorado, but in Minnesota, ermines cycle in abundance with the voles upon which they feed. Population densities of about four individuals per square kilometer have been reported from Canada, but the animals do not seem to be that abundant anywhere in Colorado.

Ermines are mostly nocturnal and they are active throughout the year. In winter, they often forage beneath the snow. As with the long-tailed weasel, the gait is a bounding, "inch-worm" affair, with leaps to two meters long. The hindfeet land nearly in the tracks made by the forefeet. Enemies of the ermine include owls, eagles, and fur trappers. Most individuals seen by people are those killed by automobiles.

A litter of four to eight young is born in April or May. The animals breed in May or June, thus exhibiting a total gestation period in excess of 10 months. However, development is not active for the entire period. Rather, it proceeds for about two months and then is suspended until implantation occurs in late winter. Ovulation is spontaneous. The altricial young are reared in a nest lined with fur and fine vegetation at the end of a burrow beneath tree roots or a boulder. Neonates are flesh-colored, scantily haired (except for a conspicuous "mane" on the neck), and weigh less than 2 g. The eyes open at about 35 days. The animals first breed as yearlings.

Selected References—C. King (1983).

Long-tailed Weasel
Mustela frenata

Description—When full-grown, long-tailed weasels are 300 to 450 mm in total length, of which the tail comprises about one-third. The animals are slender and weigh only 100 to 200 g. Males average about 20 percent larger

Long-tailed Weasel *(Fi Rust)*

than females. In summer the animals are a rich brown above and sulfur-yellow to orangish below. In winter, however, the pelage is uniformly snow white except for the tip of the tail, which remains black throughout the year. By comparison, the marten is larger, heavier, and arboreal; the ermine is smaller and has a notably shorter tail. *Field Recognition*—Small size, slender body with tail half as long as head and body; bounding, "inch-worm" gait.

Distribution and Habitat—The long-tailed weasel occurs from coast to coast in the United States, except for the Desert Southwest, and from southern Canada southward to Bolivia. The range in Colorado is statewide and these opportunistic animals occupy the full range of terrestrial habitats in the park—from brushland to dense forests and from montane parks to alpine tundra. Perhaps they are most abundant in riparian areas and in rocky, brush-covered terrain, where the rodents that provide the bulk of their diet are most abundant.

Natural History—The long-tailed weasel is probably more abundant and more nearly ubiquitous than any other carnivore in the park, and—being partially diurnal—it is among those most frequently seen. We often describe the readily visible mammals, many squirrels for example, as "bold" or "curious." The long-tailed weasel is neither; it is simply oblivious. Often, one can watch a long-tailed weasel for some time unnoticed because the animals are preoccupied with their more immediate concerns (more often meals than men). The bounding, "inch-worm" gait of weasels is distinctive. The back is arched so high that the hindfeet come down nearly in the tracks left by the forefeet. Only when "puzzling" over a trail or entering a burrow does a weasel walk in any conventional sense. Long-tailed weasels are largely terrestrial, but they can climb and swim well if necessary.

Weasels are highly efficient predators. By reputation they are "vicious," but by nature they are merely hungry. The long, slender body means that there is an extensive radiative surface per unit of heat-producing volume. To maintain a high and constant body temperature in the face of this unfavorable surface-to-volume ratio, weasels consume one-fourth to one-third or more of their own weight in food each day. There is some basis in fact for the widespread belief that, when circumstances allow, weasels kill more prey than they can eat at a given time. In autumn, some provisioning may occur. Furthermore, a weasel frequently kills its prey, feeds on it until satiated, and then becomes drowsy. After an interval of sleep, the weasel then returns to its meal. Discovering a partially eaten carcass, one might conclude that the killing had been "wanton," whereas in fact the weasel has simply dozed off for a "mid-meal nap." The diet consists mostly of small mammals—mice and voles, chipmunks, ground squirrels, pocket gophers, and shrews—with occasional larger mammals such as woodrats and young rabbits. After a short chase, the prey is wrestled to the ground and dispatched with a strong bite to the base of the skull. The legs of the weasel are short, and the supple, sinuous body helps to grasp the prey. The slender build allows the weasel to follow many small mammals into their own burrows and to pursue winter meals beneath the snow. The diet is supplemented with small birds, amphibians, snakes, insects, and even occasional plant matter, especially berries.

When not foraging, weasels retire to a simple burrow system. Frequently a remodeled hand-me-down excavated originally by a ground squirrel or pocket gopher, the burrow commonly is 8 to 10 cm in diameter and about 30 cm deep. A "latrine" littered with droppings marks the entrance of the burrow. Often the scat consists mostly of matted hair.

Weasels occasionally are preyed upon by owls and other larger carnivorous vertebrates. No predator specializes in eating weasels (or other carnivores), however, and predation is probably not an important check on populations. In the first place—like other mustelids—weasels have musk glands, which give them a rather strong odor (and presumably an even stronger taste). Secondly, preying on carnivores is just poor economics. At best, transfers of energy between levels of the terrestrial food web are only about 10 percent efficient. Hence, 100 g of plant makes 10 g of mouse makes 1 g of weasel. Even if mouse and weasel tasted equally good (which I sincerely doubt), mouse is at least a ten-fold better investment from the viewpoint of ecological efficiency. Parasitism and disease may exact a toll, and many weasels are killed by automobiles (which are particularly indiscriminate "predators").

Two molts occur annually, allowing seasonal color change. Spring molt begins in March and may take two months to complete. Brown hairs begin to appear over the shoulders and head and then new hair appears progressively down the back and tail. The autumnal molt to snow-white pelage begins in October. The pattern is the reverse of that seen in spring.

Weasels mate in summer, from June through August. Ovulation is induced by copulation. Gestation takes about 280 days, but during most of that time the development of the embryos is suspended. Implantation of the early embryo (the blastula) is delayed until spring and the interval between actual implantation and parturition is only about 27 days. The four to nine young are born in April. They are sparsely haired and weigh only about 3 g, but already they are weasel-shaped. The young are reared in a nest chamber lined with chopped grass and hair. There is some evidence that the male has a role in the care of the young, at least early in postnatal life. The eyes open at about five weeks of age and weaning begins soon thereafter. Ensuing development is rapid and females may breed their first summer (although implantation, development, and birth do not occur until the following spring).

Selected References—Hall (1951); Sheffield and Thomas (1997); Svendsen (1982, 2003).

Black-footed Ferret
Mustela nigripes

Doubtless the rarest mammal in North America, this is a medium-sized mustelid, larger than the long-tailed weasel. It surely does not occur today in Rocky Mountain National Park or immediately adjacent areas. However, it may once have occurred in what is now Arapaho National Recreation Area. This speculation is based on the fact that the Denver Museum of Nature and Science has a specimen of the black-footed ferret taken in Middle Park in 1888.

Sagebrush habitat suitable for ferrets is present now (and was then) around Granby and Grand Lake. However, white-tailed prairie dogs, the principal food of black-footed ferrets in the general vicinity, were not reported in Middle Park by the early naturalists. Hence, the ferret population that once apparently lived there may not have been particularly prosperous.

Selected References—Hillman and Clark (1980).

American Mink
Neovison vison

Description—The mink is a medium-sized, semiaquatic carnivore, thickset for a weasel but still of slender build. Males are 500 to 600 mm in total length, with tails 150 to 200 mm long; females average about 50 mm shorter. Males may weigh 1.5 kg, but average weight is closer to 1 kg, and females weigh about 675 g. The fur is mostly dark brown, grading to black toward the end of the tail. Variable white patches often mark the belly and chin. The outer hairs, long and shiny, overlie a dense, soft, gray-based underfur. The ears are short. The toes are webbed at their bases and weakly clawed. *Field Recognition*—Brownish color above and below; semiaquatic habit. Some observers confuse mink with river otters. For comparisons, see the account of the latter species.

Distribution and Habitat—The mink is a wide-ranging carnivore, living in Alaska, most of Canada, and throughout the United States except for the Desert Southwest. Although present statewide, the mink is more abundant in the mountains of Colorado than on the plains. These are semiaquatic mammals, commonly occurring in marshes, about lakes and beaver ponds, and along streams. Mink are not common in Rocky Mountain National Park, despite an abundance of seemingly suitable habitat. They are known from both sides of the Continental Divide. Most observations, however, are in the Glacier Creek drainage, especially about Bear and Nymph Lakes. Of course, this may reflect the density of human observers rather than the density of mink.

American Mink *(Chase Swift)*

Natural History—The mink is a secretive species, mostly nocturnal. Days are spent in dens beneath piles of brush or driftwood, beneath rocks, in hollow logs, or in houses or dens abandoned by beaver or muskrats. The animals forage by night.

The diet consists almost entirely of animal food. Fish and small mammals are staples, and frogs, insects, and birds are important components. Some carrion is eaten. The diet changes with seasonal abundance of prey. There is some evidence that preferred prey-size differs between sexes, which hardly is surprising, because males are nearly twice as heavy as females. In winter, excess food may be placed in "cold storage" in the den. Mink are excellent swimmers, easily capturing aquatic prey. On land, the gait is much like that of the true weasels, when due allowance is made for the mink's somewhat stockier build.

Except in severely cold, snowy weather, mink are active throughout the year. There is a tendency for males to wander widely, ranging along 2 to 5 km of a stream, whereas females tend to remain near a single den and range over a smaller area.

Breeding is promiscuous, commencing in mid-winter. Females are polyestrous, coming into heat again if the first estrus does not result in pregnancy, but a single litter per year is the rule. Ovulation is induced by mating, and implantation is delayed. Gestation takes 40 to 75 days, depending upon when implantation occurs; active pregnancy lasts about four weeks. The litter of about four young (range, one to eight) is born in April or May. The young are altricial, weighing only about 10 g. However, they develop very rapidly, attaining 40 percent of adult body weight by age seven weeks. They apparently breed their first year.

Numerous parasites are known to infest mink. Beyond that, direct and indirect human influences are the most important checks on numbers. Environmental pollutants such as mercury, PCBs, and chlorinated hydrocarbon biocides are documented hazards to these carnivores, owing to their partial dependence on fish as food. Outside the national park, trapping and destruction of habitat probably are the most effective mortality factors.

Selected References—Larivière (2003); Linscombe et al. (1982).

Wolverine
Gulo gulo

Description—The wolverine is the largest terrestrial member of the weasel family, with a total length of 700 to 1,050 mm. The short, full tail is 175 to 250 mm long. Females weigh to 11 kg (about 25 pounds), males to perhaps 18 kg (40 pounds). This is a large mustelid, and the abundant, coarse pelage makes the wolverine appear even larger than it actually is. Dorsally, the animals are dark brown. The sides are marked with a distinct, pale yellowish stripe, which begins over the shoulder, broadens posteriorly, and narrows to a "V" over the tail. The belly is pale brown. The face is dark brown to blackish, often with a paler "mask" about the eyes. *Field Recognition*—Large size and obvious pale lateral stripe.

Distribution and Habitat—The wolverine is a Holarctic mammal, occurring both in Eurasia and in boreal North America. It ranges southward from

Wolverine *(Chase Swift)*

the Arctic islands through the Colorado Rockies, but its present status at the southern limits of its range is quite uncertain. Perhaps extirpated from the park, the wolverine once occurred at least sparingly there. Abner E. Sprague saw a wolverine on the south side of Moraine Park in 1878, and pioneer trappers of wide experience and credibility reported the animals from the mountains about North and Middle Parks in the 1880s and 1890s. Wolverines occur mostly in heavy forest, but they may range past treeline into alpine or Arctic tundra. In the wildlife observation database maintained at Park Headquarters there are over sixty reports of wolverines in and near the national park over the past fifty years. It is gratifying to think that wolverines might occur in the park, but unfortunately none of these reports is documented with photographs, casts of tracks, samples of hair, or scat—any of which could provide a suitable voucher for the observation. Most years bring reports of supposed wolverines from the higher parts of the park. One must hesitate to dismiss from his armchair reports from observers in the field, but sight records of wolverines—as those of any other scarce and furtive species—should be subjected to the closest scrutiny. Dr. Tom Andrews conducted an intensive survey for wolverine and Canada lynx in Rocky Mountain National Park and adjacent national forests in 1990–1991. No sign of wolverine was found. Considering changes elsewhere in Colorado, that effort probably should be repeated, perhaps supplemented by baited track stations, perhaps with remote cameras.

Natural History—Wolverines are among the least known of our larger mammals. Not that there is any paucity of literature concerning the "glutton," but the ratio of verbiage to knowledge is frightfully high; wolverines have inspired a reputation larger than life. They have been cast as "devils of the North" since humans first ventured into the taiga. Old-timers in the high Sierra Nevada were convinced that any mammal would yield to the wolverine. Stories abound of wolverines killing lynx and cougars as well as deer, caribou, and even moose; of cabins torn apart with seeming malice; of traplines raided systematically for bait and for captive furbearers. At least some of this pervasive reputation must have some basis in reality. Part of the reality seems to be that, although not especially aggressive, wolverines are fiercely defensive and virtually fearless. They have no traditional enemies other than humans.

The animals are opportunistic feeders. They are solitary and neither fast nor agile—the gait is a rolling walk, midway between that of the weasel and that of a bear—and scavenging is more important than is active hunting. The powerful jaws crush bones easily. Wolverines are not truly fossorial, but they can excavate marmots and ground squirrels from their burrows. They climb well, using the sharp front claws. Senses of hearing and smell are acute, but sight is less so. Mostly nocturnal, wolverines will hunt by day if need be. They are usually silent, but sometimes utter a low, hoarse growl or grunt.

Wolverines are active throughout the year. In winter the feet are fitted with "snowshoes"—coarse hairs between the toe-pads and around the margins of the foot. Much of the wolverine's reputation for ferocity may be founded on its winter exploits. Snow cover makes travel difficult for many larger animals. It buries browse and weakens herds. Under such circumstances, a healthy wolverine can readily overpower an ungulate ten times its size.

Females are monoestrous, breeding in summer. Implantation is delayed, however, until January, as in many other mustelids. Total gestation is about nine months, active gestation only about five weeks. Studies in Alaska indicate that one to four young are born about March and leave the nursery den in April or May.

Selected References—Andrews (1991); Copeland and Whitman (2003); Pasitschniak-Arts and Larivière (1995); Wilson (1982).

American Badger
Taxidea taxus

Description—Badgers are stocky, short-legged mustelids. Males are 650 to 750 mm long, the short tail comprising 110 to 150 mm of the total length. Females average about 50 mm shorter. Weights vary widely with season, to about 10 kg (average, 4.5 to 5 kg, 10 to 12 pounds). The name "badger" apparently derives from the conspicuous "blaze" or "badge" of white on the forehead, which may extend well down the back. The face is black with pale (buffy to nearly white) markings. The pelage of the back is grizzled and highly variable in color, ranging from rich reddish brown to pale buff, variously overlaid with black-tipped hairs. In our area, paler animals predominate. The feet are blackish and the venter is buffy to white. *Field Recognition*—Low, flat profile; waddling gait; white middorsal stripe.

Distribution and Habitat—The badger occupies a wide range in central and western North America, from California to the Great Lakes region and from northern Alberta southward to central Mexico. Badgers are mammals of open, upland situations, and they occur statewide in Colorado. In Rocky Mountain National Park, they frequent all of the larger mountain parks and some smaller, isolated meadows as well. Reports are scattered widely in the area, from dry meadows at lowest elevations to alpine tundra. The common denominator among these habitats is an abundance of burrowing rodents, whether ground squirrels or pocket gophers.

Natural History—The badger is the most fossorial of local mustelids, and it is strongly adapted for its burrowing habit. The forefeet have heavy, elongate claws, and the shoulder region is massively developed. The limbs are short and powerful, and the profile is remarkably flat. The tail is quite short

American Badger *(Fi Rust)*

for a weasel. Burrows are recognizable by their shape—20 to 30 cm across and broadly elliptical, with a flattened bottom—in short, badger-shaped in cross-section. Denning burrows most often are on open slopes rather than in valley bottoms or swales, and they commonly have a southeastern exposure.

In marked contrast to the rather tidy dens are the excavations made by foraging badgers. Re-excavating burrows of fossorial rodents is the typical foraging tactic. The site of such feeding looks like it might have been produced by a minor explosion. Drawn by the scent of a tender meal of ground squirrel or pocket gopher, the badger digs with a vengeance, sometimes laying waste an area two meters or more in diameter. Over the long term, the badger's activity (which mixes materials from various horizons) is a boon to the evolution of the soil

Locally, Wyoming ground squirrels probably constitute the bulk of the diet. Other ground squirrels and chipmunks are taken, as are pocket gophers. Insects are important in summer, especially for young animals not yet fully able to exploit burrowing mammals. Eggs, nestling birds, and young rabbits are eaten when the badger happens upon them. Mice are an important resource in winter, when hibernating ground squirrels enjoy the partial protection of a layer of frozen ground. As is true of most carnivores, the badger is active throughout the year, although particularly cold and snowy spells—when foraging might be counterproductive in terms of energy expenditure—may be spent in the den. Badgers are active mostly at night, when they catch their largely diurnal prey napping. However, one sometimes sees the animals about by day as well, especially early and late in the day.

Except briefly during the mating season, badgers are solitary. More antisocial than shy, they usually shuffle off to the burrow when confronted by humans. The usual gait is a waddling walk, accentuated by the sway of the abundant pelage from side to side. When pressed, the badger stretches its legs to their meager limit and runs. Cornered, they become ferocious: snarling, snapping, baring the teeth, and flattening the body against the ground. Badgers have no habitual enemies except numerous parasites, armed humans, and motor vehicles; thick hide and abundant fur combined with an unsavory disposition protect the badger from larger carnivores.

Badgers mate in late summer and implantation is delayed until February. One to four (occasionally five) young are born in late March or April and reared in an unlined den. The young develop quickly and by early summer, they are one-third grown and are eating rodents caught by the mother. By late summer or autumn, the young are on their own. Reproductive maturity is attained the second autumn.

Selected References—Lindzey (1982, 2003); Long (1973).

Northern River Otter
Lontra canadensis

Description—This is a large, torpedo-shaped, aquatic mammal, with a long, round tail. Adults range in total length from 1,000 to 1,300 mm, and the tail is about half the length of the head and body, 350 to 500 mm in length. The well-webbed hindfoot is 110 to 140 mm long, and the short ears are obscured by the fur. Adult otters weigh 5 to 10 kg. The dense fur of the upper parts is rich brown in color, and the venter is paler, to grayish or silvery brown.

Observers might confuse the semiaquatic mink with the otter. The otter is the much larger of the two (about twice the size of a mink and five or more times the weight). The color is dark brown above and silvery white below. The feet are more extensively webbed, and the tail is notably thickened at the base, tapering to the end. The slippery trails common near beaver ponds sometimes are thought to be the well-known "slides" used by river otters. However, such trails are worn by beavers and used by a number of other species, including muskrats and mink. *Field Recognition*—Large size, aquatic habitat.

Distribution and Habitat—The river otter once ranged from Alaska southward through most of Canada and the United States (except for parts of the Desert Southwest) to the northern border of Mexico. The species has been extirpated from much of its former range.

Natural History—Early records of this large, aquatic mustelid are scattered throughout Colorado on most major drainage systems. E. R. Warren— Colorado's pioneer mammalogist—speculated that the seasonally variable flow of the state's streams might explain the otter's historical rarity here.

In the 1970s, the Colorado Division of Wildlife began to restore otters to the state, using stocks obtained from Louisiana, Minnesota, Wisconsin, New York, Michigan, and Arkansas. One of the sites for restoration was the Kawuneeche Valley, on the west side of Rocky Mountain National Park. From 1978 to 1984, forty-three otters were transplanted to the area. Several of those animals were fitted with radio transmitters. The otters moved an average of about 13 km (range 1 to 47) to establish home ranges averaging 18 km long in summer, 7 km long in winter. A reproducing population has been established in the park. Observations of otters in the national park are almost all from the Colorado River drainage, as would be expected. The animals should also be expected on the upper Poudre River drainage. Care must be taken to distinguish otters from mink. Both animals would be expected mostly about beaver ponds or lakes; both use "slides" to enter the water quietly; both are generally rich brown in color. However, otters have webbed feet and a nota-

Northern River Otter *(Chase Swift)*

bly thick tail, especially heavy at its base. Otters are nearly twice the size of mink, 880 to 1300 mm (35 to 52 inches) versus the mink's 490 to 720 mm (20 to 29 inches) in total length. The smallest female otter is larger than the largest male mink.

Otters are active both day and night. They are largely restricted to aquatic and subaquatic habitats, such as streamside marshes and willow thickets. Fish provide the bulk of the diet in all seasons, occurring in all otter scats found in the park. Fish to thirty-eight centimeters long were taken; suckers were eaten more often than were trout. Rodents and invertebrates also are eaten.

Otters breed in spring, but the blastocysts do not implant until the following January or February, and one to four young (typically twins) are born in March or April. Females breed again while lactating. Females breed first as yearlings, most males at two or more years of age. The young are rather altricial, being born blind and toothless, although fully furred. The eyes open at five weeks.

Selected References—Larivière and Walton (1997); Mack (1985); Melquist et al. (2003); Toweill and Tabor (1982).

FAMILY MEPHITIDAE—SKUNKS

Skunks resemble weasels (Mustelidae) in many respects, but in recent years an emerging consensus places skunks in their own family, along with the Old World stink badgers (*Mydaus*). There are twelve species in the Mephitidae, arrayed in four genera.

Selected References—Dragoo and Honeycutt (1997); Rosatte and Larivière (2003); Wilson and Reeder (2005).

Western Spotted Skunk
Spilogale gracilis

Description—The spotted skunk (sometimes erroneously called "civet cat," for it is neither a civet—a kind of mongoose—nor a cat) is notably smaller than its more familiar cousin, the striped skunk. Males are 375 to 450 mm in total length, and females range about 50 mm shorter. The tail is about one-third of the total length. Males weigh about 625 g, females about 450. The color is distinctly patterned black with variable white spots. *Field Recognition*—Small size; pattern of discontinuous white stripes on black background.

Distribution and Habitat—The western spotted skunk is a species of western North America, ranging from southern British Columbia to southern

Western Spotted Skunk *(Alden M. Johnson/California Academy of Sciences)*

Mexico and from the Pacific Coast eastward to Colorado and central Texas, where they live in rocky, broken terrain with brushy cover. Rocky Mountain National Park provides little suitable habitat, but the species is known from the western margins of Estes Park and it occurs eastward through the foothills, especially along the major canyons, such as those of the Big Thompson, Cache la Poudre, and Saint Vrain.

Natural History—The petite spotted skunk invites comparison with its larger, more widely known relative, the striped skunk. The spotted skunk is better adapted to dry environments, more decidedly nocturnal, more weasel-like in shape and progression, less social and less parasite-ridden, a more graceful and agile climber, and (admittedly a personal judgment) smellier.

These are secretive animals. Often they live in quite close proximity to people—even beneath occupied buildings—but escape all but olfactory surveillance. Away from people they den in rock shelters; in burrows abandoned by ground squirrels, badgers, or coyotes; beneath brushpiles, and in hollow logs. They do not hibernate, but they may den up to avoid extended periods of adverse winter weather.

Spotted skunks are opportunistic feeders on small mammals, insects, birds and their eggs, and fruit of various kinds. Seasonal abundance is a stronger determinant of diet than is preference. Carrion is important in winter. A taste for garbage and their small size mean that they are sometimes trapped in trash cans.

As other skunks, these animals are adequately protected from all but the hungriest predators by powerful secretions of anal musk glands. Owls sometimes prey on spotted skunks, and traffic takes a toll where the animals are abundant. Parasite load may be heavy, and nematode damage is frequent in the frontal sinuses of the skull.

Western spotted skunks breed in September. Development is suspended at an early stage, and the blastocysts float free in the uterus for six to seven months until implantation occurs in April. A litter of about four young is born in May, the total duration of pregnancy being 210 to 230 days. The young are altricial. Covered with fine hair, the characteristic pattern of markings is distinctive. Eyes and ears are closed, but the claws are developed and neonates can crawl about feebly. At about four weeks the eyes open, and the teeth erupt a week later. Thereafter, growth is rapid, with full size being attained at three months. Females typically are reproductively active their first autumn, and at least some males are also.

Selected References—Howard and Marsh (1982); Verts et al. (2001).

Striped Skunk
Mephitis mephitis

Description—The striped skunk is familiar beyond any need for description. Adult males are 625 to 750 mm in total length, of which the full tail comprises over one-third (235 to 325 mm). Females range about 40 mm shorter. Weights of males range to 4.5 kg (10 pounds) or more, with an average near 3 kg; females average about 2.5 kg. As in many other mammals, seasonal change in weight may be great. The ground color is jet black (sometimes wearing or bleaching to deep reddish brown) with a pair of continuous white lateral stripes that extend from the back of the head to the base of the bushy black and white tail. *Field Recognition*—Large size; continuous white stripes on black background.

Distribution and Habitat—The striped skunk occurs throughout most of the United States, in Canada south of Great Slave Lake and Hudson Bay, and in northern Mexico. In Colorado, the species occurs essentially statewide, and it may be expected throughout Rocky Mountain National Park, except at highest elevations. Striped skunks utilize a wide variety of habitats. Locally, they occur about the margins of parks and meadows, in streamside woodlands, and in aspen groves. They are probably most abundant in and around human settlements, including resort villages and campgrounds.

Natural History—Striped skunks are nearly omnivorous, eating insects, small mammals, birds and their eggs, amphibians, and fruit, as well as carrion and garbage. Although mostly nocturnal, they sometimes are seen by day. The den may be a hand-me-down from another mammal or it may be excavated anew. Dens under rocks, logs, and buildings are common. A nest is built of grasses and leaves. Southeast-facing slopes typically are selected for dens, to catch the first warming rays of morning sun. (This sense for the value of solar energy is a behavioral trait common to many kinds of mammals.) Striped skunks are not hibernators and they may be active year-around, but they often spend extended periods asleep during cold, snowy weather. If stored fat is depleted, striped skunks will dig out through a cover of snow to feed.

For protection, skunks are highly dependent upon the educability of potential predators. Most vertebrates show skunks a decided deference. Skunks are fitted with paired anal musk glands that fill muscular reservoirs with fluid.

In situations calling for active defense, the skunk raises its tail and relaxes the anal muscles to expose the ducts. Fluid is expelled in a double stream that spreads to a fine mist. The spray is controlled with disconcerting accuracy. The musk is an effective deterrent because of its odor and painful—if short-term—effect on the eyes. Once initiated, would-be predators seldom have need for a refresher course. Although perhaps less audacious than the diminutive spotted skunk, striped skunks show no fear of other species. They thus are unwary of traffic—a menace against which their defense is obviously inappropriate—and frequently they become casualties on the highway. Indeed, their disproportionate frequency as roadkill probably leads us to imagine them to be much more abundant than they actually are. Occasional skunks fall prey to especially hungry foxes, coyotes, and large raptorial birds, but their malodorous carcass is staple fare for no predator. Internal and external parasites are abundant, and skunks are important carriers of rabies. These maladies all stem in part from the striped skunk's gregarious denning habits.

Striped skunks breed in March or early April. Mating is accompanied by complex "pacification" behavior. Gestation takes about two months and two to ten (average about five) altricial young are born in May or June. The young develop rapidly and are weaned within two months. Although independent by fall, they may den with their mother through the first winter, breeding first as yearlings.

Selected References—Godin (1982); Rosatte and Larivière (2003); Verts (1967); Wade-Smith and Verts (1982).

FAMILY FELIDAE—CATS

From an evolutionary and structural standpoint, the cat family is a very tight group, nearly all species being active carnivores that hunt by stealth. Three species of native cats occur in Colorado. All of them are known from Rocky Mountain National Park. There are some forty species in the family, which is distributed throughout the world except for Australia and Antarctica. How many genera of cats there are is mostly a matter of taxonomic taste; the range from one classification to another is from two to nearly two dozen. The uncertainty even reaches to the local fauna. Some authorities place all three local species of cats in a single genus, *Felis*.

Mountain Lion
Puma concolor

Description—When full-grown, female mountain lions may be 2 meters in total length and weigh 35 to 60 kg (80 to 130 pounds), whereas males may

Mountain Lion *(Gene Putney)*

be 2.5 meters long and weigh in excess of 90 kg. The tail is long, round, and slender, comprising 30 to 40 percent of the total length.

The color is variable both individually and geographically. In our area, the upper parts range from grayish to reddish brown, darkest on the ears and the tip of the tail. The belly is white. Unlike the smaller, short-tailed bobcat and lynx, the upper parts are not spotted (hence the specific epithet, *concolor*). The young are marked with irregular grayish to blackish spots, but the obviously long tail readily distinguishes mountain lions of any age from other local cats. **Field Recognition**—Solid-colored back; long, rounded tail.

Distribution and Habitat—The mountain lion—also called puma or cougar—once enjoyed the largest geographic range of any native American mammal—from northern British Columbia southward to Argentina. From large parts of their former range they have retreated in the face of civilization. Occasional individuals are reported from Rocky Mountain National Park, mostly in summer. Most lions probably follow the deer herds into the lower canyons outside the park to winter. Mountain lions are not particularly rare in parts of southern and western Colorado, and they appear to be making a gratifying comeback in the foothills of the Eastern Slope, even in the face of an expanding human population. Most recent reports in the park are from lower elevations, on either side of the Continental Divide. Mountain lions are most abundant in broken rimrock country with good cover of brush or woodland. Extensive stands of heavy timber are avoided, perhaps in part because large herbivores, the preferred diet, are relatively scarce in such communities. Also, open grasslands provide inadequate cover for a large predator that hunts largely by stealth. Mountain lions move through virtually any kind of habitat in search of suitable hunting grounds, and at one time they must have been present—at least occasionally—throughout the park, although they doubtless were more common at lower elevations.

Natural History—In the minds of many, the mountain lion is the ultimate American predator. Although smaller than the bears, less fleet than the wolf, and less audacious than the coyote, the cougar's stealth, its majestic silence, inspires awe. And for good reason, for the strength and grace of the mountain lion are impressive by any standard. It is little wonder that fact and fancy are so thoroughly mixed wherever the puma is concerned.

The dietary staple of Colorado pumas is venison, provided by the abundant and ubiquitous mule deer. A study in Utah and Nevada indicated that some 75 percent of the diet was provided by deer and that an adult puma required an average of one deer per week for its sustenance. Occasional elk and bighorn sheep are also taken, as are smaller mammals, including beaver and porcupines. Newly weaned kittens and very old individuals may prey on smaller animals, including rabbits, small rodents, and birds, and they may eat some carrion. Where domestic livestock is grazed untended in mountain lion range, some loss should be expected. (The subspecific name of our local race is *F. c. hippolestes,* derived from Greek roots meaning "horse thief.")

Mountain lions may travel 40 km in a single night in search of a meal. The animals track their prey by "following their noses," although with their rather short muzzles, the sense of smell seems to be less developed than among some members of the dog family. Most hunting is done at night. The basic tactic is that of a house cat on a grand scale. The lion stalks silently to within a few meters of the prey. The approach may be at ground level or from the vantage point of overhanging rocks. As the puma eyes its prey, the tip of the tail twitches from side to side. A single furious but graceful leap usually immobilizes the prey. The crushing force of the leap or a piercing bite to the nape of the neck dispatches the quarry. Cats are highly adapted to this style of predation. The jaw is hinged tightly in the skull, providing good leverage, and the mandible can be lowered to provide a very wide gape. The canine teeth grasp and puncture the prey. The cheekteeth are very sharp, and the movement of the jaw is tightly limited to a single plane, so the cheekteeth (last premolar over first molar, the so-called carnassial teeth) function almost exclusively as shears.

The propulsive force for the prodigious leap comes from the hind limbs, and the shoulders are constructed to cushion the landing. The collarbone of felids is well developed as a shock-absorber. It also allows the front limbs some lateral mobility. These specializations preclude sustained, rapid running, but the bounding rush of an adult mountain lion can overcome a fleeing deer over a distance of about 50 meters.

The lion often moves its prey to a secluded spot before feeding. Larger prey is dragged, and smaller prey is carried in the mouth. The ability of pumas so laden to jump into trees or high onto boulders is legendary. There is a tendency to dine from a carcass and then to cover the leftovers with leaves, snow, or soil. The lion may return to take a meal from the carcass several times until it is consumed or until it begins to spoil. This practice is especially true of a female confined to a small area with her young. Males, on the other hand, tend to wander more widely and may eat but little from a single carcass. Overall, the economy is one of "feast or famine"—after gorging, an individual may retreat to rest in an inaccessible spot for three or four days. While eating, the animals are nervous and assertive, and there is little sharing of prey, except by a mother with her cubs. The animals lap blood eagerly and are known to subsist without free water for lengthy periods in dry areas.

Rock shelters, shallow caves, heavy thickets, and eroded banks provide suitable dens, which are not "improved" by the occupant. Perhaps because no nest is built and dens are used only a short time, cougars usually harbor a light load of external parasites. Fleas and ticks do inhabit pumas, however, as does a variety of endoparasitic worms. Other than parasites, adult cougars have no serious enemies other than humans. Some rabies is known. Occasional fights among mountain lions cause death, and males have been known to kill young abandoned by their mothers. Otherwise, natural mortality probably results mostly from starvation due to ineffective hunting (because of broken or age-worn teeth) or from injury inflicted by other pumas or by the antlers or hooves of intended prey.

The breeding structure is promiscuous, and males may fight for dominance and the right to mate with a particular female. The animals breed first at two to three years of age. One to six (mode about three) kittens compose a litter, born after a gestation period of 13 to 14 weeks. Births occur mostly in summer, with a peak in July, but have been reported from every month of the year. The 400-gram young is blind at birth, but the eyes open by about two weeks of age. They nurse for about four to five weeks, and then milk is replaced gradually by fresh meat. Kittens reach a weight of about 4.5 kg (10 pounds) in eight weeks; at six months of age, they weigh 12 to 20 kg, and yearlings may weigh over 24 kg. The pelage of juveniles is variously spotted and the tail is ringed. Kittens play together near the maternal den. Injury is fairly common during these bouts of play, and spinal damage in pumas is rather common. The young may remain with the mother for two years. If a litter of cubs is lost at birth, estrus occurs almost immediately. Otherwise, females probably breed only every other year.

Mountain lions are extremely wary of humans, and settlement would have had an adverse effect on their numbers even if there had not been deliberate attempts to control or eliminate mountain lions over much of their range. When fleeing danger, pumas head for rough, inaccessible country. Pursued, they readily take to the trees. One can hardly say that they climb trees; the first "step" is often a graceful leap of 3 to 5 meters to the lowest branch. Unprovoked attacks on humans are reported very rarely. Indeed, the fear of humans is so strong that a mother may abandon her kittens to flee. Only disturbing a feeding individual is predictably dangerous. Mountain lions do kill domestic pets such as dogs and house cats.

There are about 250 reports of mountain lion observations on file at Park Headquarters over the period 1997–2003. A majority are based on sightings of individual lions, and some are based on observations of tracks or scat. Of those, about a quarter are from west of the Continental Divide and about two-thirds are from the Big Thompson watershed. That bias probably reflects several factors: the distribution of ideal foraging habitat (rocky sites with open woodland or brushy habitats), the preferred habitat of their preferred prey (the mule deer), and the concentration of human observers.

Mountain lions are large predators and should be considered dangerous. Lion attacks on humans are very rare. Nonetheless, in July 1997, a female lion attacked and killed a ten-year-old boy in the Summerland Park area, northeast of Grand Lake. In 1999, a three-year-old child apparently was killed by a mountain lion along the Big South Trail in the Comanche Peak Wilderness, just north of the national park.

The Colorado Division of Wildlife has extensive experience with human-lion interactions. Their good advice is to stop and think. Remain calm. Speak calmly yet firmly to the lion. Raise your arms and your walking stick to appear larger. Move slowly and back away slowly. Do not turn and do not run If the lion behaves aggressively, throw stones, branches, or whatever is available. If a lion attacks, fight back. In short, to prevent becoming prey, do not act like prey.

Selected References—A. Anderson et al. (1992); Armstrong (2006); Colorado Division of Wildlife (2006); Currier (1983); Dixon (1982); Logan and Sweanor (2000); Pierce and Bleich (2003); Young and Goldman (1946).

Canada Lynx
Lynx canadensis

Description—Because of the similarity of the two species, this description is made as a comparison between the Canada lynx and the bobcat. The lynx is the decidedly larger animal -825 to 950 mm or more in total length and up to 16 kg (35 pounds) in weight, with longer legs, a shorter tall (100 to 125 mm long), and larger feet. In color, the lynx is paler, tending toward grayish white rather than reddish. The markings overall are less pronounced and the forelimbs lack prominent black markings. The tail has a solid-black tip rather than an incomplete black ring. Furthermore, the ears have loose, black tassels, nearly as long as the ear itself, rather than a well-defined point. Habitats of the animals also differ, the lynx being a species of heavy forest, the bobcat living in woodland or shrubland on broken terrain. The Canada lynx is considered by some taxonomists to be a subspecies of the Old World lynx, *Lynx lynx*. *Field Recognition*—Tail black-tipped; ears with long, open tassel; habitat heavy forest.

Distribution and Habitat—The Canada lynx is a boreal animal, ranging from subarctic Canada southward in the United States along the Rockies to southern Colorado, at least formerly. The present status of the species in Rocky Mountain National Park is uncertain. The lynx ranks with the wolverine as our least known carnivore. Lynx apparently once occurred here regularly if sparingly, but records are difficult to authenticate. The mountain bobcat, being large and pale, looks more like a lynx than does any other subspecies of

Canada Lynx *(Lee Kline)*

bobcat. Nearly every summer, some observer—familiar with reddish-colored bobcats elsewhere in the country—reports the local bobcat as a lynx. Careful attention to detail is essential if we are to establish the presence of the lynx in the park. There are about a dozen reports of lynx on file at Park Headquarters over the past fifty years. Most of those are equivocal and predate lynx restoration efforts in Colorado. Two reports from 2006, however, are of particular interest. In June, park biologist Jeff Connor observed a lynx along the Grand Ditch above the Holzworth Historic Site; the animal was fitted with a radio collar. In December, a park visitor observed what may well have been a lynx near Bear Lake. Lynx restoration has been concentrated in the San Juan Mountains of southern Colorado, but the animals are known to have dispersed widely after release, and their reestablishment in Rocky Mountain National Park probably is just a matter of time. No sign of the Canada lynx was encountered in intensive winter survey of Rocky Mountain National Park and adjacent national forest lands in 1990–1991.

Natural History—Differences in habitat between the lynx and the bobcat are profound, and they go far to explain the minor differences in habits. Snowshoe hares are a dietary staple for lynx in the north and in the Southern Rockies as well. Squirrels, mice, and birds are also eaten, as is carrion in poor years. Food caching behavior is known. The lynx is active throughout the year. Individuals have a home range of 15 to 20 square kilometers, more or less dependent on the productivity of prey populations.

The reliance of the lynx on the snowshoe hare is widely known. Snowshoe hares are subject to wide, periodic fluctuations in numbers. The reproductive success of the lynx seems to be tied to these fluctuations. Kittens are produced each year, but only in years of peak production of hares do the young survive to weaning. An average litter of four young is produced in April or May after a gestation period of about two months.

Selected References—E. Anderson and Lovallo (2003); Andrews (1991); Glick (2006); McCord and Cardoza (1982); Ruggiero et al. (2000); Tumlison (1987).

Bobcat
Lynx rufus

Description—The bobcat is the smallest of Colorado's native cats. Males range from 825 to 925 mm in total length, the stubby tail being 130 to 160 mm long. Females average smaller, total length ranging from 730 to 975 mm, with a tail 120 to 150 mm long. As is true in many other mammals, the full pelage gives the bobcat a deceptively large appearance. This is heightened by the presence of a "ruff" on the face. Weights range from about 5.5

Bobcat *(Lee Kline)*

to 8 kg (12 to 20 pounds), with exceptionally large males weighing in excess of 10 kg.

The color of bobcats is highly variable in our area because this is a region of contact between rather distinctive geographic races: a reddish foothills race and a paler mountain subspecies. In both forms, grayish hairs predominate, the amount of reddish-tipped hairs in the pelage being the principal variable. Strong black markings are present. The ears are pale in front, rimmed with black behind, and come to a sharp point. The end of the tail has incomplete rings of black above and a distinct white "pencil" at the very tip. The bobcat can be confused with no local species other than the lynx; for comparisons, see the account of the latter species. *Field Recognition*—Tail with incomplete black rings; ears without obvious tuft or tassel, coming to definite point; habitat open woodland or shrubland.

Distribution and Habitat—Bobcats range from coast to coast and from southern Canada to northern Mexico. Permanent settlement has altered the overall range very little, although the animals do avoid human populations, with their attendant dog populations. Bobcats range virtually statewide in Colorado and are present at least occasionally in suitable habitat throughout Rocky Mountain National Park. This is an animal of "patchy" country—forest edge, woodland, and shrubland. Unbroken forest and open parkland are traversed only to reach areas of better game.

Natural History—Bobcats are legendary for their ferocity, and perhaps rightfully so, but their secrecy is at least as noteworthy. The animals often are fairly common in an area where they are thought to be nonexistent. Nocturnal habits and a penchant for rough country make them hard to spot. Keen eyes and ears, gracefully silent movements, and a thorough distrust of humans further the conspiracy. Occasional individuals freeze at the roadside in the beam of headlights and sometimes a rock-climber inadvertently flushes one from a daytime retreat. The best evidence of their presence is the occasional footprint, especially obvious in snow. Bobcats are active throughout the year.

Bobcats are highly specialized predators, pound-for-pound as capable as any. The long, retractable claws are sharpened continually. The canine teeth are long, thin, and rapier-sharp. The cheekteeth oppose each other in a scissorlike cutting action. Single bobcats occasionally kill deer that may outweigh them by five to ten times. The staple prey under most conditions is rabbits and hares, sometimes comprising three-quarters of the diet. A rabbit is a package of food large enough to make serious hunting worthwhile. The bobcat waits motionless beside a game trail or stalks the unsuspecting prey, slinking on its belly, the tail twitching like a furry metronome. Then, with one or two bounds, the prey is surprised and overcome. Although rabbits are a staple, about anything beaver-sized or smaller that moves is taken occasionally—shrews, mice, woodrats, squirrels, marmots, birds (songbirds as well as ground dwellers), and even porcupines. Pocket gophers are eaten but rarely are excavated actively. Most hunting is done on the ground although bobcats climb well and swim readily. Carrion is taken when other food is scarce. A circuitous route 8 to 15 km long is an evening's foraging round. Days are passed in unimproved shelter—rocky clefts, caves, wind-thrown trees—usually a new retreat each day. Only females with kittens have a permanent den. The usual gait is an erratic bounding run. When focused, they can move quickly, but they rely mostly on stealth, rather than speed, while hunting.

There is a justifiable tendency to compare the bobcat with its domesticated cousin, the house cat. They are similar in structure, function, and spirit. Both are beautifully adapted predators, both are curious but cautious, and both are mostly aloof (one prudently, the other arrogantly) from humans. Bobcats sharpen their claws and bury their dung; they even purr. Both are furiously defensive, snarling and hissing, rolling on their backs to rake the adversary's belly with the claws.

Bobcats harbor parasites, including fleas, nematodes, and tapeworms, although their transient lifestyle and their typical independence of carrion make them less prone to parasitism than are some other carnivores. Bobcats have few serious, habitual enemies other than humans. Larger carnivores can hardly afford the "expense" involved in preying actively on other carnivorous species. They are too few in number to be a dependable resource, and the usual (and ecologically sounder) course is to get solar energy via the shortest route possible—from a primary consumer, a vegetarian. The best bet—and the most common situation in the wild—is for carnivores to avoid each other, even other individuals of the same species. Mutual avoidance eventually spaces bobcats across available habitat. These are solitary animals, a solitude compromised only during the breeding season.

Females are polyestrous and may breed any month, although most breeding occurs from January through September, with a distinct peak in March and April. With a gestation period of about 60 days, most young—altricial and weighing less than 500 g—are born in May and June. Litters average three to four kittens, although the range is one to six. The eyes open at nine days of age. At about two weeks, the kittens begin to play among themselves, an important learning activity that continues until the litter separates. The young are weaned at about two months. The father has no part in the care of the kittens (although rare exceptions have been noted). A mother with kittens is dangerous to a person or to the kittens' sire. If the litter is disturbed, the den is abandoned and the young are moved. Nursery dens may be under rocks, roots, brushpiles, or even old buildings; any hollow, in fact, that is well concealed and needs little or no excavating.

Selected References—E. Anderson and Lovallo (2003); Larivière and Walton (1997); Makar (1980); McCord and Cardoza (1982); Van Wormer (1963); Young (1958).

Mule Deer *(Gene Putney)*

11

ORDER ARTIODACTYLA
Even-toed Hoofed Mammals

The artiodactyls include our largest extant native mammal, the wapiti, or American elk, and are some of the most familiar and conspicuous members of our fauna. Four species are resident in the area, the bison once lived here, and the moose—deliberately introduced to Colorado—is becoming fairly common in parts of Rocky Mountain National Park.

Artiodactyls are members of a large—and diverse—group of mammals, the ungulates, so-called because they walk on their ungules ("nails," or hooves). Ungulates are adapted to covering long distances with minimal effort. In so doing, they have sacrificed the versatility of the ancestral, five-toed mammalian foot.

Our native ungulates are all ruminants, a subgroup of artiodactyls with a complex digestive system. The ruminant "stomach" is composed of four compartments, termed (from front to back) rumen, reticulum, omasum, and abomasum. The rumen is the largest compartment. Rumen and reticulum knead the food; bacteria in these compartments begin the breakdown of cellulose by fermentation. From the reticulum, the partially digested food—now called "cud"—is regurgitated, and the animal "chews its cud," a process more properly called rumination. Then the cud is re-swallowed and passed (via a shortcut) to the omasum, where muscular walls rework the food mechanically. From there the food passes to the abomasum, where the food is processed chemically by secretions of gastric glands. Close examination of the tissues of the ruminant "stomach" reveals that only the abomasum has a structure comparable to the stomach of other mammals. The anterior three compartments actually are elaborate modifications of the esophagus.

A structure as complex as the ruminant "stomach" must have considerable adaptive significance. What might that be? Obviously, the apparatus serves to maximize the nutrients derived from plant material by allowing separate compartments for specialized bacterial action, but that is not the whole story. The ruminant gut also allows the animal to harvest large amounts of forage rapidly. Then the individual can retreat to the safety of cover (or the safety of its herd), regurgitate the meal a little at a time, and process the material properly at a leisurely pace. The ruminant digestive apparatus is surely a major key to the evolutionary success of the artiodactyls. Overall, the order includes about 240 living species, arranged in some eighty-nine genera representing ten families. The six families of ruminants include 90 percent of the species.

FAMILY CERVIDAE—DEER AND ALLIES

Deer occur throughout the northern continents and in South America, but they are absent from Australia and Sub-Saharan Africa. (In Australia, wallabies fill the role of deer and in Africa, antelope and other bovids do the same.) There are about fifty recent species of deer, four of which occur in Rocky Mountain National Park.

Wapiti, or Elk
Cervus canadensis

Description—The wapiti, or elk, is second in size only to the moose among members of the deer family. Bulls stand 1.5 m (5 feet) tall at the shoulder and weigh 340 kg (750 pounds) or more; mature cows are smaller, weighing about 225 kg (500 pounds). In fresh fall pelage, the rump-patch and tail are yellowish tan and the sides are gray-brown. In striking contrast, the head and neck are blackish brown. Females usually show less contrasting coloration than

Wapiti, or Elk *(Gene Putney)*

do bulls. The pelage bleaches and wears through the winter and is replaced in spring by a shorter, more reddish summer coat. *Field Recognition*—Large size; dark colored head and paler body; tail narrow and without black tip.

Distribution and Habitat—The wapiti once ranged across North America from the eastern seaboard to the West Coast and from northern British Columbia, central Ontario, and New York southward to New Mexico, Texas, Louisiana, and Georgia. The American elk is considered by some to be a member of a Holarctic species, *Cervus elaphus,* the "red deer" of Eurasia. Except for small, restored populations in the eastern United States, the wapiti now is restricted to the western part of the continent where, subject to careful management, the animals are assured a secure future, wherever their habitat is not degraded further by habitat conversion.

In Rocky Mountain National Park, the wapiti once lived mostly in forest edge situations with lush herbage, where they feed in openings, staying near enough to the trees to retreat to cover if necessary. Today, absent wolves, they spend more time in open parks than they once did. Alpine tundra is grazed in summer, and large open parks at moderate elevations (Horseshoe, Moraine, and Hollowell Parks, for example) provide winter range. There are distinct seasonal migrations.

Natural History—The wapiti is less elusive and more abundant than the bighorn sheep but certainly is second to none of our fauna in its thoroughly regal mien. "Wapiti" is a word of Amerindian derivation. Unfortunately, it is mostly a "textbook name," rare in popular usage. The result is some minor international confusion. In Eurasia, the name "elk" is applied to the animal we call "moose" (*Alces alces*), and the "wapiti" of the Old World are called "red deer."

Wapiti have not always been abundant in the park. According to the memoirs of Milton Estes, when permanent Euroamerican settlers established themselves in Estes Park in 1860, "great bands of elk . . . were everywhere." But in the half century that followed, the wapiti was nearly extirpated by market-hunting (to which these large, gregarious was animals were especially susceptible) and by competition with domestic livestock for winter range. Strict protection and active restoration (from the Yellowstone area of northwestern Wyoming) reestablished the herds. Acquisition of Beaver Meadows and Horseshoe and Moraine Parks provided some winter range within Rocky Mountain National Park. Now, overpopulation is a chronic problem. Over the past decade, numbers of elk in the national park and adjacent Estes Park have ranged from 1,700 to 3,500.

Unlike mule and white-tailed deer, the wapiti is mostly a grazer, feeding on grasses and forbs rather than shrubs. A study on Specimen Mountain indicated that grasses provided 85 percent of the diet. Diet changes with the season, the principal forage at any given time being the fastest-growing, most succulent (and often the most nutritious) species. Some browse is taken, especially in winter, when shrubs may comprise 90 percent of the diet for brief periods. Bark and twigs of aspen are eaten commonly. Evidence of this habit is widespread in the park; look for stunted saplings and for long, deep "claw marks" on the bark of mature aspen, 2 m or more above ground. These marks are not made by bears but by the teeth of the wapiti.

The animals feed mostly just after dawn and near dusk, with intervals of grazing and resting occupying the daylight hours. At night, they retire to the cover of forest. The same trails are used continually, becoming quite worn. The bed-ground is used repeatedly, but a given individual seems not to lie in the same spot on successive nights.

The wapiti is a gregarious animal. Herding behavior is strong evidence that the animals' present-day predilection for forested country is something of an innovation. Herding is a defensive strategy typical of mammals of open country—recall the herds of bison on the prairie, muskoxen or caribou on the tundra, and dolphins in the oceans. Forest-dwelling ungulates tend to live alone or in small bands. Winter herds of elk are large, including fifty to several hundred individuals of both genders. Winter herds disband as bulls move first to summer range, following the retreating snowline and the advance of green herbage. Cows and calves follow bulls to summer range, and the great herds of winter break up into smaller bands. Copious forage allows more leisurely feeding than in winter, but summer heat and insects seem to cause more discomfort than does the cold of winter, impelling the animals to wallow in mudholes and snowbanks.

The wapiti is alert with keen senses. They usually are not fast-moving, the typical gait being a walk. When startled, however, they will run, covering ground rapidly with long, graceful strides. Obstacles are hurdled deer-like, with an agility and ease surprising for an animal of such size.

The antlers of a mature bull may weigh 12 kg (25 pounds) or more, with a total spread of nearly 1.5 m. (This is considerably wider than the average distance between trees in the subalpine forest—another hint that these animals are adapted to open country.) Antlers are made of bone. They are shed (or "cast") in late winter, and replacement begins within two weeks. By early August, the antlers are nearly full-grown and covered with "velvet"—tender skin overlying abundant blood vessels. When growth is complete, the mineral-rich blood supply is curtailed and the velvet is shed, usually by vigorous rubbing against trees. This rubbing colors the antlers with pigments from the bark.

Cast antlers are found surprisingly seldom. When "sheds" are found in the national park, they must be left in place. For other members of the fauna—especially the rodents—the concentrated mineral resource of a cast antler is a bonanza. An old antler is recycled quickly, as gnawing mice and other animals funnel the minerals back into the resource web of the biotic community. The chemical salts that compose bone tend to be scarce in mountain ecosystems. Water flows downhill, after all, carrying dissolved substances with it.

One cannot age a bull directly by its antlers, but rough estimates are possible. There is no antler development during a calf's first autumn. The second autumn, "spikes" are present. The third year, three- to five-point antlers are typical. The fourth season and thereafter, a six-point rack is typical, the base generally becoming more massive each year. Damage to the base of the antler may cause aberrant growth in subsequent years. Bulls past their prime may show more than six points, but often they are poorly formed or asymmetric. Antlers of bulls on inadequate range are stunted.

In autumn, profound changes occur among the wapiti. The crisp air of late September carries the bugling of the bulls. The rut is beginning. Bugling actually starts well before the actual mating. Although commonly described as a "challenge" or a "threat," bugling is apparently not quite either of those. In part, at least, bugling is a sort of safety valve that releases the tension of the bull's seasonal physiological changes. With the rut, shoulders and neck swell. Antlers are sharpened. Bugling peaks in early October, and the most aggressive bulls assert authority over bands of five to fifteen cows. Another bull may challenge that authority. Sparring with the massive antlers follows. This activity is more analogous to arm-wrestling than to all-out combat, but the bouts can result in broken antlers and occasionally contestants are gored, even fatally. Usually, however, ritual sparring does the trick, and the vanquished bull retires to temporary bachelorhood.

Gestation takes about 250 days, and a single calf, weighing about 15 kg (33 pounds), is born in June. No special calving ground is used; calves are dropped in snow-free, forested areas around the open parks that constitute the winter range or they arrive while their mothers are migrating, even as high as alpine tundra. The calf is reddish buff, marked with pale buffy spots. With an odor seemingly detectable only by the mother, the calf remains motionless and is left alone as the cow forages. As is typical of ungulates, the calves are mobile—if haltingly so—within hours of birth. The calf develops quickly and usually is weaned by late summer. At six months of age, it may weigh 120 kg (265 pounds). Cows are reproductively mature their second autumn, and usually calve first at three years of age. Because of the social structure, bulls do not generally manage to acquire a harem and breed until their fourth or fifth year.

As the largest member of our extant fauna, the wapiti is subject to few enemies. On good range, a cow may live fifteen years or more; males have a somewhat shorter life expectancy.

Native hunters drove elk to the kill along game walls that still mark the tundra in the national park. At one time gray wolves preyed on them, and mountain lions still take a few. A pack of coyotes can kill a weakened elk or one immobilized on glaze ice or in deep snow, and coyotes—and likewise bobcats and bears—may kill calves when they happen upon them, but they do not tangle with cows over them. As with other ungulates, the elk harbors parasites, including flukes, tapeworms and roundworms, lice, botflies, and mites, the latter being the contagion of scabies. Chronic wasting disease (CWD) is known in elk in and near Rocky Mountain National Park. Colorado big game management units north and east of the park have reported incidence over 5 percent. Current status reports on CWD are available online from the Colorado Division of Wildlife.

Selected References—Benedict (1996); Harrington (1978); Murie (1951); Rocky Mountain National Park (2006); Olmstead (1979); Peek (2003); Van Wormer (1969); Wisdom and Cook (2000).

Mule Deer
Odocoileus hemionus

Description—The mule deer stands about a meter high at the shoulder. Bucks weigh to 120 kg (265 pounds) or more, does usually 45 to 70 kg (100 to 155 pounds). Overall, then, a mule deer is barely half the size of a wapiti. In color, mule deer are reddish tan in summer, tending to grayish brown in winter. The ears are disproportionately large and the tail is narrow, its bushy black tip contrasting with the white rump patch.

The mule deer differs from the white-tailed deer in its narrow, black-tipped (rather than broad, white, and "flag-like") tail, its conspicuously large ears, and its dichotomous antlers, which branch into equal Y-shaped parts rather than sprouting several tines off a single main stem. *Field Recognition*—Dichotomous antlers; moderate size; relatively large ears; head and neck colored much like body.

Distribution and Habitat—The mule deer is a western species, ranging from the Great Plains to the Pacific Coast and from the Canadian territories southward to Baja California, Durango, and Veracruz, Mexico. Mule deer are most abundant in brushy situations, about the margins of meadows, in canyons, and in streamside woodlands. Any opening that supports shrubs will be occupied. Successional shrublands on burned-over areas provide good habitat. Some individuals, especially bucks, summer at or above timberline, especially favoring willow thickets. In short, expect to find mule deer throughout the park, except in the heaviest forest or the most open country.

Mule Deer *(Gene Putney)*

Natural History—The mule deer is a large mammal that all but the most hurried visitor may expect to see. Today they are abundant throughout the Southern Rockies. As with our other ungulates, however, this has not always been true. As plentiful as they are today, it is hard to imagine the situation described by Merritt Cary (1911) in his *A Biological Survey of Colorado*: "[A] few mule deer [were reported] in the Estes Park region in 1895, but I heard of none in the foothills of Boulder and Larimer Counties in 1906." This is in dramatic contrast to Milton Estes's description of the situation in 1860, when "deer were everywhere." Today, they are everywhere once again. Over their range, mule deer have proved remarkably resilient when unregulated hunting is curtailed. Unlike many other ungulates, deer thrive in close proximity to humans, and being browsers, they compete very little with domestic livestock.

The diet consists of shrubbery and herbage. A study conducted on Specimen Mountain indicated that shrubs contributed 73 percent of the diet and broad-leafed herbs about 26 percent. Therefore, on good range there is little or no competition with elk and bighorn sheep, both of which are grazers, or with domestic livestock outside the park. Food preference shifts with the season, emphasizing species that are growing most actively and thus are most succulent. Actively growing tissues also are the most nutritious, so selectivity goes beyond mere taste. Conifers are browsed on poor range, especially in winter, when competition with elk may become severe. Mule deer feed mostly at night, seemingly oblivious to weather, and retire to heavy cover to spend the day.

Seasonal migrations occur between summer and winter ranges, but this is somewhat less marked than in the wapiti (perhaps because the animals move in smaller groups). Snow seems to drive the animals down for the winter, and snow's retreat draws them back to summer range. Bucks often summer at or above timberline, whereas does and fawns occupy subalpine forest edge situations. In autumn, about October, they move down, many wintering outside the national park in the lower foothills of the Front Range or around Middle Park on the Western Slope.

Mule deer have acute senses of smell and hearing. They see moving objects at great distances but may be oblivious to a motionless observer at close range. When startled, the deer moves with a mechanical, bounding gait that is gracefully effortless almost beyond belief. Under more secure circumstances, they move with a stately high-stepping walk.

Bucks shed the antlers in December or January and renew them annually. Young-of-the-year do not produce antlers; the second fall, a light, two-point set is typical. The third fall—when the buck is just over two years old—weak, three- or four-point antlers are produced. Older bucks usually have four principal points on either side, and the rack becomes progressively heavier each year. In old age (beyond 10 years) or when injured, asymmetric racks often form. Most mature racks have a spread of 60 to 90 cm (about 2 to 3 feet). Occasional antlered does are reported; these are hormonal "freaks."

Deer are important primary consumers in local ecosystems. A strong deer population can support good populations of the larger carnivores. The browsing strategy taps a rich food resource, and the deer converts its dietary intake into a package of animal protein of convenient size for a larger predator. Hunting rabbits and marmots is a poor investment for a mountain lion. In an energetic sense, deer are purveyors of vegetation to his majesty, the cougar. Coyotes and bobcats also prey on them, especially young, weak, or snowbound animals, and wolves once took them as well. Black bears kill a few fawns each year, probably stumbling upon them rather than actively hunting them down. Traffic takes a heavy toll of deer. Maximal longevity is about 20 years. Chronic wasting disease (CWD) is an emerging disease of deer, elk, and moose, related to scrapie in sheep. It was first discovered in captive and free-ranging deer and elk in northeastern Colorado and adjacent Wyoming. Like so-called mad cow disease, CWD is a transmissible spongiform encephalopathy (TSE) caused by a prion, a sort of rogue protein. Chronic wasting disease is present in and near Rocky Mountain National Park, especially in Larimer and Boulder Counties, where incidence exceeds 5 percent. West of the park, in Grand County, incidence is somewhat lower. For current status of CWD, consult the Colorado Division of Wildlife on the Internet.

Deer molt in mid-September, and about that same time the antlers of the bucks mature. In November, the rut begins. With neck and shoulders swollen, mature bucks joust furiously for mating rights, a behavior like that of the wapiti but without the bugling and without forming a cohesive harem. Mating is completed by late December. Then bucks, their seasonal belligerence exhausted, may band together loosely or they may spend the winter in seclusion. Does and young form winter herds separate from the bucks.

Gestation takes about 200 days, and the 4.5 kg (10-pound) young are born from June to early July. After the first pregnancy—usually as a two-year-old—does typically produce twins, achieving an average litter size of about 1.6. In common with other kinds of deer, fawns are spotted and without obvious odor. Twin siblings usually are hidden separately, the mother approaching them only to nurse. Within a few weeks, fawns are strong enough to follow their mother. They are weaned in autumn at about 22.5 kg (50 pounds).

Selected References—A. Anderson and Wallmo (1984); Harrington (1978); Kie and Czech (2000); Loveless (1967); Mackie et al. (2003); Wallmo (1978, 1981).

White-tailed Deer
Odocoileus virginianus

Description—The white-tailed deer is a handsome animal, reddish to grayish brown in general color, with a white muzzle and eye ring, and a white rump patch. The animals carry the broad, flag-like tail erect while running. Bucks are larger than does; mature males average about 2 m in total length, with a tail 300 mm long, and they weigh about 200 kg (440 pounds). Does are about 1.7 m long and weigh about 100 kg (220 pounds). The only species with which the white-tailed deer might be confused is the mule deer; for

White-tailed Deer *(Lee Kline)*

comparison, see the account of that species. *Field Recognition*—White-edged, flag-like tail.

Distribution and Habitat—The white-tailed deer is a widespread species, ranging from central Canada throughout most of the United States (except the Great Basin, the Colorado Plateau, and much of the Pacific Coast) and as far south as Peru and Bolivia. The animals apparently have arrived in Rocky Mountain National Park only recently. Around the turn of the century, Merritt Cary reported the species from the foothills of the Big Thompson drainage and from the Laramie River drainage north of the national park. From then until the 1950s, white-tailed deer were rare or even absent from Colorado. Then increasingly frequent reports of the species began to be received from the irrigated bottomlands of the eastern plains. In the 1970s, white-tailed deer became increasingly abundant along the foothills of the Front Range. The first records of the species from Rocky Mountain National Park were in 1984. They now have been reported from both sides of the Continental Divide, but they are not common.

White-tailed deer are animals of forest edge situations. In eastern Colorado, they appear to occur mostly in riparian communities along major streams. Habitat relationships with mule deer have not been studied. Seasonal movements are to be expected but have yet to be investigated in Colorado.

Natural History—White-tailed deer are mostly crepuscular, active at dawn and dusk. As with the mule deer, this is a browser, feeding mostly on woody vegetation. One would predict competition with the mule deer for food or cover, but this has yet to be investigated in Colorado. A large deer needs 2 to 3 kg of dry-weight forage per day. Food items are selected on the basis of nutritive value rather than species; hence, diet changes with the season and the growth stage of particular plants.

The rut occurs in October and November, with the promiscuous males following does in estrus. Normally, all mature females are bred. One to three fawns are born in late May or June after a gestation period of about 200 days. The fawns grow quickly, doubling their 2.5 kg birth weight by two weeks, and doubling it again by five weeks. The spotted fawns molt to adult pelage at three months. Thereafter there are two molts annually. Does usually breed first as yearlings, after their second summer, and yearling males participate in the rut. Antlers begin to grow in April and are completed by August; the velvet is shed by September, and the antlers are cast in February.

The basic social unit is a doe with fawns of two ages. Adult bucks tend to be solitary or to form bachelor herds. In the mating season, females may become more solitary, driving off the young. After the rut, fairly large herds may form, sometimes including both adult does and bucks. Even within these herds, most interaction is between the doe and her own offspring.

Predators include coyotes, bobcats, and humans. (In terms of annual harvest and number of hunters, this is the most important big game animal in North America.) Where white-tailed deer are abundant, many are killed by vehicles. Maximal longevity in the wild is about 10 years.

Selected References—Demarais et al. (2000); Hesselton and Hesselton (1982); Miller et al. (2003); W. Smith (1979).

Moose
Alces alces

The moose is a circumboreal species. It is not a native resident of Colorado, but occasional individuals have wandered in on their own over the past century, perhaps from northern Utah or northwestern Wyoming. Moose are wide ranging animals and they occasionally herd with elk or even domestic cattle. In the early 1860s, Milton Estes shot a moose (from among a band of elk) in the park that bears his family's name. Other early Coloradan moose records

Moose *(Gene Putney)*

are from the vicinity of Steamboat Springs and from southwest of Meeker. In 1978, the Colorado Division of Wildlife introduced moose to North Park, northwest of Rocky Mountain National Park, partly in an attempt to control the encroachment of willows into irrigated hayfields. The largest expanse of suitable habitat for moose in the national park is the wet willow community of the Kawuneeche Valley, at the headwaters of the Colorado River. In the wildlife observation files at RMNP Headquarters there are over 500 reports of moose from RMNP, dated between 1988 and 2006. Over 80 percent of reports are from prior to 1998. It appears that within a decade of their arrival in the park, the moose had become commonplace and thus less frequently reported by visitors and staff. About 89 percent of observations on file are from the Western Slope. Reports from east of the Continental Divide are concentrated in the Big Thompson Watershed, especially the Glacier Creek drainage.

    Selected References—Bowyer et al. (2003); Coady (1982); Franzmann (1981, 2000).

FAMILY ANTILOCAPRIDAE—PRONGHORN

The pronghorn is the sole surviving member of an endemic American family (sometimes ranked as a subfamily of the Bovidae). Antilocaprids had a greater diversity in the geologic past than they do today, with perhaps a dozen genera, all but one of which became extinct before the end of the Pleistocene ice ages.

Pronghorn
Antilocapra americana

    The pronghorn probably is not resident in Rocky Mountain National Park, and its early status in the area is poorly known. North Park remains a stronghold of these fleet and beautiful animals, and Middle Park once was prime pronghorn range. Milton Estes, in his memoirs of the early 1860s, mentioned the pronghorn among game species hunted in Estes Park for sale in the Denver markets. Given the human development in and near the town of Estes Park, restoration of these animals on the east side of the national park is impractical. A pronghorn was observed in June 2002 on Harbison Meadow, on the west side of the national park, the first individual known inside the park since its establishment in 1915. With predicted drying and warming over coming years, habitat for this species in Middle Park may be expected to expand eastward and upslope.

    Selected References—Byers (1997, 2003); Kitchen and O'Gara (1982); O'Gara (1978); Yoakum and O'Gara (2003).

Pronghorn *(Fi Rust)*

FAMILY BOVIDAE—CATTLE, SHEEP, GOATS, AND ALLIES

The Bovidae includes the majority of living artiodactyls, the greatest diversity being among the antelope of the Old World. The family is native worldwide except for South America and Australia, and several domestic species are cosmopolitan. Colorado has two native bovids. The bighorn sheep persists in Rocky Mountain National Park and the bison once occurred here. Mountain goats have been introduced near the national park and occasionally wander across the park boundary. Because they are an exotic species they are removed from the park as quickly as humanely practicable.

Bison
Bos bison

The last native bison in Colorado were killed in the Lost Park area (in Park County, southeast of Jefferson) in 1897. The last known native bison in eastern Colorado was killed near Springfield in 1889, and the last remnant animal in northwestern Colorado was killed at Cedar Springs (west of Craig) in 1884. Today, bison occur in the state only in semidomestication, classified by state law as livestock, not wildlife.

The history of the bison in Rocky Mountain National Park is rather poorly known. Certainly these magnificent animals were not abundant in the area by the time literate settlers arrived to report on the native fauna. Milton Estes made no mention of bison or their remains in his memoirs of Estes Park in the early 1860s. Abner Sprague came to the area in 1868, about eight years after Estes arrived. He noted bison remains near the north end of Estes Park, while en route to the North Fork of the Big Thompson River near the site of present-day Glen Haven. In about 1878, Sprague found a bison skull on Hagues Peak, above 3,550 m (12,000 feet). About the same time, he found the nearly fresh carcass of a bison at the south end of North Peak.

Other early localities of bison remains include Horseshoe Park, east of Marys Lake, McCreery Gulch (south of Gem Lake), Moraine Park, Dunraven Meadows, Lost Lake (near the headwaters of the North Fork of the Big Thompson), Tuxedo Park, and Grand Lake. Thatchtop Mountain was known to the Arapaho as "the Buffalo Climb," and Buffalo Pass—to the north of the national park—was so-named by Indians. Long Gulch (near Mount Olympus) was used by the Arapaho as a buffalo trap. In 1981, two skulls and other remains of bison melted out of the snowfield below Icefield Pass, on the headwaters of the Big Thompson River at an elevation of 11,600 feet. With ongoing climatic warming, bison skulls are melting out of the receding glaciers of the Colorado Front Range with increasing frequency.

Bison *(Gene Putney)*

Obviously, the bison was once important in the mountain ecosystems of our region. Apparently the animals were migratory. The Arapaho found them to be a rather undependable resource in the area. Occasional individuals or bands ranged above timberline, and greater concentrations lived at intervals on open parklands. The bison is a rightful member of the native fauna. However, the present-day national park has too little range to support the animals as anything but captives and is far too small to accommodate the animals' migratory habits.

Selected References—Benedict (1993, 1999); Fryxell (1928); Isenberg (2000); Lee et al. (2006); Meagher (1986); Reynolds et al. (2003); Shaw and Meagher (2000).

Mountain Goat
Oreamnos americanus

Mountain goats were introduced to the Southern Rocky Mountains by the Colorado Division of Wildlife beginning in 1949. There is no evidence that the modern species of mountain goat is a member of the native fauna of Colorado (although fossils of an extinct species of mountain goat, *Oreamnos harringtoni,* have been reported from interglacial Pleistocene deposits some 650,000 to 800,000 years old excavated at Porcupine Cave in South Park). On several occasions over the past decade, mountain goats have been observed at scattered locations in Rocky Mountain National Park, mostly at higher elevations. With their long white coats and black horns and hooves, mountain goats are unmistakeable. Visitor observations of mountain goats should be reported to Park Service personnel. Rocky Mountain National Park is committed to the preservation of natural conditions. Mountain goats that are located in the national park are captured humanely and removed from the area.

Selected References—Barnosky and Bell (2004); Côté and Festa-Bianchet (2003); Peek (2000).

Mountain, or Bighorn, Sheep
Ovis canadensis

Description—Mountain sheep vary widely in color over their range. In our area, adults are a rich brown above in fresh spring pelage and then pale gradually through the season to grayish brown or almost white. The prominent rump patch is white and continues uninterrupted down the hind legs. The backs of the forelegs are also white. Both sexes have horns. Those of the ewes are spikelike. The massive, spiraling horns of the ram taper gradually.

Mountain, or Bighorn, Sheep *(Gene Putney)*

Unlike the antlers of the deer family, horns are not shed but grow continually from the base, laying down annual rings, which permit the approximate aging of individuals. A ram with a three-quarter curl is about 10 years old.

Mature males stand a meter (about 40 inches) high at the shoulder and weigh about 180 kg (400 pounds). Ewes are about 88 cm (35 inches) high and weigh less than half as much as rams, usually less than 70 kg (about 155 pounds). *Field Recognition*—Both sexes with horns; white rump and legs.

Distribution and Habitat—Within historic times, bighorn sheep ranged in western North America from central British Columbia southward to Baja California and from the Sierra Nevada eastward to the badlands and pine-clad escarpments of the Dakotas and Nebraska. Existing populations are scattered within those historical limits, restricted by human encroachment to the more remote parts of the West.

Over its wide range, the mountain sheep lives in a wide variety of habitats, from desert valleys (including Death Valley), canyons, and arid mountain ranges to alpine tundra in the Rockies. The animals generally prefer open situations. In Colorado, they now occur mostly at higher elevations—usually avoiding forested country—but once they migrated in winter to lower elevations, even to the edge of the Great Plains.

Natural History—Bighorn sheep rightfully have come to be the animal symbol of Rocky Mountain National Park, and they are the official state mammal of Colorado. Mountain sheep are impressive mammals indeed. In their rugged native haunts they portray a wild grandeur to match their majestic home. But despite their majesty as silhouettes against the alpine skyline, the bighorns' erratic behavior permits occasional moments of amusingly informal abandon. The scrambling play of lambs among the rocks and the headlong running of their startled elders down the most precipitous slopes hardly suggest a thorough composure.

Except during the breeding season—which extends from November to January with a peak in December—the daily round of activity consists of alternate periods of feeding and rest (and rumination). At midday the entire band usually stops grazing for siesta. As is true of other mammals of open country, bighorns have keen eyesight and detect the slightest movement at great distances. No one individual serves as sentinel; all are alert for danger, real or imagined.

Bighorn bands are variable in size and composition, ranging from a few individuals to several dozen. Rams band together in summer and forage at higher elevations than do ewes and lambs. Bighorns are mostly grazers, the bulk of the diet, under good range conditions, being grasses and sedges. In a study of food habits of bighorn sheep, elk, and mule deer on Specimen Mountain, grasses provided 88 percent of the diet of bighorns and forbs only

12 percent. Browsing was minimal. As a result there was little dietary overlap with mule deer, whose diet emphasized woody vegetation. The bighorns' predilection for ridgeline tundra meadows takes them out of potential competition with elk, which tend to graze in Krummholz stands and subalpine parks and meadows. Sheep may ingest mud for its salt content, as at Sheep Lakes in Horseshoe Park or on Specimen Mountain. At dusk the animals retire for the night to a bedding ground in a rocky area. Often the same ground is used continually for long periods, and especially favored sites may be used year after year.

During the fall breeding season, the usually disorderly and nervous behavior of bighorns gives way to utter chaos. Usually a single ewe comes into estrus at a time. She is singled out by mature rams for attention. As the ram approaches, the ewe runs off for a few meters and then stops. The ram follows, but if another ram joins the chase, the budding romance gives way to dueling between rams. Fighting consists mostly of head-on butting, the massive horns absorbing most of the shock. No holds are barred, however, and kicking the flanks and butting about the shoulders are not uncommon. The victor earns the right to mate. But at times a third ram will mate with the ewe while she watches the principals in their pugilistic ritual. Under these promiscuous conditions, virtually all ewes are bred. Females breed first their third year; males mature their fourth but typically do not actually manage to breed until seven or eight years old.

The gestation period is about 6 months, and lambing peaks in late May and early June. Lambing grounds typically are on remote, precipitous slopes providing the precocial young with protection. Single births are the general rule, although twinning has been recorded. Lambs play near the ewes. Milk is supplemented by occasional herbage as early as two weeks after birth and the young are weaned in mid- to late autumn. Lambing grounds mostly are protected from human encroachment.

Before permanent human settlement in the region, bighorns made rather lengthy seasonal migrations, wintering in the foothills and along the western margin of the plains. In some parts of Colorado they still winter mostly on south-facing slopes at moderate elevations and follow the retreating snowline to summer range in the alpine tundra, rams preceding ewes and young. In the vicinity of Rocky Mountain National Park, however, civilization has interrupted the migrations of the typically wary sheep.

Prior to the mid-nineteenth century, mountain sheep apparently were abundant in what is now Rocky Mountain National Park. By 1900, however, they had been virtually eliminated by market hunters and trophy hunters, by habitat disturbance (especially by competition with domestic livestock for winter range), and by introduced sheep diseases, such as scabies. With the establishment of the national park, the population began to recover, partly because of an actual recovery of the local population and partly because sheep from surrounding areas concentrated in the newly established wildlife sanctuary. In the 1920s, a new decline began, owing to concentration of the animals year-around on what had been high-elevation summer range. The addition of Horseshoe Park to the national park provided mineral-rich winter range, although sheep sporadically return to the alpine to winter. Horseshoe Park is a place where many visitors first observe bighorns. Crowding apparently led to mineral and protein deficiencies and an increase in lungworm and other endoparasitic diseases.

In 1977, twenty bighorns were moved to the Cow Creek drainage from the Tarryall Range near Pikes Peak. Bighorns now occur chiefly in two areas: along the Continental Divide and the Never Summer Range, and on the east side of the park, moving between the Mummy Range and the vicinity of Sheep Lake. Visitors frequently see sheep along Fall River Road east of the park entrance, at the foot of MacGregor Mountain. Excess animals from that band were moved in the late 1980s to the mouth of the Big Thompson Canyon, with the hope of restoring the long-distance migrations once typical of this species.

Extensive game walls on the tundra suggest that mountain sheep (as well as elk and deer) were hunted by Native people in what is now Rocky Mountain National Park. Today, coyotes prey on lambs, and wolves certainly took a toll formerly. Mountain lions prey on bighorns, but they probably are not sufficiently abundant to cause appreciable mortality on a long-term basis. Despite their broad hooves and remarkable agility, accidents—including avalanches—claim sheep from time to time. Most mortality today is from disease, especially lungworm and associated pneumonia. Poor nutrition on inadequate range weakens the bands and increases their susceptibility to infection. Other parasites weaken the animals further. Persistent crowding of bands by visitors can cause stress in bighorns, which may predispose them to death from otherwise sublethal disease. Maximum longevity in the wild is 15 to 20 years.

Selected References—Benedict (1996); Geist (1971); Goodson (1978); Harrington (1978); Krausman and Bowyer (2003); Krausman and Shackleton (2000); Lawson and Johnson (1982); Moser (1962); Packard (1946); Shackleton (1985); Stevens and Hanson (1986).

APPENDIX I
Key to Mammals of Rocky Mountain National Park and Vicinity

This is a "dichotomous key," so-called because it is based on pairs of choices. Pairs of alternatives are called "couplets." From each couplet, select the alternative description that best applies to the mammal in question. The alternative will lead either to another couplet or to the name of a species or group of species. An attempt has been made to use both external and cranial characters. This allows the user to identify whole animals observed in the field as well as odd skulls that might be picked up.

Here is a prudent rule of thumb: *never trust a key*. Any key may use some characters that are difficult to observe or involve some subjective judgment. Follow the key through to reach a preliminary best guess at the identity of an organism. Then refer to accounts of species to make certain that the description fits the mammal in question. Illustrations and characteristics of habitat may also be important at this point.

KEY TO ORDERS OF MAMMALS

1. Forelimbs modified as wings . . . . BATS, KEY B
   Forelimbs not modified as wings 2

2. Stance bipedal; body mostly hairless; tail absent; snout reduced; eyes directed forward; thumb apposable; digits with nails; cerebral cortex greatly enlarged; metabolic energy augmented with fossil fuels; communication between non-overlapping generations cultural as well as genetic . . . .
   . . . . PRIMATES—Humankind—*Homo sapiens*, **p.** 72
   Stance quadrupedal; body well-haired; tail present; snout prominent; eyes directed more or less laterally; thumb (if present) not apposable; digits with claws or hooves; cerebral cortex not markedly developed; metabolic energy not augmented with fossil fuels; communication between non-overlapping generations genetic only 3

3. Upper incisors absent; males, at least, with horns or antlers . . . .
   . . . . ARTIODACTYLS, KEY F
   Upper incisors present; without horns or antlers 4

4. Canine teeth present; no pronounced gap (diastema) present between incisors and cheekteeth 5
   Canine teeth absent; pronounced gap (diastema) present between incisors and cheekteeth 6

5. Canine teeth not markedly longer than adjacent teeth . . . .
   . . . . INSECTIVORES, KEY A
   Canine teeth markedly longer than adjacent teeth . . . CARNIVORES, KEY E

6. Incisors 2 / 1; tail shorter than hindfoot . . . . LAGOMORPHS, KEY C
   Incisors 1 / 1; tail longer than hindfoot . . . . RODENTS, KEY D

KEY A—SORICOMORPHS

1. Total length greater than 150 mm; greatest length of skull, 20 mm or more; hindfoot with conspicuous fringe of stiff hairs; color grayish black . . . .
   . . . . **American Water Shrew** (*Sorex palustris*), **p.** 46
   Total length less than 120 mm; greatest length of skull, 18 mm or less; hindfoot without conspicuous fringe of stiff hairs; dorsal color variously brownish, never black 2

2. Only three unicuspid teeth conspicuous in lateral view; dorsal color dark brown . . . . **Pygmy Shrew** (*Sorex hoyi*), **p.** 42
   Four or five unicuspid teeth conspicuous in lateral view; dorsal color medium brown to pale brown 3

3. Third unicuspid tooth obviously smaller than fourth 4

Third and fourth unicuspid teeth of approximately equal size 5

4. Total length usually 100 mm or greater; habitat primarily moist, boggy situations . . . . **Montane Shrew** (*Sorex monticolus*), p. 43

Total length less than 100 mm; habitat sometimes as above but also in drier rocky or shrubby areas . . . . **Dwarf Shrew** (*Sorex nanus*), p. 45

5. Unicuspid teeth markedly robust; color pale grayish above, whitish below, tail usually markedly bicolored; habitat relatively dry woodland or brushland . . . .

. . . . **Merriam's Shrew** (*Sorex merriami*), p. 43

Unicuspid teeth not markedly robust; color medium brown above, brownish to buffy below; tail indistinctly bicolored to unicolored; habitat moist, boggy situations . . . . **Masked Shrew** (*Sorex cinereus*), p. 40

KEY B—BATS

1. Ear relatively long (30 mm or greater), pale, nearly translucent, with prominent, transverse ridges; folded back in resting animal . . . .

. . . . **Townsend's Big-eared Bat** (*Corynorhinus townsendii*), p. 67

Ear short to moderate in length (25 mm or less), dark, not translucent; in resting animal, may be folded forward but not back 2

2. Hairs of back with whitish or silvery tips, at least in part 3

Hairs of back without whitish tips 4

3. Upper surface of uropatagium densely furred to posterior border; ears short, rounded, well-furred, rimmed with black; size large; forearm greater than 50 mm; total teeth, 32; flight late, swift . . . . **Hoary Bat** (*Lasiurus cinereus*), p. 60

Upper surface of uropatagium not densely furred to posterior border; ears relatively long, pointed, dark, and naked; size moderate; forearm less than 45 mm; total teeth, 36; flight early, very slow . . . .

. . . . **Silver-haired Bat** (*Lasionycteris noctivagans*), p. 63

4. Size large, forearm greater than 45 mm; total teeth, 32 . . . .

. . . . **Big Brown Bat** (*Eptesicus fuscus*), p. 65

Size small to moderate, forearm about 40 mm or less; total teeth, 38 5

5. Ear relatively long, extending past end of nose when laid forward . . . .

. . . . **Long-eared Myotis** (*Myotis evotis*), p. 55

Ear relatively short, not extending past end of nose when laid forward 6

6. Body fur extending on underside of wing to level of elbow; calcar keeled . . . .

. . . . **Long-legged Myotis** (*Myotis volans*), p. 59

Body fur extending little or not at all onto underside of wing; calcar not keeled 7

7. Size smaller; forearm about 33 mm; hindfoot about 8 mm . . . .
. . . . **Western Small-footed Myotis** (*Myotis ciliolabrum*), **p. 53**
Size larger; forearm about 40 mm; hindfoot about 10 mm **8**

8. Posterior border of interfemoral membrane with conspicuous fringe of stiff
hairs . . . . **Fringed Myotis** (*Myotis thysanodes*), **p. 58**
Posterior border of interfemoral membrane without conspicuous fringe of
stiff hairs . . . . **Little Brown Bat** (*Myotis lucifugus*), **p. 56**

KEY C—LAGOMORPHS

1. Ear as broad as long; no visible tail; five upper cheekteeth on each side of jaw
. . . . **American Pika** (*Ochotona princeps*), **p. 76**
Ear much longer than broad; tail short but obvious; six upper cheekteeth on
each side of jaw **2**

2. Hindfoot less than 105 mm; ear relatively short, usually less than 65 mm; interparietal bone distinct; pelage dark throughout year . . . .
. . . . **Mountain, or Nuttall's, Cottontail** (*Sylvilagus nuttallii*), **p. 79**
Hindfoot more than 135 mm; ear relatively long, usually more than 65 mm;
interparietal bone indistinct; pelage dark in summer, white in winter **3**

3. Size moderate; ear less than half the length of hindfoot; hindfoot remarkably
long; greatest length of skull less than 80 mm; habitat willow thickets and
brushy openings in dense forest . . . . **Snowshoe Hare** (*Lepus americanus*), **p. 82**
Size large; ear about two-thirds as long as hindfoot; greatest length of skull
greater than 90 mm; habitat open country (mountain parks, tundra) . . . .
. . . . **White-tailed Jackrabbit** (*Lepus townsendii*), **p. 85**

KEY D—RODENTS

1. Pelage of back in part modified to form stout quills; infraorbital foramen larger than foramen magnum . . . .
. . . . **North American Porcupine** (*Erethizon dorsatum*), **p. 144**
Pelage of back not modified to form quills; infraorbital foramen various but
smaller than foramen magnum **2**

2. Tail broad, flattened, nearly hairless; nostrils and ears valvular; length of skull
greater than 120 mm . . . . **American Beaver** (*Castor canadensis*), **p. 118**
Tail not broadly flattened; nostrils and ears not valvular; length of skull less
than 100 mm **3**

3. External, fur-lined cheek pouches present; lips closing behind incisors; fore-feet strongly clawed; ears and eyes reduced . . . .
. . . . **Northern Pocket Gopher** (*Thomomys talpoides*), **p. 115**
External, fur-lined cheek pouches absent; lips closing over incisors; forefeet not obviously strongly clawed; eyes and ears generally prominent **4**

4. Tail long (half again as long as body); hindfoot elongate; hind limb modified for jumping; upper incisor grooved . . . .
. . . . **Western Jumping Mouse** (*Zapus princeps*), **p. 142**
Tail short (no longer than head and body); hind limb not modified for jumping; upper incisors not grooved **5**

5. Total teeth 20 or 22, four or five upper cheekteeth on each side of jaw; animals diurnal, mostly conspicuous **6**
Total teeth 16, three upper cheekteeth on each side of jaw; animals nocturnal (or if diurnal, inconspicuous and secretive) **15**

6. Tail short, less than one-fourth total length; length of skull greater than 90 mm . . . . **Yellow-bellied Marmot** (*Marmota flaviventris*), **p. 97**
Tail relatively long, more than one-fourth total length; length of skull less than 80 mm . . . .   , ... **7**

7. Habitat mostly woodland or forest; habit arboreal; crown of second upper molar as long as wide **8**
Habitat mostly open, rocky, or brushy areas; habit mostly terrestrial or fossorial; crown of second upper molar notably wider than long **10**

8. Size smaller (total length less than 350 mm); ear tufts small to moderate; color grayish to reddish brown above, grayish white below; third upper premolar reduced or lacking . . . .
Pine Squirrel, Chickaree, or Red Squirrel (*Tamiasciurus hudsonicus*), **p. 112**
Size larger (total length greater than 450 mm); color reddish, black, brown, or gray; three upper premolars **9**

9. Ears with prominent tufts; dorsal color black, brown, or "salt-and-pepper" gray; habitat mostly in ponderosa pine woodlands . . . .
. . . . **Abert's Squirrel** (*Sciurus aberti*), **p. 108**
Ears without prominent tufts; dorsal color reddish, buffy, or white below; habitat mostly riparian woodlands and ornamental plantings . . . .
. . . . **Eastern Fox Squirrel** (*Sciurus niger*), **p. 111**

10. Upper parts striped, the stripes continuing onto the head; posterior border of cheekbone opposite first molar **11**
Upper parts dappled, or if striped, the stripes not continuing onto the head; posterior border of cheekbone opposite third premolar **13**

11. Size small, total length usually less than 210 mm; hindfoot 32 mm or less . . . . .
. . . . **Least Chipmunk** (*Neotamias minimus*)**, p. 90**
Size larger, total length usually greater than 210 mm; hindfoot greater than 32
mm **12**

12. Dorsal color dusky, paler stripes rather obscure; habitat mostly above 2,400 m
(8,000 ft) . . . . **Uinta Chipmunk** (*Neotamias umbrinus*)**, p. 95**
Dorsal color bright, stripes well defined; habitat usually below 2,250 m (7,500
ft) . . . . **Colorado Chipmunk** (*Neotamias quadrivittatus*)**, p. 93**

13. Upper parts striped . . . .
. . . . **Golden-mantled Ground Squirrel** (*Spermophilus lateralis*)**, p. 103**
Upper parts not striped **14**

14. Size larger, total length 450 mm or greater; tail long, rather bushy; habitat in
rocky canyons . . . . **Rock Squirrel** (*Spermophilus variegatus*)**, p. 107**
Size moderate, total length less than 350 mm; tail relatively short, narrow;
habitat meadows, parklands, forest edge . . . .
. . . . **Wyoming Ground Squirrel** (*Spermophilus elegans*)**, p. 100**

15. Size large (total length greater than 450 mm); tail scaly, nearly naked, laterally
flattened; hindfoot partially webbed; length of skull greater than 65 mm . . . . .
. . . . **Muskrat** (*Ondatra zibethicus*)**, p. 139**
Size moderate to small (total length less than 450 mm); tail haired, not scaly,
not laterally flattened; hindfoot not webbed; length of skull less than 55 mm
. . . . **16**

16. Underparts and feet white; ears prominent, not obscured by dense fur; skull
not abruptly constricted just anterior to braincase **17**
Underparts and feet dark gray to silvery gray, not truly white; ears not prominent, obscured by dense fur; skull abruptly constricted just anterior to brain-
case **20**

17. Size relatively large, total length greater than 300 mm; cheekteeth without
true cusps **18**
Size relatively small, total length 200 mm or less; cheekteeth cusped **19**

18. Size smaller, total length 360 mm or less; tail narrow, not bushy, with black
medial stripe; length of skull less than 45 mm; habitat mostly in horizontal
rock outcrops in foothills . . . . **Mexican Woodrat** (*Neotoma mexicana*)**, p. 130**
Size larger, total length 375 mm or greater; tail bushy, grayish above; habitat
mostly among granitic rocks of mountains . . . .
. . . . **Bushy-tailed Woodrat** (*Neotoma cinerea*)**, p. 128**

19. Tail relatively short, obviously less than 20 mm; dorsal color buffy to reddish brown; greatest length of skull less than 27 mm . . . .
. . . . **Deer Mouse** (*Peromyscus maniculatus*), **p.** 123
Tail relatively long, nearly or quite as long as head and body; ears relatively large, 20 mm or longer; dorsal color grayish brown; greatest length of skull greater than 28 mm . . . . **Northern Rock Mouse** (*Peromyscus nasutus*), **p.** 126

20. Hairs of back deep reddish brown, sides buffy or yellowish brown; underparts silvery gray to buffy . . . . . **Southern Red-backed Vole** (*Myodes gapperi*), **p.** 131
Hairs of back, sides, and dorsum gray to grayish brown or black 21

21. Tail usually greater than one-third total length . . . .
. . . . **Long-tailed Vole** (*Microtus longicaudus*), **p.** 134
Tail usually less than one-third total length 22

22. Tail markedly short but little longer than hindfoot; color pale gray . . . .
. . . . **Sagebrush Vole** (*Lemmiscus curtatus*), **p.** 138
Tail longer, markedly longer than hindfoot; color grayish brown to brown . . .
. . . . 23

23. Size smaller, usually less than 150 mm; tail 35 mm or less; tail speckled with white above; when viewed from above, inner angles of lower molars deeper than outer angles . . . .
. . . . **Western Heather Vole** (*Phenacomys intermedius*), **p.** 133
Size larger, usually greater than 150 mm; tail usually 40 mm or longer; tail not speckled white above; when viewed from above, inner and outer angles of lower molars of equal depth . . . . . **Montane Vole** (*Microtus montanus*), **p.** 136

KEY E—CARNIVORES

1. Hindfoot with five toes 2
Hindfoot with four toes 15

2. Tail shorter than hindfoot; size large; total teeth, 42 3
Tail longer than hindfoot; size small to medium; total teeth 40 or fewer . . . 4

3. Forehead distinctly concave; shoulders distinctly humped; front claws distinctly longer than rear claws; length of maxillary toothrow greater than 110 mm . . . . **Grizzly, or Brown, Bear** (*Ursus arctos*), **p.** 164
Forehead not concave; shoulders not humped; front and rear claws of about equal length; length of maxillary toothrow less than 110 mm . . . .
. . . . **Black Bear** (*Ursus americanus*), **p.** 160

4. Tail with banded pattern; musk glands absent; molars 2/2, total teeth, 40 . . .
. . . . 5

Tail without banded pattern; musk glands present; molars 1/2, total teeth, 39 or fewer 6

5. Dark bands on upper surface of tail only; tail approximately equal to head and body; length of skull 100 mm or less . . . . **Ringtail (*Bassariscus astutus*), p. 166**
Dark bands on tail complete; tail obviously shorter than head and body; length of skull 110 mm or more . . . .
. . . . **Northern Raccoon (*Procyon lotor*), p. 167**

6. Body relatively stout; tail less than one-third length of head and body 7
Body relatively slender, or if heavier-bodied, tail greater than one-third length of head and body 8

7. General color dark, blackish brown above and below, with pale stripe on sides; no stripe on forehead; premolars 4/4 . . . . **Wolverine (*Gulo gulo*), p. 180**
General color pale, upper parts grayish buff to reddish brown, muzzle and feet black; prominent white stripe on head, continuing for variable distance onto back; premolars 3/3 . . . . **American Badger (*Taxidea taxus*), p. 183**

8. Toes webbed; size large, total length greater than 1000 mm; condylobasal length of skull greater than 90 mm . . . .
. . . . **Northern River Otter (*Lutra canadensis*), p. 186**
Toes not webbed; size small to moderate, total length less than 800 mm; condylobasal length of skull less than 85 mm 9

9. Color of back a pattern of white on black throughout the year; auditory bullae small, flat **10**
Color of back not patterned, usually a shade of white or brown; auditory bullae inflated **11**

10. Back marked with two continuous white stripes; size large, total length 600 mm; length of skull greater than 70 mm . . . .
. . . . **Striped Skunk (*Mephitis mephitis*), p. 190**
Back marked with four or more lines of irregular white spots; size smaller, total length less than 500 mm; length of skull less than 70 mm . . . .
. . . . **Western Spotted Skunk (*Spilogale gracilis*), p. 188**

11. Tail brown to tip; condylobasal length of skull usually greater than 65 mm . . .
. . . . **12**
Tail with prominent black tip; condylobasal length of skull usually less than 55 mm **13**

12. Color golden brown above, pale brown to orangish below; habitat forest; habit arboreal; premolars 4/4 . . . . **American Marten** (*Martes americana*), **p. 170**

Color brownish above, brown below; habitat riparian; habit semiaquatic; premolars 3/3 . . . . **American Mink** (*Neovison vison*), **p. 178**

13. Size smaller, total length less than 250 mm; tail less than 70 mm; condylobasal length of skull less than 40 mm . . . .
. . . . **Ermine, or Short-tailed Weasel** (*Mustela erminea*), **p. 172**

Size larger, total length greater than 300 mm; tail greater than 100 mm; condylobasal length of skull greater than 40 mm **14**

14. Body and tail yellowish white; face marked with prominent black mask; feet black . . . . **Black-footed Ferret** (*Mustela nigripes*), **p. 178**

Body and tail brownish in summer, orangish to brownish below, pure white in winter; face without prominent black mask; feet not black . . . .
. . . . **Long-tailed Weasel** (*Mustela frenata*), **p. 174**

15. Claws not retractable; muzzle elongate **16**

Claws retractable; muzzle foreshortened **17**

16. Tail with mane or crest of stiff, black-tipped hairs; temporal ridges pronounced, lyre-shaped . . . . **Gray Fox** (*Urocyon cinereoargenteus*), **p. 158**

Tail without mane of stiff, black-tipped hairs; temporal ridges indistinct or V-shaped **17**

17. Color usually reddish-yellow above; tip of tail white; postorbital process thin, concave; length of skull less than 150 mm . . . . **Red Fox** (*Vulpes vulpes*), **p. 155**

Color reddish gray to black above; tip of tail black; postorbital process thick, convex; length of skull greater than 170 mm **18**

18. Color generally gray to blackish; size larger, total length greater than 1.4 m; greatest length of skull greater than 230 mm; tail held high while running . . .
. . . . **Gray Wolf** (*Canis lupus*), **p. 153**

Color generally buffy to reddish gray; size smaller; total length less than 1.4 m; greatest length of skull less than 230 mm; tail "tucked," held low while running . . . . **Coyote** (*Canis latrans*), **p. 150**

19. Tail long, more than one-third total length; length of skull greater than 150 mm . . . . **Mountain Lion** (*Puma concolor*), **p. 192**

Tail short, less than one-fifth total length; length of skull less than 130 mm . .
. . . . **20**

20. Tip of tail black above and below; ears with prominent black tufts; feet notably large . . . . **Canada Lynx** (*Lynx canadensis*), **p. 197**

Tip of tail black above, white below; ears at most slightly tufted; feet not notably large . . . . **Bobcat** (*Lynx rufus*), **p. 199**

KEY F—ARTIODACTYLS

1. Frontal appendages horns (keratinous sheath over a bony core) 2
   Frontal appendages antlers (branching structure of bone) 5

2. Horns branched . . . . **Pronghorn** (*Antilocapra americana*), **p. 218**
   Horns not branched 3

3. Horns smooth, without annular ridges . . . . **Bison** (*Bos bison*), **p. 220**
   Horns rough, with annular ridges 4

4. Horns of males robust (increasingly so with age), strongly curved into posteriorly directed helix; lacrimal pits present; coat not shaggy; color brown with
   white rump patch . . . .
   . . . . **Mountain, or Bighorn, Sheep** (*Ovis canadensis*), **p. 222**
   Horns of both sexes of moderate size; slightly curved posterolaterally; lacrimal pits absent; coat shaggy, white, without contrastingly colored rump patch
   . . . . **Mountain Goat** (*Oreamnos americanus*), **p. 222**

5. Antlers palmate (the branches flattened), rounded at the tips; nasal bones noticeably short; profile humped at shoulders; throat with prominent dewlap . . .
   . . . . **Moose** (*Alces alces*), **p. 217**
   Antlers not palmate, pointed at tips; nasal bones relatively long; profile not
   humped at shoulders; throat without prominent dewlap 6

6. Antlers with prominent brow tine; upper canines present . . . .
   . . . . **Wapiti, or Elk** (*Cervus canadensis*), **p. 206**
   Antlers without prominent brow tine; upper canines absent 7

7. Tail narrow, white with black terminal tuft; antlers branching dichotomously,
   anterior and posterior beams nearly equal . . . .
   . . . . **Mule Deer** (*Odocoileus hemionus*), **p. 211**
   Tail broad, brown above, white beneath; antlers with single main beam, not
   branching dichotomously . . . .
   . . . . **White-tailed Deer** (*Odocoileus virginianus*), **p. 215**

APPENDIX II
Glossary

agonism: contesting behavior among individuals of same species.

altricial: born at a relatively undeveloped and helpless stage of development (compare *precocial*).

alveolus: socket in jaw in which mammalian tooth is set.

ambulatory: walking locomotion.

antler: bony derivative of frontal bone of skull typical of males of deer family (compare *horn*).

arboreal: tree-dwelling.

auditory bulla: bony case enclosing sensory apparatus of ear.

baculum: stiffening rod of bone in penis of many mammalian groups; also called *os penis*.

bicolored: of two distinct colors.

biocides: chemicals developed to kill living things; a near synonym of "pesticide" but preferable because term "pesticide" presumes objective definition of "pest," which is probably impossible.

boreal: northern.

bristle: short, stiff hair.

caecotrophy: consumption of specialized, nutritive "fecal" pellets (= reingestion).

calcar: spur of cartilage or bone that projects inward from ankle of some species of bats, forming partial support for uropatagium.

canine: anterior-most tooth in maxillary bone; tooth specialized for piercing and/or grasping; primitive mammals have one canine tooth on either side of jaw, above and below.

carrion: remains of dead animals.

cheek pouch: distensible storage space in cheeks of some rodents.

cheekteeth: collective term for molars and premolars; i.e., all teeth posterior to canine.

circumboreal: occurring around the Northern Hemisphere.

cloaca: common chamber for products of urogenital and digestive tracts; from the Latin for "sewer."

commensal: the beneficiary of commensalism, a kind of symbiosis in which one species benefits while a second species (the host) is neither harmed nor benefited.

convergence: evolutionary phenomenon in which organisms of separate ancestry come to resemble each other in some way.

cranial: pertaining to the skull.

crepuscular: active at dawn and/or dusk (compare *diurnal, nocturnal*).

cursorial: running locomotion.

deciduous: capable of being shed (said of teeth, antlers, placentae, leaves of woody plants).

delayed implantation: suspension of embryonic development after first few cell divisions and prior to embedding (implantation) in wall of uterus.

diastema: gap between teeth in jaw due to evolutionary loss of teeth and/or elongation of jaw bone.

dichotomous: branching into two equal parts; Y-shaped branch.

digitigrade: standing on the digits (toes, fingers).

dispersal: movement of individuals from place of birth to place of reproduction (compare *migration*).

distichous: arrangement of hairs of tail in lateral rows, producing flattened appearance.

diurnal: active by day (compare *crepuscular, nocturnal*).

dormancy: extended, deep sleep, often during periods of resource scarcity or severe weather.

dorsal: pertaining to back (compare *ventral*).

ecotone: area of overlap between adjacent distinctive biotic communities.

ectoparasite: external parasite (usually insect, mite, tick).

endemic: restricted in occurrence to a particular place.

endoparasite: internal parasite (usually roundworm, flatworm, protist, bacterium).

endothermy: "warm bloodedness"; maintenance of constant body temperature despite variation in environmental temperature.

epithet: a name; in biological taxonomy usually used in the context of "specific epithet." The scientific name of a species consists of two words, the name of the genus and the specific epithet. In the name *Canis latrans*, "*latrans*" is the specific epithet.

estrous: of, relating to, or characteristic of estrus.

estrus: "heat"; period of maximal sexual receptivity of female.

extirpation: local extinction.

family: taxonomic category above genus and below order; familial names of animals end in suffix -idae.

feces: solid wastes of digestive processes.

fellfield: stone-strewn ground.

feral: pertaining to domestic animal reverted to wild state, or at least escaped from domestication into native ecosystems.

foramen: "hole"; opening in skull or other bone, usually for passage of nerves and/or muscles.

foramen magnum: large opening connecting cranial cavity and spinal column, through which spinal cord enters brain.

forbs: "forest herbs"; broad-leafed herbaceous plants.

form: shallow depression, usually beneath shrub or other cover, occupied by rabbits and hares.

genus: taxonomic category comprising one or more closely related species.

gestation: period between fertilization and parturition, or birth.

guard hairs: stiffer, longer, outer hairs of pelage; overlie underfur.

hectare: metric unit of land area, a square 100 meters on a side, 10,000 square meters; there are 100 hectares to the square kilometer; a hectare equals about 2.47 acres.

heterodont: teeth of several kinds within toothrow (incisors, canines, premolars, molars in primitive mammal) specialized for various functions (compare *homodont*).

hibernaculum: place in which hibernation is passed.

hibernation: regulation of physiology to minimum, especially in winter.

Holarctic: occurring in the Northern Hemisphere, both New and Old Worlds.

holotype: type specimen; specimen to which name of a species or subspecies is tied.

home range: area covered by an individual in its daily round of activities (compare *territory*).

homodont: teeth all roughly the same; no specialization within toothrow (compare *heterodont*).

horn: covering of keratin (the structural protein of hair and nails) over bony growth of skull; typical of family Bovidae (compare *antler*).

implantation: burial of early embryo in wall of uterus prior to development of placenta.

incisor: nipping or gnawing tooth; in primitive mammals, three on either side of jaw, above and below.

infraorbital foramen: opening in skull below orbit, or eye socket.

interfemoral membrane: flap of skin between hind limbs of many bats, including tail (= uropatagium).

interparietal: bone forming posterior part of skull cap, bounded laterally by parietals, posteriorly by occipital.

Krummholz: woodland of stunted, crooked trees at upper treeline; from German.

lactation: process of milk production in mammary glands.

lateral: pertaining to the sides of the body (compare *medial*).

mammary gland: milk-producing gland of female mammals (and source of name of class).

mean: arithmetic average.

medial: pertaining to the midline of the body (compare *lateral*).

metabolism: sum of chemical processes in an organism.

migration: movement of individuals, mostly to access new feeding grounds or hibernacula, usually seasonal, cyclic (compare *dispersal*).

mode: in a series of values for a particular variable, the most common value.

molar: most posterior cheekteeth, usually adapted to grinding; not present in deciduous ("milk") dentition; in primitive mammals, three in each toothrow, above and below.

molt: normal loss and replacement of hair; typically seasonal.

monoestrous: having one estrous cycle (and hence, one breeding period) annually (compare *polyestrous*).

monogamous: mating system in which individual (of either sex) has single mate.

natatorial: locomotion by swimming.

occlusion: functional contact between upper and lower teeth.

order: taxonomic category above level of family and below level of class.

ovulation: release of egg cell from follicle of ovary.

parasite: consumer organism that derives its nourishment from another organism (the "host") but normally does not actually kill the host.

parturition: act of giving birth.

pelage: coat of hair and derivative structures (quills, bristles, vibrissae, etc.).

placenta: composite structure produced by female mammal and developing embryo, across which nutrients, gases, and wastes move between maternal and fetal bloodstreams.

plantigrade: standing on sole of foot, with toes, foot bones, and distal parts of ankle in contact with ground.

polyandrous: mating system in which female has more than one mate (compare *polygamous, polygynous*).

polyestrous: having more than one estrous cycle (hence, the possibility of more than one breeding period) annually (compare *monoestrous*).

polygamous: mating system in which individuals have more than one mate; a general term in which gender is not specified (compare *monogamous, polyandrous, polygynous*).

polygynous: mating system in which one male mates with several females (compare *polyandrous, polygamous*).

postorbital process: projection of temporal bone behind eye socket (orbit).

postpartum estrus: estrus immediately following parturition.

precocial: born in relatively well-developed and independent state (compare *altricial*).

premolar: cheekteeth of variable structure and function located ahead of molars; present in deciduous ("milk") dentition; in primitive mammals, four in each toothrow, above and below.

prevernal: "before spring"; usually used in reference to molting.

rabies: infectious viral disease of nervous system.

raptor: bird of prey; general term for eagles, hawks, falcons, and owls.

reingestion: consumption of specialized, nutritive "fecal" pellets (= caecotrophy).

riparian: river or streamside habitat.

saltatory: referring to locomotion by jumping.

scabies: contagious disease caused by burrowing of certain mites beneath skin.

scansorial: locomotion by scampering or climbing.

scat: droppings, feces.

scrotum: sac in which testes of most mammals are carried during active spermatogenesis.

species: group of actually or potentially interbreeding individuals reproductively isolated from other such groups.

spermatogenesis: sperm production.

supraorbital shield: bony projection of frontal bone above eye socket.

taiga: coniferous forest; derived from the Russian.

talus: slope of fragmented rock.

taxonomy: scientific study of classifications.

temporal ridges: prominences on temporal bones serving as points of attachment for temporal muscles that close the jaw.

territory: portion of home range defended (actively or passively) by an individual against other individuals of same species (compare *home range*).

thecodont: teeth set in sockets (alveoli).

torpor: partial suspension of physiologic activity; deep sleep.

tularemia: contagious bacterial disease typified by intermittent fever.

type locality: place at which holotype (type specimen) was collected.

type specimen: holotype; specimen to which name of a species or subspecies is tied.

underfur: short, often dense, insulating coat beneath guard hairs of many mammals.

unguligrade: standing on the hooves.

unicuspid: tooth having a single cusp or point.

urogenital tract: the common ducts and openings of the urinary and reproductive systems.

uropatagium: interfemoral membrane; flap of skin between hind limbs of many bats, including tail.

uterus: "womb"; muscular organ of female mammal in which young are carried before birth; lining of uterus participates in formation of placenta.

valvular: capable of being closed.

ventral: pertaining to belly or underside (compare *dorsal*).

vestigial: nonfunctional remnant of former structure or function.

vibrissae: "whiskers"; stiff, touch-sensitive hairs.

APPENDIX III
Derivation of Scientific Names

The formal names of science are invaluable in classifying and retrieving information. Noting that two species have the same generic name (*Peromyscus maniculatus* and *Peromyscus nasutus,* for example) makes an evolutionary statement, suggesting that these are closely related species. At least part of what we know about the biology of the abundant, widespread, and well-studied deer mouse is probably true as well for the scarcer, less widespread, and relatively poorly studied rock mouse.

For most people, however, actually learning scientific names of organisms is a waste of time and energy; it is quite enough to know where to look up the names. A few persons need know zoological names for professional purposes, because they use them all the time. A few others actually enjoy knowing their biological acquaintances on a formal basis. It is for the last-named few that this section is included.

One of the easiest ways to remember scientific names is to know their derivation. Scientific names are Latin or have a Latinized form (or at the very least are treated grammatically as if they were Latin). Many are classical names for the animals to which they apply (*alces, felis, lupus*). Other names are commemorative, honoring naturalists of note (*hoyi, merriami, townsendii*). Others are descriptive of the animals (*nanus, cinereus*), their habitat (*palustris*), or their geographical range (*canadensis*). Some are even humorous (the specific epithet for the blue whale, the largest animal that has ever lived on Earth, is *musculus*, "little mouse").

Because scientific names of genera and species are written in a foreign language, they are underlined in manuscript and italicized in print. (By convention, proper names of higher taxonomic categories—families, orders, classes, phyla— are not underlined.) A useful reference for tracking down the etymology of scientific names is Borror (1971).

The following list of derivations is included because knowing the source of a name often helps one to remember it. Please do not mistake this mnemonic device, however, for anything else. Despite the Latin name, individuals of the species *Homo sapiens* are not necessarily wise, either individually or collectively, and *Lasionycteris noctivagans* does not mean "night-flying shaggy bat" any more than everyone named Smith is a metalworker or everyone named Fletcher makes arrows. Rather, the scientific name means the biological entity to which it is applied. (Abbreviations, L = Latin, G = Greek.)

aberti: for J. W. Abert (1820–1897), military explorer-naturalist of the Southwest.
Alces: "elk" (L).
americana: Latinized form pertaining to America.
americanus: Latinized form pertaining to America.
Antilocapra: compound of two other generic names, *Antilope* (the Old World blackbuck) and *Capra* (goats).
arctos: "bear" (G).
astutus: "skilled" (L).
Bassariscus: diminutive form of *bassaris*, "fox" (G).
Bison: "bison," from Germanic *wisent*, "bison."
canadensis: Latinized form pertaining to Canada.
Canis: "dog" (L).
Castor: "beaver" (G).
Cervus: "deer" (L).
ciliolabrum: *cilio-*, "small hair" (L), + *-labrum*, "lip" (L).
cinereoargenteus: *cinereo-*, "ashen" (L), + *-argenteus*, "silvery" (L).
cinereus: "ashen," "gray" (L).
concolor: *con-*, "together" (L), + *-color*, "color" (L).
Corynorhinus: *coryno-*, "club-like" (G), + *-rhinus*, "snout" (G).
curtatus: "short" (L).
dorsatum: pertaining to the dorsum (L), or back.

elegans: "elegant" (L).

Erethizon: *erethi-*, "irritate" (G), + *-zon*, "animal" (G).

erminea: Latinized form of French *hermine*, "ermine."

evotis: *ev-*, "good" (G), + *-otis*, "ear" (G).

flaviventris: *flavi-*, "yellow" (L), + *-ventris*, "belly" (L).

frenata: "brindle" (L).

fuscus: "brown" (L).

Gulo: "glutton" (L).

hemionus: *hemi-*, "one-half" (G), + *-onus*, "ass," "mule" (L).

Homo: "self" (G).

hoyi: for P. R. Hoy (1816–1892), pioneer naturalist in Wisconsin.

hudsonicus: pertaining to Hudson Bay.

intermedius: "between" (L).

Lagurus: *lag-*, "rabbit" (G), + *-urus*, "tail" (G).

Lasionycteris: *lasio-*, "shaggy" (G), + *-nycteris*, "bat" (G).

Lasiurus: *lasio-*, "shaggy" (G), + *-urus*, "tail" (G).

lateralis. pertaining to "side" (L).

latrans: "barking" (L).

Lemmiscus: diminutive form based on *Lem-*, "plague" (G).

Lepus: "hare" (L).

longicaudus: *longi-*, "long" (L), + *caudus*, "tail" (L).

lotor: "washing" (L).

lucifugus: *luci-*, "light" (L), + *-fugus*, "flee" (L).

lupus: "wolf" (L).

Lutra: "otter" (L).

Lynx: "cat" (G).

maniculatus: pertaining to *manicula*, "little hands" (L).

Marmota: Latinized form of French *marmotte*, from Late Latin *musmontanus*, "mountain mouse."

Martes: "marten" (L).

Mephitis: "foul odor" (L).

merriami: for C. Hart Merriam (1855–1942), first chief of the Bureau of Biological Survey, U.S. Department of Agriculture, and first president of the American Society of Mammalogists.

mexicana: pertaining to Mexico.

Microtus: *micr-*, "small" (G), + *-otus*, "ear" (G).

montanus: "mountain" (L).

Mustela: "weasel" (L).

Myodes: *my-*, "mouse" (G), + *-odes*, "like" (G).

Myotis: *my-*, "mouse" (G), + *-otis*, "ear" (G).

nanus: "small" (G).

nasutus: "big-nosed" (L).

Neotamias: *neo-*, "new" (G), + *-tamias*, "distributor" (L)—perhaps a reference to the food-hoarding habit of chipmunks.

Neotoma: *neo-*, "new" (G), + *-toma*, "cut" (G).

niger: *nigri-*, "black" (L).

nigripes: *nigri-*, "black" (L), + *-pes*, "foot" (L).

noctivagans: *nocti-*, "night" (G), + *-vagans*, "wandering" (L).

nuttallii: for Thomas Nuttall (1786–1859), pioneer American naturalist.

Ochotona: Latinized form of *ochodona*, the Mongol name for pika.

Odocoileus: *odo-*, "tooth" (G), + *-coileus*, "hollow" (G).

Ondatra: Latinized form of Huron name for muskrat.

Oreamnos: *oreo-*, "mountain" (G), + *-amnos*, "lamb" (G).

Ovis: "sheep" (L).

palustris: pertaining to swamp or marsh (L).

Peromyscus: *pero-*, "defective" (G), + *-myscus*, "mouse" (G).

Plecotus: *plec-*, "folded" (G), + *-otus*, "ear" (G).

princeps: "first," "chief" (L).

Procyon: *pro-*, "before" (G), + *-cyon*, "dog" (G).

Puma: mountain lion, cougar (Spanish, borrowed from the Inca language, Quechua)

quadrivittatus: *quadri-*, "four" (L), + *-vittatus*, "stripe" (L).

rufus: "red" (L).

sapiens: "wise" (L).

Sciurus: *sci-*, "shade" (G), + *-urus*, "tail" (G).

Sorex: "shrew" (L).

Spermophilus: *spermo-*, "seed" (G), + *-philus*, "lover" (G).

Spilogale: *spilo-*, "spotted" (G), + *-gale*, "weasel" (G).

Sylvilagus: *sylvi-*, "forest" (L), + *-lagus*, "rabbit" (G).

talpoides: *talpo-*, "mole" (L), + *-id*, "like" (G).

Tamiasciurus: compound of two other generic names, *Tamias* and *Sciurus*.

Taxidea: possibly a derivative of *taxus* (see below).

taxus: "badger" (L).

Thomomys: *thomo-*, "heap" (G), + *-mys*, "mouse" (G).

thysanodes: *thysan-*, "fringed" (G), + *-odes*, "like" (G).

townsendii: for J. K. Townsend (1809–1851), explorer and naturalist of the American Northwest.

umbrinus: "shady" (L).

Urocyon: *uro-*, "tail" (G), + *-cyon*, "dog" (G).

Ursus: "bear" (L).

variegatus: "variegated," "variously colored" (L).

virginianus: pertaining to Virginia.

vison: French for mink.

volans: "flying" (L).

Vulpes: "fox" (L).

Zapus: *za-*, "excessive" (G), + *-pus*, "foot" (G).

zibethicus: from *zibeth*, an Indian civet.

LITERATURE CITED

Adams, R. A. 1997. Onset of juvenile volancy and foraging patterns of little brown bats. Journal of Mammalogy 78:239–246.

Adams, R. A. 2003. Bats of the Rocky Mountain West: Natural history, ecology, and conservation. University Press of Colorado, Boulder.

Allen, G. M. 1939. Bats. Harvard University Press, Cambridge, Massachusetts.

Anderson, A. E., D. C. Bowden, and D. M. Kattner. 1992. The puma on Uncompahgre Plateau, Colorado. Technical Publication, Colorado Division of Wildlife 40:viii + 1–116.

Anderson, A. E., and O. C. Wallmo. 1984. *Odocoileus hemionus*. Mammalian Species 219:1–9.

Anderson, E. M., and M. J. Lovallo. 2003. Bobcat and lynx (*Lynx rufus* and *Lynx canadensis*). Pp. 758–786 in Wild mammals of North America: Biology, management, and conservation, 2nd edition (G. A. Feldhamer, B. C. Thompson, and J. A. Chapman, eds.). Johns Hopkins University Press, Baltimore, Maryland.

Anderson, S., and J. K. Jones Jr., eds. 1984. Orders and families of recent mammals of the world. John Wiley and Sons, New York.

Andrews, T. 1991. A survey of Rocky Mountain National Park and surrounding areas of Arapaho and Roosevelt national forests for wolverine and lynx, winter 1990–1991. Unpublished report, Lyons, Colorado.

Armitage, K. B. 1991. Social and population dynamics of yellow-bellied marmots: Results from long-term research. Annual Review of Ecology and Systematics 22:379–407.

Armitage, K. B. 2003. Marmots (*Marmota monax* and allies). Pp. 188–210 in Wild mammals of North America: Biology, management, and conservation, 2nd edition (G. A. Feldhamer, B. C. Thompson, and J. A. Chapman, eds.). Johns Hopkins University Press, Baltimore, Maryland.

Armstrong, D. M. 1972. Distribution of mammals in Colorado. Monograph, University of Kansas Museum Natural History 3:x + 1–415.

Armstrong, D. M. 1975. Rocky Mountain mammals. Rocky Mountain Nature Association, Estes Park, Colorado.

Armstrong, D. M. 1977. Ecological distribution of small mammals in the Upper Williams Fork Basin, Grand County, Colorado. Southwestern Naturalist, 22:289–304.

Armstrong, D. M. 1982. Mammals of the Canyon Country. Canyonlands Natural History Association, Moab, Utah.

Armstrong, D. M. 1987. Rocky Mountain mammals: A handbook of mammals of Rocky Mountain National Park and vicinity, revised edition. Colorado Associated University Press, Boulder.

Armstrong, D. M. 1993. Effects of the Lawn Lake Flood on local distribution and abundance of mammals. Pp. 170–191 in Ecological effects of the Lawn Lake flood of 1982, Rocky Mountain National Park. Scientific Monograph, National Park Service, United States Department of the Interior, NPS/NRROMO/NRSM-93/21: vi + 214 pp.

Armstrong, D. M. 1996. Northern limits of mammals of northern interior Mexico. Pp. 261–283 in Contributions in mammalogy: A memorial volume honoring Dr. J. Knox Jones Jr. Museum of Texas Tech University (H. H. Genoways and R. J. Baker, eds.), il + 315 pp.

Armstrong, D. M. 2006. Lions, ferrets & bears: A guide to the mammals of Colorado, 2nd edition. Colorado Division of Wildlife, Denver, Colorado.

Armstrong, D. M., R. A. Adams, S. J. Bissell, J. Freeman, and K. W. Navo. 1995. Bats of Colorado: Shadows in the night. Colorado Division of Wildlife, Denver, Colorado.

Armstrong, D. M., and J. Amoroso. 2002. Wolves in the Southern Rockies: Principles, problems, and prospects. National Wildlife Federation and Colorado Wildlife Federation, Boulder, Colorado.

Armstrong, D. M., B. H. Banta, and E. J. Pokropus. 1973. Altitudinal distribution of small mammals along a cross-sectional transect through the Arkansas River watershed, Colorado. Southwestern Naturalist 17:315–317.

Armstrong, D. M., and J. K. Jones Jr. 1971. *Sorex merriami*. Mammalian Species 2:1–2.

Baker, B. W., and E. P. Hill. 2003. Beaver (*Castor canadensis*). Pp. 288–310 in Wild mammals of North America: Biology, management, and conservation, 2nd edition (G. A. Feldhamer, B. C. Thompson, and J. A. Chapman, eds.). Johns Hopkins University Press, Baltimore, Maryland.

Baker, R. J., R. D. Bradley, and L. R. McAliley Jr. 2003. Pocket gophers (Geomyidae). Pp. 276–287 in Wild mammals of North America: Biology, management, and conservation, 2nd edition (G. A. Feldhamer, B. C. Thompson, and J. A. Chapman, eds.). Johns Hopkins University Press, Baltimore, Maryland.

Baker, R. J., L. C. Bradley, R. D. Bradley, J. W. Dragoo, M. D. Engstrom, R. S. Hoffman, C. A. Jones, F. Reid, D. W. Rice, and C. Jones. 2003. Revised checklist of North American mammals north of Mexico, 2003. Occasional Papers, Museum of Texas Tech University 229:1–23.

Ballard, W. B., and P. S. Gipson. 2000. Wolf. Pp. 321–346 in Ecology and management of large mammals of North America (S. Demarais and P. R. Krausman, eds.). Prentice Hall, Upper Saddle River, New Jersey.

Barbour, R. W., and W. B. Davis. 1969. Bats of America. University of Kentucky Press, Lexington, Kentucky.

Barnosky, A. D., and C. J. Bell. 2004. Age and correlation of key fossil sites in Porcupine Cave. Pp. 64–73 in Biodiversity response to climate change in the Middle Pleistocene: The Porcupine Cave Fauna from Colorado (A. D. Barnosky, ed.). University of California Press, Berkeley.

Bartels, M. A., and D. P. Thompson. 1993. *Spermophilus lateralis* Mammalian Species 440:1–8.

Bear, G. H., and R. M. Hansen. 1966. Food habits, growth and reproduction of the white-tailed jackrabbit in southern Colorado. Technical Bulletin, Agricultural Experiment Station, Colorado State University 90:viii + 1–59.

Bekoff, M. 1977. *Canis latrans*. Mammalian Species 79:1–9.

Bekoff, M. 1982. Coyote. Pp. 447–459 in Wild mammals of North America: Biology, management, and economics (J. A. Chapman and G. A. Feldhamer, eds.). Johns Hopkins University Press, Baltimore, Maryland.

Bekoff, M., and E. M. Gese. 2003. Coyote (*Canis latrans*). Pp. 467–481 in Wild mammals of North America: Biology, management, and conservation, 2nd edition (G. A. Feldhamer, B. C. Thompson, and J. A. Chapman, eds.). Johns Hopkins University Press, Baltimore, Maryland.

Bekoff, M., and M. C. Wells. 1980. The social ecology of coyotes. Scientific American 242:130–148.

Bekoff, M., and M. C. Wells. 1986. Social ecology and behavior of coyotes. Advances in the Study of Behavior 16:251–338.

Benedict, J. B. 1992. Footprints in the snow: High-altitude cultural ecology of the Colorado Front Range, U.S.A. Arctic and Alpine Research 24:1–16.

Benedict, J. B. 1993. Excavations at Bode's Draw: A women's work area in the mountains near Estes Park, Colorado. Research Report, Center for Mountain Archaeology 6:ix + 1–42.

Benedict, J. B. 1996. The game drives of Rocky Mountain National Park. Research Report, Center for Mountain Archaeology 7:xiii + 1–110.

Benedict, J. B. 1999. Effects of changing climate on game-animal and human use of the Colorado high country (U.S.A.) since 1000 BC. Arctic, Antarctic, and Alpine Research 31:1–15.

Beneski, J. T., and D. W. Stinson. 1987. Sorex palustris. Mammalian Species 296:1–6.

Bergstrom, B. J. 1988. Home ranges of three species of chipmunks (*Tamias*) as assessed by radiotelemetry and grid trapping. Journal of Mammalogy 69:190–193.

Best, T. L., S. L. Burt, and J. L. Bartig. 1994. Tamias quadrivittatus. Mammalian Species 466:1–7.

Bittner, S. L., and O. J. Rongstad. 1982. Snowshoe hare and allies (*Lepus americanus* and allies). Pp. 146–163 in Wild mammals of North America: Biology, management, and economics (J. A. Chapman and G. A. Feldhamer, eds.). Johns Hopkins University Press, Baltimore, Maryland.

Black, H. L. 1974. A northern temperate bat community: Structure and prey population. Journal of Mammalogy 55:138–157.

Borror, D. J. 1971. Dictionary of word roots and combining forms. Mayfield Publishing Co., Palo Alto, California.

Bowyer, R. T., V. Van Ballenberghe, and J. G. Kie. 2003. Moose (*Alces alces*). Pp. 931–964 in Wild mammals of North America: Biology, management, and conservation, 2nd edition (G. A. Feldhamer, B. C. Thompson, and J. A. Chapman, eds.). Johns Hopkins University Press, Baltimore, Maryland.

Brown, L. N. 1967a. Ecological distribution of six species of shrews, and comparison of sampling methods in the central Rocky Mountains. Journal of Mammalogy 48:617–623.

Brown, L. N. 1967b. Seasonal activity patterns and breeding of western jumping mice (*Zapus princeps*) in Wyoming. American Midland Naturalist 78:460–470.

Brown, L. N. 1969. Reproductive characteristics of the Mexican woodrat at the northern limit of its range in Colorado. Journal of Mammalogy 50:536–541.

Brown, L. N. 1970. Population dynamics of the western jumping mouse (*Zapus princeps*) during a four-year study. Journal of Mammalogy 51:651–658.

Buchholtz, C. W. 1983. Rocky Mountain National Park, a history. Colorado Associated University Press, Boulder.

Byers, J. A. 1997. American pronghorn, social adaptations and the ghosts of predators past. University of Chicago Press, Chicago, Illinois.

Byers, J. A. 2003. Pronghorn (*Antilocapra americana*). Pp. 998–1008 in Wild mammals of North America: Biology, management, and conservation, 2nd edition (G. A. Feldhamer, B. C. Thompson, and J. A. Chapman, eds.). Johns Hopkins University Press, Baltimore, Maryland.

Callisher, C. H., J. N. Mills, J. J. Root, and B. J. Beaty. 2003. Hantaviruses: Etiologic agents of rare, but potentially life-threatening zoonotic diseases. Journal of the American Veterinary Medicine Association 222:163–166.

Carleton, M. D. 1989. Systemtics and evolution. Pp. 7–141 in Advances in the Study of *Peromyscus* (Rodentia). (G. L. Kirkland Jr. and J. N. Layne, eds.). Texas Tech University Press, Lubbock, Texas.

Carleton, W. M. 1966. Food habits of two sympatric Colorado sciurids. Journal of Mammalogy 47:91–103.

Carroll, L. E., and H. H. Genoways. 1980. *Lagurus curtatus*. Mammalian Species 124: 1–6.

Cary, M. 1911. A biological survey of Colorado. North American Fauna 33:1–256.

Cassells, E. S. 1997. The archaeology of Colorado, revised edition. Johnson Books, Boulder, Colorado.

Chapman, J. A. 1975. *Sylvilagus nuttallii*. Mammalian Species 56:1–3.

Chapman, J. A., J. G. Hockman, and W. R. Edwards. 1982. Cottontails. Pp. 83–123 in Wild mammals of North America: Biology, management, and economics (J. A. Chapman and G. A. Feldhamer, eds.). Johns Hopkins University Press, Baltimore, Maryland.

Chapman, J. A., and J. A. Litvaitis. 2003. Eastern Cottontail (*Sylvilagus floridanus* and allies). Pp. 101–125 in Wild mammals of North America: Biology, management, and conservation, 2nd edition (G. A. Feldhamer, B. C. Thompson, and J. A. Chapman, eds.). Johns Hopkins University Press, Baltimore, Maryland.

Cinq-Mars, R. J., and L. N. Brown. 1969. Reproduction and ecological distribution of the rock mouse, Peromyscus difficilis, in northern Colorado. American Midland Naturalist 81:205–217.

Clark, T. W., E. Anderson, C. Douglas, and M. Strickland. 1987. *Martes americana*. Mammalian Species 289:1–8.

Coady, J. W. 1982. Moose. Pp. 902–922 in Wild mammals of North America: Biology, management, and economics (J. A. Chapman and G. A. Feldhamer, eds.). Johns Hopkins University Press, Baltimore, Maryland.

Colorado Division of Wildlife. 2006. Living with wildlife in lion country. http://wildlife.state.co.us/WildlifeSpecies/LivingWithWildlife/Mammals/LionCountry.htm.

Conaway, C. H. 1952. Life history of the water shrew (Sorex palustris navigator). American Midland Naturalist 48:219–248.

Copeland, J. P., and J. S. Whitman. 2003. Wolverine (*Gulo gulo*). Pp. 672–682 in Wild mammals of North America: Biology, management, and conservation, 2nd edition (G. A. Feldhamer, B. C. Thompson, and J. A. Chapman, eds.). Johns Hopkins University Press, Baltimore, Maryland.

Cornely, J. E., and R. J. Baker. 1986. *Neotoma mexicana*. Mammalian Species 262:1–7.

Costello, D. F. 1966. The world of the porcupine. J. B. Lippincott, Philadelphia, Pennsylvania.

Côté, S. D., and M. Festa-Bianchet. 2003. Mountain goat (*Oreamnos americanus*). Pp. 1061–1075 in Wild mammals of North America: Biology, management, and conservation, 2nd edition (G. A. Feldhamer, B. C. Thompson, and J. A. Chapman, eds.). Johns Hopkins University Press, Baltimore, Maryland.

Craighead, J. J., and J. A. Mitchell. 1982. Grizzly bear. Pp. 515–556 in Wild mammals of North America: Biology, management, and economics (J. A. Chapman and G. A. Feldhamer, eds.). Johns Hopkins University Press, Baltimore, Maryland.

Currier, M.J.P. 1983. *Felis concolor*. Mammalian Species 200:1–7.

Cypher, B. L. 2003. Foxes (*Vulpes* species, *Urocyon* species, and *Alopex lagurus*). Pp. 511–546 in Wild mammals of North America: Biology, management, and conservation, 2nd edition (G. A. Feldhamer, B. C. Thompson, and J. A. Chapman, eds.). Johns Hopkins University Press, Baltimore, Maryland.

Demarais, S., K. V. Miller, and H. A. Jacobson. 2000. White-tailed deer. Pp. 601–628 in Ecology and management of large mammals of North America (S. Demarais and P. R. Krausman, eds.). Prentice Hall, Upper Saddle River, New Jersey.

Dixon, K. R. 1982. Mountain lion. Pp. 711–727 in Wild mammals of North America: Biology, management, and economics (J. A. Chapman and G. A. Feldhamer, eds.). Johns Hopkins University Press, Baltimore, Maryland.

Dodge, W. E. 1982. Porcupine. Pp. 355–366 in Wild mammals of North America: Biology, management, and economics (J. A. Chapman and G. A. Feldhamer, eds.). Johns Hopkins University Press, Baltimore, Maryland.

Douglas, C. L. 1969. Comparative ecology of pinyon mice and deer mice in Mesa Verde National Park, Colorado. University of Kansas Publications, Museum of Natural History 18:421–504.

Dragoo, J. W., and R. L. Honeycutt. 1997. Systematics of mustelid-like carnivores. Journal of Mammalogy 78:426–443.

Drummond, A. 1995. Enos Mills: Citizen of nature. University Press of Colorado, Boulder.

Dunn, J. P., J. A. Chapman, and R. E. Marsh. 1982. Jackrabbits. Pp. 124–145 in Wild mammals of North America: Biology, management, and economics (J. A. Chapman and G. A. Feldhamer, eds.). Johns Hopkins University Press, Baltimore, Maryland.

Edwards, J., M. Ford, and D. Guynn. 2003. Fox and gray squirrels (*Sciurus niger* and *S. carolinensis*). Pp. 248–267 in Wild mammals of North America: Biology, management, and conservation, 2nd edition (G. A. Feldhamer, B. C. Thompson, and J. A. Chapman, eds.). Johns Hopkins University Press, Baltimore, Maryland.

Eisenberg, J. F. 1981. The mammalian radiations. University of Chicago Press, Chicago, Illinois.

Elias, S. A. 2002. Rocky Mountains. Smithsonian Institution. Washington, District of Columbia.

Erb, J., and J. R. Perry Jr. 2003. Muskrats (*Ondatra zibethicus* and *Neofiber alleni*). Pp. 311–348 in Wild mammals of North America: Biology, management, and conservation, 2nd edition (G. A. Feldhamer, B. C. Thompson, and J. A. Chapman, eds.). Johns Hopkins University Press, Baltimore, Maryland.

Errington, P. L. 1963. Muskrat populations. Iowa State University Press, Ames, Iowa.

Estes, M. 1939. The memoirs of Estes Park. Bulletin, Colorado State College Library 6:1–14.

Fagerstone, K. A. 1988. The annual cycle of Wyoming ground squirrels in Colorado. Journal of Mammalogy 69:678–687.

Farentinos, R. C. 1972. Social dominance and mating activity in the tassel-eared squirrel (*Sciurus aberti ferreus*). Animal Behavior 20:316–326.

Feldhamer, G. A., L. C. Drickamer, S. H. Vessey, and J. F. Merritt. 2004. Mammalogy: Adaptation, diversity, and ecology, 2nd edition. McGraw-Hill, New York.

Fenton, M. B., and R.M.R. Barclay. 1980. *Myotis lucifugus*. Mammalian Species 142:1–8.

Finley, R. B. 1969. Cone caches and middens of *Tamiasciurus* in the Rocky Mountain Region. Miscellaneous Publications, University of Kansas Museum Natural History 51:233–273.

Finley, R. B., Jr. 1958. The wood rats of Colorado. University of Kansas Publications, Museum of Natural History 10:213–552.

Fitzgerald, J. P., C. A. Meaney, and D. M. Armstrong. 1994. *Mammals of Colorado.* Denver Museum of Natural History, Denver, and University Press of Colorado, Boulder.

Flinders, J. T., and J. A. Chapman. 2003. Black-tailed jackrabbit (*Lepus californicus* and allies). Pp. 126–146 in Wild mammals of North America: Biology, management, and conservation, 2nd edition (G. A. Feldhamer, B. C. Thompson, and J. A. Chapman, eds.). Johns Hopkins University Press, Baltimore, Maryland.

Forsyth, D. J. 1976. A field study of growth and development of nestling masked shrews (*Sorex cinereus*). Journal of Mammalogy 57:708–721.

Franzmann, A. W. 1981. *Alces alces.* Mammalian Species 154:1–7.

Franzmann, A. W. 2000. Moose. Pp. 578–600 in Ecology and management of large mammals of North America (S. Demarais and P. R. Krausman, eds.). Prentice Hall, Upper Saddle River, New Jersey.

Frase, B. A., and R. S. Hoffmann. 1980. *Marmota flaviventris.* Mammalian Species 135: 1–8.

Friedrichsen, T. T. 1977. Responses of rodent populations to visitors in a national park. MS thesis, Colorado State University, Fort Collins.

Fritzell, E. K., and K. J. Haroldson. 1982. *Urocyon cinereoargenteus.* Mammalian Species 189:1–8.

Fryxell, F. M. 1928. The former range of the bison in the Rocky Mountains. Journal of Mammalogy 9:129–139.

Gannon, W. L. 2003. Bats (Vespertilionidae, Molossidae, Phyllostomidae). Pp. 56–74 in Wild mammals of North America: Biology, management, and conservation, 2nd edition (G. A. Feldhamer, B. C. Thompson, and J. A. Chapman, eds.). Johns Hopkins University Press, Baltimore, Maryland.

Gehrt, S. D. 2003. Raccoon (*Procyon lotor* and allies). Pp. 611–634 in Wild mammals of North America; Biology, management, and conservation, 2nd edition (G. A. Feldhamer, B. C. Thompson, and J. A. Chapman, eds.). Johns Hopkins University Press, Baltimore, Maryland.

Geist, V. 1971. Mountain sheep: A study in behavior and evolution. University of Chicago Press, Chicago, Illinois.

Glick, D. 2006. Of lynx and men, scenes from a homecoming. National Geographic, January, pp. 56–67.

Godin, A. J. 1982. Striped and hooded skunks (*Mephitis mephitis* and allies). Pp. 674–687 in Wild mammals of North America: Biology, management, and economics (J. A. Chapman and G. A. Feldhamer, eds.). Johns Hopkins University Press, Baltimore, Maryland.

Goodson, N. J. 1978. Status of bighorn sheep in Rocky Mountain National Park. MS thesis, Colorado State University, Fort Collins.

Halfpenny, J. C. 1986. A field guide to mammal tracking in western America. Johnson Publishing Co., Boulder, Colorado.

Hall, E. R. 1951. American weasels. University of Kansas Publications, Museum of Natural History 4:1–466.

Hall, E. R. 1981. The mammals of North America, 2nd edition. John Wiley and Sons, New York.

Hansen, R. M. 1960. Pocket gophers in Colorado. Bulletin, Experiment Station, Colorado State University 508-S:1–26.

Hansen, R. M., and J. T. Flinders. 1969. Food habits of North American hares. Science Series, Range Science Department, Colorado State University 1:1–18.

Hansen, R. M., and A. L. Ward. 1966. Some relations of pocket gophers to rangelands on Grand Mesa, Colorado. Technical Bulletin, Agricultural Experiment Station, Colorado State University 88:1–20.

Harrington, F. A., Jr. 1978. Ecological segregation of ungulates in alpine and subalpine communities. PhD dissertation, Colorado State University, Fort Collins.

Hart, E. B., M. C. Belk, E. Jordan, and M. W. Gonzalez. 2004. *Zapus princeps*. Mammalian Species 749:1–7.

Hatt, R. T. 1927. Notes on the ground squirrel, Callospermophilus. Occasional Papers, University of Michigan Museum of Zoology 185:1–22.

Hatt, R. T. 1943. The pine squirrel in Colorado. Journal of Mammalogy 24:311–345.

Hayes, J. P. 2003. Habitat ecology and conservation of bats in western coniferous forests. Pp. 81–119 in Mammal community dynamics: Management and conservation in the coniferous forests of western North America (C. J. Zabel and R. G. Anthony, eds.). Cambridge University Press, Cambridge, United Kingdom.

Hennings, D., and R. S. Hoffmann. 1977. A review of the taxonomy of the *Sorex vagrans* complex from western North America. Occasional Papers, Museum of Natural History, University of Kansas 68:1–35.

Herrero, S. 2002. Bear attacks, their causes and avoidance, revised edition. Lyons Press, Guilford, Connecticut.

Hesselton, W. T., and R. T. Hesselton. 1982. White-tailed deer. Pp. 878–901 in Wild mammals of North America: Biology, management, and economics (J. A. Chapman and G. A. Feldhamer, eds.). Johns Hopkins University Press, Baltimore, Maryland.

Hill, E. P. 1982. Beaver. Pp. 256–281 in Wild mammals of North America: Biology, management, and economics (J. A. Chapman and G. A. Feldhamer, eds.). Johns Hopkins University Press, Baltimore, Maryland.

Hill, J. E., and J. D. Smith. 1984. Bats: A natural history. University of Texas Press, Austin, Texas.

Hillman, C. W., and T. W. Clark. 1980. *Mustela nigripes*. Mammalian Species 126:1–3.

Hoffmann, R. S., and J. G. Owen. 1980. *Sorex tenellus* and *Sorex nanus*. Mammalian Species 131:1–4.

Hoffmeister, D. F., and V. E. Diersing. 1978. Review of the tassel-eared squirrels of the subgenus *Otosciurus*. Journal of Mammalogy 59:402–413.

Holloway, G. L., and R.M.R. Barclay. 2001. *Myotis ciliolabrum*. Mammalian Species 670:1–5.

Howard, W. E., and R. E. Marsh. 1982. Spotted and hog-nosed skunks. Pp. 664–673 in Wild mammals of North America: Biology, management, and economics (J. A. Chapman and G. A. Feldhamer, eds.). Johns Hopkins University Press, Baltimore, Maryland.

Humphrey, S. R. 1982. Bats, Vespertilionidae and Molossidae. Pp. 52–70 in Wild mammals of North America: Biology, management, and economics (J. A. Chapman and G. A. Feldhamer, eds.). Johns Hopkins University Press, Baltimore, Maryland.

Humphrey, S. R., and T. H. Kunz. 1976. Ecology of a Pleistocene relict, the western big-eared bat (*Plecotus townsendii*) in the southern Great Plains. Journal of Mammalogy 57:470–494.

Husar, S. L. 1976. Behavioral character displacement: Evidence of food partitioning in insectivorous bats. Journal of Mammalogy 57:331–338.

Isenberg, A. C. 2000. The destruction of the bison. Cambridge University Press, Cambridge, United Kingdom.

Jenkins, S. H., and P. E. Busher. 1979. *Castor canadensis*. Mammalian Species 120:1–8.

Johnson, D. R. 1967. Diet and reproduction of Colorado pikas. Journal of Mammalogy 48:311–315.

Johnson, K. 1981. Social organization of a colony of rock squirrels (*Spermophilus variegatus*, Sciuridae). Southwestern Naturalist 26:237–242.

Jones, J. K., Jr., D. M. Armstrong, and J. R. Choate. 1985. Guide to mammals of the Plains States. University of Nebraska Press, Lincoln.

Jones, J. K., Jr., D. M. Armstrong, R. S. Hoffmann, and C. Jones. 1983. Mammals of the Northern Great Plains. University of Nebraska Press, Lincoln.

Kaufmann, J. H. 1982. Raccoon and allies. Pp. 567–585 in Wild mammals of North America. Biology, management, and economics (J. A. Chapman and G. A. Feldhamer, eds.). Johns Hopkins University Press, Baltimore, Maryland.

Keith, J. O. 1965. The Abert squirrel and its dependence on ponderosa pine. Ecology 46:150–163.

Kie, J. G., and B. Czech. 2000. Mule and black-tailed deer. Pp. 629–657 in Ecology and management of large mammals of North America (S. Demarais and P. R. Krausman, eds.). Prentice Hall, Upper Saddle River, New Jersey.

King, C. M. 1983. *Mustela erminea*. Mammalian Species 195:1–8.

King, J. A., ed. 1968. The biology of *Peromyscus* (Rodentia). Special Publications, American Society of Mammalogists 2:viii + 1–593.

Kitchen, D. W., and B. W. O'Gara. 1982. Pronghorn. Pp. 960–971 in Wild mammals of North America: Biology, management, and economics (J. A. Chapman and G. A. Feldhamer, eds.). Johns Hopkins University Press, Baltimore, Maryland.

Koprowski, J. L. 1994. *Sciurus niger*. Mammalian Species 479:1–9.

Krausman, P. R., and R. T. Bowyer. 2003. Mountain sheep (*Ovis canadensis* and *O. dalli*). Pp. 1095–1115 in Wild mammals of North America: Biology, management, and conservation, 2nd edition (G. A. Feldhamer, B. C. Thompson, and J. A. Chapman, eds.). Johns Hopkins University Press, Baltimore, Maryland.

Krausman, P. R., and D. M. Shackleton. 2000. Bighorn sheep. Pp. 517–544 in Ecology and management of large mammals of North America (S. Demarais and P. R. Krausman, eds.). Prentice Hall, Upper Saddle River, New Jersey.

Kunz, T. H. 1974. Reproduction, growth, and mortality of the vespertilionid bat, *Eptesicus fuscus*, in Kansas. Journal of Mammalogy 55:1–13.

Kunz, T. H. 1982a. *Lasionycteris noctivagans*. Mammalian Species 172:1–5.

Kunz, T. H., ed. 1982b. Ecology of bats. Plenum, New York.

Kunz, T. H., and R. A. Martin. 1982. *Plecotus townsendii*. Mammalian Species 175:1–6.

Kurta, A., and R. H. Baker. 1990. *Eptesicus fuscus*. Mammalian Species 356:1–10.

Kurtén, B. 1971. The Age of Mammals. Columbia University Press, New York.

Kurtén, B., and E. Anderson. 1980. Pleistocene Mammals of North America. Columbia University Press, New York.

Larivière, S. 2001. *Ursus americanus*. Mammalian Species 647:1–11.

Larivière, S. 2003. Mink (*Mustela vison*). Pp. 662–671 in Wild mammals of North America: Biology, management, and conservation, 2nd edition (G. A. Feldhamer, B. C. Thompson, and J. A. Chapman, eds.). Johns Hopkins University Press, Baltimore, Maryland.

Larivière, S., and M. Pasitschniak-Arts. 1996. *Vulpes vulpes*. Mammalian Species 537: 1–11.

Larivière, S., and L. R. Walton. 1997. *Lynx rufus*. Mammalian Species 563:1–8.

Lawson, B., and R. Johnson. 1982. Mountain sheep. Pp. 1036–1055 in Wild mammals of North America: Biology, management, and economics (J. A. Chapman and G. A. Feldhamer, eds.). Johns Hopkins University Press, Baltimore, Maryland.

Lechleitner, R. R. 1969. Wild mammals of Colorado. Pruett Publishing Co., Boulder, Colorado.

Lee, C. M., J. B. Benedict, and J. B. Lee. 2006. Ice patches and remnant glaciers: Paleontological discoveries and archeological possibilities in the Colorado high country. Southwestern Lore 72:26–43.

Lim, B. K. 1987. *Lepus townsendii*. Mammalian Species 288:1–6.

Lindzey, F. G. 1982. Badger. Pp. 653–663 in Wild mammals of North America: Biology, management, and economics (J. A. Chapman and G. A. Feldhamer, eds.). Johns Hopkins University Press, Baltimore, Maryland.

Lindzey, F. G. 2003. Badger (*Taxidea taxus*). Pp. 683–691 in Wild mammals of North America: Biology, management, and conservation, 2nd edition (G. A. Feldhamer, B. C. Thompson, and J. A. Chapman, eds.). Johns Hopkins University Press, Baltimore, Maryland.

Linscombe, G., N. Kinler, and R. J. Aulerich. 1982. Mink. Pp. 629–643 in Wild mammals of North America: Biology, management, and economics (J. A. Chapman and G. A. Feldhamer, eds.). Johns Hopkins University Press, Baltimore, Maryland.

Logan, K. A., and L. L. Sweanor. 2000. Puma. Pp. 347–377 in Ecology and management of large mammals of North America (S. Demarais and P. R. Krausman, eds.). Prentice Hall, Upper Saddle River, New Jersey.

Long, C. A. 1973. *Taxidea taxus*. Mammalian Species 26:1–4.

Long, C. A. 1974. *Microsorex. hoyi* and *Microsorex thompsoni*. Mammalian Species 33:1–4.

Lopez, B. H. 1978. Of wolves and men. Touchstone, New York.

Lotze, J. H., and S. Anderson. 1979. *Procyon lotor*. Mammalian Species 119:1–8.

Loveless, C. M. 1967. Ecological characteristics of a mule deer winter range. Technical Publication, Colorado Game, Fish and Parks Department 20:1–124.

MacClintock, D. 1970. Squirrels of North America. Van Nostrand Reinhold Co., New York.

Mack, C. M. 1985. River otter restoration in Grand County, Colorado. MS thesis, Colorado State University, Fort Collins.

Mackie, R. J., J. G. Kie, D. F. Pac, and K. L. Hamlin. 2003. Mule deer (*Odocoileus hemionus*). Pp. 889–905 in Wild mammals of North America: Biology, management, and conservation, 2nd edition (G. A. Feldhamer, B. C. Thompson, and J. A. Chapman, eds.). Johns Hopkins University Press, Baltimore, Maryland.

Makar, P. W. 1980. Bobcat and coyote food habits and habitat use in Rocky Mountain National Park. MS thesis, Colorado State University, Fort Collins.

Manning, R. W., and J. K. Jones Jr. 1989. *Myotis evotis*. Mammalian Species 329:1–5.

Martin, P. S. 2005. Twilight of the mammoths: Ice Age extinctions and the rewilding of America. University of California Press, Berkeley.

McAllister, J. A., and R. S. Hoffmann. 1988. *Phenacomys intermedius*. Mammalian Species 305:1–8.

McCord, C. M., and J. E. Cardoza. 1982. Bobcat and lynx. Pp. 728–766 in Wild mammals of North America: Biology, management, and economics (J. A. Chapman and G. A. Feldhamer, eds.). Johns Hopkins University Press, Baltimore, Maryland.

McKeever, S. 1964. The biology of the golden-mantled ground squirrel. Ecological Monographs 34:383–401.

Meagher, M. 1986. *Bison bison*. Mammalian Species 266:1–8.

Meaney, C. A. 1983. Olfactory communication in pikas (*Ochotona princeps*). PhD dissertation, University of Colorado, Boulder.

Mech, L. D. 1974. *Canis lupus*. Mammalian Species 37:1–6.

Melquist, W. E., P. J. Polechla Jr., and D. Toweill. 2003. River otter (*Lontra canadensis*). Pp. 708–734 in Wild mammals of North America: Biology, management, and conservation, 2nd edition (G. A. Feldhamer, B. C. Thompson, and J. A. Chapman, eds.). Johns Hopkins University Press, Baltimore, Maryland.

Merritt, J. F. 1981. *Clethrionomys gapperi*. Mammalian Species 146:1–9.

Merritt, J. F., and J. M. Merritt. 1978a. Population ecology and energy relationships of *Clethrionomys gapperi* in a Colorado subalpine forest. Journal of Mammalogy 59:576–598.

Merritt, J. F., and J. M. Merritt. 1978b. Seasonal home ranges and activity of small mammals of a Colorado subalpine forest. Acta Theriologica 23:195–202.

Merritt, J. F., and J. M. Merritt. 1980. Population ecology of the deer mouse (*Peromyscus maniculatus*) in the Front Range of Colorado. Annals of the Carnegie Museum 49:113–130.

Miller, K. V., L. I. Muller, and S. Demarais. 2003. White-tailed deer (*Odocoileus virginianus*). Pp. 906–930 in Wild mammals of North America: Biology, management, and conservation, 2nd edition (G. A. Feldhamer, B. C. Thompson, and J. A. Chapman, eds.). Johns Hopkins University Press, Baltimore, Maryland.

Mills, E. A. 1911. The spell of the Rockies. Houghton Mifflin, Boston, Massachusetts.

Mills, E. A. 1914. The story of Estes Park, 3rd edition. Privately published, Estes Park, Colorado.

Mills, E. A. 1915. The Rocky Mountain wonderland. Houghton Mifflin, Boston, Massachusetts.

Mills, E. A. 1919. The grizzly, our greatest wild animal. Riverside Press, Cambridge, Massachusetts.

Mills, E. A. 1922. Watched by wild animals. Doubleday Page & Company, New York.

Monty, A., and R. E. Emerson. 2003. Eastern woodrat (*Neotoma floridana* and allies). Pp. 381–393 in Wild mammals of North America: Biology, management, and conservation, 2nd edition (G. A. Feldhamer, B. C. Thompson, and J. A. Chapman, eds.). Johns Hopkins University Press, Baltimore, Maryland.

Moser, C. A. 1962. The bighorn sheep of Colorado. Technical Publication, Colorado Game and Fish Department 10:1–49.

Murie, O. J. 1951. The elk of North America. Stackpole Co., Harrisburg, Pennsylvania.

Murie, O. J. 1954. A field guide to animal tracks. Houghton Mifflin Co., Boston, Massachusetts.

Murray, D. L. 2003. Snowshoe hare and other hares (*Lepus americanus* and allies). Pp. 147–175 in Wild mammals of North America: Biology, management, and conservation, 2nd edition (G. A. Feldhamer, B. C. Thompson, and J. A. Chapman, eds.). Johns Hopkins University Press, Baltimore, Maryland.

Mutel, C. F., and J. C. Emerick. 1992. From grassland to glacier, a natural history of Colorado. Johnson, Boulder, Colorado.

Muths, E. 1999. Dwarf shrew found in Rocky Mountain National Park. Park Science 19(1):1–2.

Nash, D. J., and R. N. Seaman. 1977. *Sciurus aberti*. Mammalian Species 80:1–5.

Neff, D. J. 1959. A seventy-year history of a Colorado beaver colony. Journal of Mammalogy 40:381–387.

Neubaum, D. J., T. J. O'Shea, and K. R. Wilson. 2006. Autumn migration and selection of rock crevices as hibernacula by big brown bats in Colorado. Journal of Mammalogy 87:470–479.

Neuwall-Poglayen, I., and D. E. Toweill. 1988. *Bassariscus astutus*. Mammalian Species 327:1–8.

Oaks, E. C., P. S. Young, G. L. Kirkland Jr., and D. F. Schmidt. 1987. *Spermophilus variegatus*. Mammalian Species 272:1–8.

O'Farrell, M. J., and E. H. Studier. 1980. *Myotis thysanodes*. Mammalian Species 137:1–5.

O'Gara, B. W. 1978. *Antilocapra americana*. Mammalian Species 90:1–7.

Olmstead, C. E., Jr. 1979. The ecology of aspen with reference to utilization by large herbivores in Rocky Mountain National Park. Pp. 89–97 in North American elk: ecology, behavior, and management (M. S. Boyce and L. D. Hayden-Wing, eds.). University of Wyoming, Laramie, 294 pp.

Packard, F. M. 1946. An ecological study of the bighorn sheep in Rocky Mountain National Park, Colorado. Journal of Mammalogy 27:3–28.

Paquet, P. C., and L. N. Carbyn. 2003. Gray wolf (*Canis lupus* and allies). Pp. 482–510 in Wild mammals of North America: Biology, management, and conservation, 2nd edition (G. A. Feldhamer, B. C. Thompson, and J. A. Chapman, eds.). Johns Hopkins University Press, Baltimore, Maryland.

Paradiso, J. L., and R. M. Nowak. 1982. Wolves. Pp. 460–474 in Wild mammals of North America: Biology, management, and economics (J. A. Chapman and G. A. Feldhamer, eds.). Johns Hopkins University Press, Baltimore, Maryland.

Pasitschniak-Arts, M. 1993. *Ursus arctos*. Mammalian Species 439:1–10.

Pasitschniak-Arts M., and S. Larivière. 1995. *Gulo gulo*. Mammalian Species 499:1–10.

Pasitschniak-Arts, M., and F. Messier. 2000. Brown (grizzly) and polar bears. Pp. 409–428 in Ecology and management of large mammals of North America (S. Demarais and P. R. Krausman, eds.). Prentice Hall, Upper Saddle River, New Jersey.

Peek, J. M. 2000. Mountain goat. Pp. 467–490 in Ecology and management of large mammals of North America (S. Demarais and P. R. Krausman, eds.). Prentice Hall, Upper Saddle River, New Jersey.

Peek, J. M. 2003. Wapiti (*Cervus elaphus*). Pp. 877–888 in Wild mammals of North America: Biology, management, and conservation, 2nd edition (G. A. Feldhamer, B. C. Thompson, and J. A. Chapman, eds.). Johns Hopkins University Press, Baltimore, Maryland.

Pelton, M. R. 2000. Black bear. Pp. 389–408 in Ecology and management of large mammals of North America (S. Demarais and P. R. Krausman, eds.). Prentice Hall, Upper Saddle River, New Jersey.

Pelton, M. R. 2003. Black bear (*Ursus americanus*). Pp. 547–555 in Wild mammals of North America: Biology, management, and conservation, 2nd edition (G. A. Feldhamer, B. C. Thompson, and J. A. Chapman, eds.). Johns Hopkins University Press, Baltimore, Maryland.

Pierce, B. M., and V. C. Bleich. 2003. Mountain lion (*Puma concolor*). Pp. 744–757 in Wild mammals of North America: Biology, management, and conservation, 2nd edition (G. A. Feldhamer, B. C. Thompson, and J. A. Chapman, eds.). Johns Hopkins University Press, Baltimore, Maryland.

Powell, R. A., S. W. Buskirk, and W. J. Zielinski. 2003. Fisher and marten (*Martes pennanti* and *Martes americana*). Pp. 635–649 in Wild mammals of North America: Biology, management, and conservation, 2nd edition (G. A. Feldhamer, B. C. Thompson, and J. A. Chapman, eds.). Johns Hopkins University Press, Baltimore, Maryland.

Pugh, S. R., S. Johnson, and R. H. Tamarin. 2003. Voles (*Microtus* species). Pp. 349–370 in Wild mammals of North America: Biology, management, and conservation, 2nd edition (G. A. Feldhamer, B. C. Thompson, and J. A. Chapman, eds.). Johns Hopkins University Press, Baltimore, Maryland.

Reynolds, H. W., C. C. Gates, and R. D. Glaholt. 2003. Bison (*Bison bison*). Pp. 1009–1060 in Wild mammals of North America: Biology, management, and conservation, 2nd edition (G. A. Feldhamer, B. C. Thompson, and J. A. Chapman, eds.). Johns Hopkins University Press, Baltimore, Maryland.

Rocky Mountain National Park. 2006. Elk and vegetation management plan, Rocky Mountain National Park, Colorado. Draft Environmental Impact Statement, xxxvii + 497 pp.

Rosatte, R., and S. Larivière. 2003. Skunks (genera *Mephitis, Spilogale,* and *Conepatus*). Pp. 692–707 in Wild mammals of North America: Biology, management, and conservation, 2nd edition (G. A. Feldhamer, B. C. Thompson, and J. A. Chapman, eds.). Johns Hopkins University Press, Baltimore, Maryland.

Ross, A. 1967. Ecological aspects of food habits of insectivorous bats. Proceedings of the Western Foundation for Vertebrate Zoology 2:205–263.

Roze, U., and L. M. Ilse. 2003. Porcupine (*Erethizon dorsatum*). Pp. 371–380 in Wild mammals of North America: Biology, management, and conservation, 2nd edition (G. A. Feldhamer, B. C. Thompson, and J. A. Chapman, eds.). Johns Hopkins University Press, Baltimore, Maryland.

Rue, L. L., III. 1964a. The world of the raccoon. J. B. Lippincott, Philadelphia, Pennsylvania.

Rue, L. L., III. 1964b. The world of the beaver. J. B. Lippincott, Philadelphia, Pennsylvania.

Rue, L. L., III. 1969. The world of the red fox. J. B. Lippincott, Philadelphia, Pennsylvania.

Ruggiero, L. F., K. B. Aubrey, S. W. Buskirk, G. M. Koehler, C. J. Krebs, K. S. McKelvey, and J. R. Squires. 2000. Ecology and conservation of lynx in the United States. University Press of Colorado, Boulder.

Samuel, D. E., and B. B. Nelson. 1982. Foxes. Pp. 475–490 in Wild mammals of North America: Biology, management, and economics (J. A. Chapman and G. A. Feldhamer, eds.). Johns Hopkins University Press, Baltimore, Maryland.

Schoonmaker, W. J. 1968. The world of the grizzly bear. J. B. Lippincott, Philadelphia, Pennsylvania.

Schwartz, C. C., S. D. Miller, and M. A. Haroldson. 2003. Grizzly bear (*Ursus arctos*). Pp. 556–586 in Wild mammals of North America: Biology, management, and conservation, 2nd edition (G. A. Feldhamer, B. C. Thompson, and J. A. Chapman, eds.). Johns Hopkins University Press, Baltimore, Maryland.

Sera, W. E., and C. N. Early. 2003. *Microtus montanus*. Mammalian Species 716:1–10.

Shackleton, D. M. 1985. *Ovis canadensis*. Mammalian Species 230:1–9.

Sharpe, V. A., B. Norton, and S. Donnelley, eds. 2001. Wolves and human communities, biology, politics, and ethics. Island Press, Washington, District of Columbia.

Shaw, J. H., and M. Meagher. 2000. Bison. Pp. 447–466 in Ecology and management of large mammals of North America (S. Demarais and P. R. Krausman, eds.). Prentice Hall, Upper Saddle River, New Jersey.

Sheffield, S. R., and H. H. Thomas. 1997. *Mustela frenata*. Mammalian Species 570: 1–9.

Shump, K. A., Jr., and A. U. Shump. 1982. *Lasiurus cinereus*. Mammalian Species 185: 1–5.

Skryja, D. D. 1974. Reproductive biology of the least chipmunk (*Eutamias minimus operarius*) in southeastern Wyoming. Journal of Mammalogy 55:764–795.

Smith, A. T. 1975. The distribution and dispersal of pikas: Influences of behavior and climate. Ecology 55:1368–1376.

Smith, A. T. 1978. Comparative demography of pikas (*Ochotona*): Effect of spatial and temporal age-specific mortality. Ecology 59:133–139.

Smith, A. T., and M. L. Weston. 1990. *Ochotona princeps*. Mammalian Species 352:1–8.

Smith, C. C. 1968. The adaptive nature of social organization in the genus of three [*sic*] squirrels *Tamiasciurus*. Ecological Monographs 34:383–401.

Smith, F. A. 1997. *Neotoma cinerea*. Mammalian Species 56:1–8.

Smith, M. E., and M. C. Belk. 1996. *Sorex monticolus*. Mammalian Species 528:1–5.

Smith, W. P. 1991. *Odocoileus virginianus*. Mammalian Species 388:1–13.

Smolen, M. J., and B. L. Keller. 1987. *Microtus longicaudus*. Mammalian Species 271: 1–7.

Snyder, M. A. 1992. Selective herbivory by Abert's squirrel mediated by chemical variability in ponderosa pine. Ecology 73:1730–1741.

Snyder, M. A. 1998. Abert's squirrel (*Sciurus aberti*) in ponderosa pine (*Pinus ponderosa*) forests: Directional selection, diversifying selection. Pp. 195–201 in Ecology and evolutionary biology of tree squirrels (M. A. Steele, J. F. Merritt, and D. A. Zegers, eds.). Special Publication, Virginia Museum of Natural History 6:1–320.

Sorensen, M. W. 1962. Some aspects of water shrew behavior. American Midland Naturalist 68:445–462.

Southwick, C. H., S. C. Golian, M. R. Whitworth, J. C. Halfpenny, and R. Brown. 1986. Population density and fluctuations of pikas (*Ochotona princeps*) in Colorado. Journal of Mammalogy 67:149–153.

Spencer, A. W., and D. Pettus. 1966. Habitat preferences of five sympatric species of long-tailed shrews. Ecology 47:677–683.

Steele, M. A. 1998. *Tamiasciurus hudsonicus*. Mammalian Species 586:1–9.

Stevens, D. R., and D. D. Hanson. 1986. The range use and movements of an introduced bighorn sheep population 5 years after establishment. Journal of the Colorado-Wyoming Academy of Science 18(1):51.

Stiger, M. 2001. Hunter gatherer archaeology of the Colorado high country. University Press of Colorado, Boulder.

Stinson, N., Jr. 1978. Habitat structure and species diversity on north and south-facing slopes in the Colorado Lower Montane Zone. Southwestern Naturalist 23: 77–84.

Storz, J. F., and C. F. Williams. 1996. Summer population structure of subalpine bats in Colorado. Southwestern Naturalist 41:322–324.

Strickland, M. A., C. W. Douglas, M. Novak, and N. P. Hunziger. 1982. Marten. Pp. 599–612 in Wild mammals of North America: Biology, management, and economics (J. A. Chapman and G. A. Feldhamer, eds.). Johns Hopkins University Press, Baltimore, Maryland.

Svendsen, G. E. 1979. Territoriality and behavior in a population of pikas (*Ochotona princeps*). Journal of Mammalogy 60:324–330.

Svendsen, G. E. 1982. Weasels. Pp. 613–628 in Wild mammals of North America: Biology, management, and economics (J. A. Chapman and G. A. Feldhamer, eds.). Johns Hopkins University Press, Baltimore, Maryland.

Svendsen, G. E. 2003. Weasels and black-footed ferret (*Mustela* species). Pp. 650–661 in Wild mammals of North America: Biology, management, and conservation, 2nd edition (G. A. Feldhamer, B. C. Thompson, and J. A. Chapman, eds.). Johns Hopkins University Press, Baltimore, Maryland.

Telleen, S. L. 1978. Structural niches of *Eutamias minimus* and *E. umbrinus* in Rocky Mountain National Park. PhD dissertation, University of Colorado, Boulder.

Toweill, D. E., and J. E. Tabor. 1982. River otter. Pp. 688–703 in Wild mammals of North America: Biology, management, and economics (J. A. Chapman and G. A. Feldhamer, eds.). Johns Hopkins University Press, Baltimore, Maryland.

Trimble, S. 1984. Longs Peak, a Rocky Mountain chronicle. Rocky Mountain Nature Association, Estes Park, Colorado.

Tumlison, R. 1987. *Felis lynx*. Mammalian Species 269:1–8.

Turner, R. W. 1974. Mammals of the Black Hills of South Dakota and Wyoming. Miscellaneous Publications, University of Kansas Museum of Natural History 60: 1–178.

Tuttle, M. D., and L. R. Heaney. 1974. Maternity habits of *Myotis leibii* in South Dakota. Bulletin of the Southern California Academy of Sciences 73:80–83.

Van Wormer, J. 1963. The world of the bobcat. J. B. Lippincott, Philadelphia, Pennsylvania.

Van Wormer, J. 1966. The world of the black bear. J. B. Lippincott, Philadelphia, Pennsylvania.

Van Wormer, J. 1969. The world of the American elk. J. B. Lippincott, Philadelphia, Pennsylvania.

Vaughan, T. A. 1969. Reproduction and population densities in a montane small mammal fauna. Miscellaneous Publications, University of Kansas Museum of Natural History 51:51–74.

Vaughan, T. A. 1974. Resource allocation in some sympatric subalpine rodents. Journal of Mammalogy 55:764–795.

Vaughan, T. A., J. M. Ryan, and N. J. Czaplewski. 2000. Mammalogy, 4th edition. Saunders, Fort Worth, Texas.

Verts, B. J. 1967. The biology of the striped skunk. University of Illinois Press, Urbana, Illinois.

Verts, B. J., and L. N. Carraway. 1999. *Thomomys talpoides*. Mammalian Species 618:1–11.

Verts, B. J., and L. N. Carraway. 2001. *Tamias minimus*. Mammalian Species 646:1–10.

Verts, B. J., L. N. Carraway, and A. Kinlaw. 2001. *Spilogale gracilis*. Mammalian Species 674:1–10.

Wade-Smith, J., and B. J. Verts. 1982. *Mephitis mephitis*. Mammalian Species 173:1–7.

Wallmo, O. C. 1978. Mule and black-tailed deer. Pp. 31–41 in Big game of North America (D. L. Gilbert and J. L. Schmidt, eds.). Stackpole Books, Harrisburg, Pennsylvania.

Wallmo, O. C., ed. 1981. Mule and black-tailed deer of North America. University of Nebraska Press, Lincoln.

Warner, R. M., and N. J. Czaplewski. 1984. *Myotis volans*. Mammalian Species 224:1–4.

Whitaker, J. O., Jr. 2004. *Sorex cinereus*. Mammalian Species 743:1–9.

White, J. A. 1953. Taxonomy of the chipmunks *Eutamias quadrivittatus* and *Eutamias umbrinus*. University of Kansas Publications, Museum of Natural History 5:563–582.

Willard, B. E., and S. Q. Foster. 1990. A roadside guide to Rocky Mountain National Park. Johnson Publishing Company, Boulder, Colorado.

Williams, O. 1952. New Phenacomys records from Colorado. Journal of Mammalogy 33:399.

Willner, G. R., G. A. Feldhamer, E. E. Zucker, and J. A. Chapman. 1980. *Ondatra zibethicus*. Mammalian Species 141:1–8.

Wilson, D. E. 1982. Wolverine. Pp. 644–652 in Wild mammals of North America: Biology, management, and economics (J. A. Chapman and G. A. Feldhamer, eds.). Johns Hopkins University Press, Baltimore, Maryland.

Wilson, D. E., and D. M. Reeder, eds. 2005. Mammal species of the world, a taxonomic and geographic reference. Johns Hopkins University Press, Baltimore, Maryland.

Wisdom, M. J., and J. G. Cook. 2000. North American elk. Pp. 694–735 in Ecology and management of large mammals of North America (S. Demarais and P. R. Krausman, eds.). Prentice Hall, Upper Saddle River, New Jersey.

Wishart, D. J. 1979. The fur trade in the American West 1807–1840. University of Nebraska Press, Lincoln.

Woods, C. A. 1973. *Erethizon dorsatum.* Mammalian Species 29:1–6.

Yahner, R. H. 2003. Pine squirrels *(Tamiasciurus hudsonicus* and *T. douglasii).* Pp 268–275 in Wild mammals of North America: Biology, management, and conservation, 2nd edition (G. A. Feldhamer, B. C. Thompson, and J. A. Chapman, eds.). Johns Hopkins University Press, Baltimore, Maryland.

Yensen, E., and P. W. Sherman. 2003. Ground squirrels *(Spermophilus* and *Ammospermophilus* species). Pp. 211–231 in Wild mammals of North America: Biology, management, and conservation, 2nd edition (G. A. Feldhamer, B. C. Thompson, and J. A. Chapman, eds.). Johns Hopkins University Press, Baltimore, Maryland.

Yoakum, J. D., and B. W. O'Gara. 2003. Pronghorn. Pp. 559–577 in Wild mammals of North America: Biology, management, and conservation, 2nd edition (G. A. Feldhamer, B. C. Thompson, and J. A. Chapman, eds.). Johns Hopkins University Press, Baltimore, Maryland.

Young, S. P. 1958. The bobcat of North America. Stackpole Co., Harrisburg, Pennsylvania.

Young, S. P., and E. A. Goldman. 1944. The wolves of North America. American Wildlife Institute, Washington, District of Columbia.

Young, S. P., and E. A. Goldman. 1946. The puma, mysterious American cat. American Wildlife Institute, Washington, District of Columbia.

Young, S. P., and H.H.T. Jackson. 1951. The clever coyote. Stackpole Co., Harrisburg, Pennsylvania.

Zegers, D. A. 1984. *Spermophilus elegans.* Mammalian Species 214:1–7.

Zwinger, A. H., and B. R. Willard. 1972. Land above the trees: A guide to American alpine tundra. Harper & Row, New York.

Approximate Conversion Factors, Metric-English Measurements

LINEAR MEASUREMENTS

To convert *inches* to *millimeters,* multiply by 25.
To convert *millimeters* to *inches,* multiply by 0.04 (that is, divide by 25).
To convert *inches* to *centimeters,* multiply by 2.5.
To convert *centimeters* to *inches,* multiply by 0.4 (that is, divide by 2.5).
To convert *feet* to *meters,* multiply by 0.3.
To convert *meters* to *feet,* multiply by 3.3.

MEASUREMENTS OF WEIGHT

To convert *ounces* to *grams,* multiply by 28.
To convert *grams* to *ounces,* multiply by 0.35 (that is, divide by 28).
To convert *pounds* to *grams,* multiply by 450.
To convert *pounds* to *kilograms,* multiply by 0.45.
To convert *kilograms* to *pounds,* multiply by 2.2.

BETTER STILL, DON'T CONVERT—JUST THINK METRIC!

A dime weighs 2.5 grams, a penny 3, a nickel 5, a quarter 6; a quart of milk weighs almost a kilogram; and that liter of bottled water weighs precisely a kilogram. The mechanical pencil in my pocket is about 14 centimeters long and 8 mm thick, and a U.S. dollar bill is 65 mm wide and 155 mm long. For comments on the use of the metric system, see pp. 5–6.